THE ARDEN SHAKESPEARE
GENERAL EDITOR: W. J. CRAIG
1891–1906: R. H. CASE, 1909

THE TRAGEDY OF HAMLET

THE WORKS

OF

SHAKESPEARE

THE TRAGEDY OF HAMLET

EDITED BY

EDWARD DOWDEN

METHUEN & CO. LTD.

36 ESSEX STREET : STRAND

LONDON

Eighth Edition, Revised

First Published . . . . . October 1899
Second Edition   . . . . December 1909
Third Edition . . . . . February 1912
Fourth Edition . . . . . July   1914
Fifth Edition . . . . . May   1920
Sixth Edition, Revised . . January   1929
Seventh Edition, Revised . January   1933
Eighth Edition, Revised . 1938

PRINTED IN GREAT BRITAIN

CONTENTS

b

INTRODUCTION

THIS edition of *Hamlet* aims in the first place at giving a trustworthy text.

Secondly, it attempts to exhibit the variations from that text which are found in the primary sources—the Quarto of 1604 and the Folio of 1623—in so far as those variations are of importance towards the ascertainment of the text. Every variation is not recorded, but I have chosen to err on the side of excess rather than on that of defect. Readings from the Quarto of 1603 are occasionally given, and also from the later Quartos and Folios, but to record such readings is not a part of the design of this edition. The letter Q means Quarto 1604[1]; F means Folio 1623.

The dates of the later Quartos are as follows :—Q 3, 1605 ;[2] Q 4, 1611 ; Q 5, undated ; Q 6, 1637. For my few references to these later Quartos I have trusted the *Cambridge Shakespeare* and Furness's edition of *Hamlet*.

Thirdly, it gives explanatory notes. Here it is inevitable that my task should in the main be that of selection and condensation. But, gleaning after the gleaners, I have perhaps brought together a slender sheaf. Thus, I am not aware that I have been antici-

---

[1] Also denoted by Q 2, in Q 2, 3, etc.
[2] Not now regarded as a separate Quarto (Q 3), but as some copies of Q 2 dated 1605 instead of 1604. R. H. C.]

pated in my explanation of Hamlet's question about
Alexander's body, in the Churchyard scene (V. i. 218) ;
of his swearing by St. Patrick (I. v. 136) ; of the name
Lamord (IV. vii. 93). I hope I may have done something
towards the solution of the " dram of eale " crux (I. iv.
36–38), and of " stand a comma 'tween their amities "
(V. ii. 42). I have noted a curious parallel between
Jonson and Shakespeare (II. ii. 210–214). With the aid
of the New English Dictionary I have perhaps removed
any doubt as to the meaning of " mortal coil " (III. i. 67),
and given its correct sense (though this is doubtful) to
" anchor's cheer " (III. ii. 231). I have perhaps explained
why Polonius classes " fencing " with drinking and drabbing (II. i. 25). I have made what I suppose to be new
—perhaps erroneous—suggestions as to " Take this from
this " (II. ii. 156) and " tender me a fool " (I. iii. 109). If
ingenuities are anywhere pardonable, it is in conjecturing
the meaning of Hamlet's riddling speeches ; it was not
his cue ever to talk sheer nonsense ; accordingly I have
ventured to throw out, doubtfully, suggestions—possibly
darkening counsel with words—on " fishmonger " (II. ii.
174), " mad . . . handsaw " (II. ii. 401–403), " suit of
sables " (III. ii. 139), " soul of Nero " (III. ii. 413), " The
body is with the king " (IV. ii. 30), " drink up eisel ? eat
a crocodile " (V. i. 298). I, very doubtfully, suggest a
new reading of " select and generous " (I. iii. 74), and a
modification of Mr. Tovey's emendation of the
" Yaughan " crux (V. i. 67). Occasionally, as in the
" Nunnery " scene with Ophelia (III. i), I have tried
to explain Hamlet's thoughts rather than verbal difficulties. When what is worthless has been sifted away,

a little that is a real addition to our knowledge of Shakespeare may remain.

For the earliest references to the legendary Hamlet the reader should consult Mr. Gollancz's interesting volume *Hamlet in Iceland* (1898). The first in date, he tells us, is found in the second section of Snorri Sturlason's *Prose Edda* (about 1230) :—" The Nine Maids of the Island Mill " (daughters of Ægir, the Ocean-god) " in ages past ground Hamlet's meal." The words occur in a quotation of Snorri from Snæbjörn, who was probably an Arctic adventurer of the tenth century. The name Amhlaide is found yet earlier. In the *Annals of Ireland by the Four Masters*, under the year 917 (=919), in a fragment of song (having reference to the battle of Ath-Cliath between the Northerners and the Irish) attributed to Queen Gormflaith, appear the words : " Niall Glundubh [was slain] by Amhlaide." Mr. Gollancz identifies this Amhlaide with Sitric, a Northerner, who first came to Dublin in 888, and hazards the conjecture that " Gaile," a cognomen applied to Sitric, may mean *mad*, and that Amhlaide may be a synonym of " Gaile." He believes that in the Scandinavian kingdom of Ireland was developed, in the eleventh century, the Northern tale of Hamlet as we know it from Saxo.[1]

[1] The *Ambales Saga*, which Mr. Gollancz prints, is in its present form "a modern production belonging to the sixteenth, or perhaps early seventeenth century," preserving possibly some elements of the pre-Saxo Hamlet legend. The Icelandic folk-tale of Brjam (first written down from oral tradition in 1705) is "nothing but a levelling down of the story of Hamlet, cleverly blended with another folk-tale of the 'Clever Hans' type" (Gollancz, Introduction, lxiv. and lxviii.). [See also the same author's *Sources of Hamlet*, 1926, and articles on the etymology of Hamlet by Professor Kemp Malone in *The Review of English Studies*, July 1927 and 1928. R. H. C.]

Probably about the opening of the thirteenth century the Danish writer Saxo Grammaticus told in Latin the story of Amlethus in the third and fourth books of his *History of the Danes*. The reader will find an English version in Mr. Elton's translation of Saxo. The Northern Hamlet legends, oral or written, are mingled by Saxo with borrowings from the old Roman story of Lucius Junius Brutus. Horwendil and his brother Feng rule Jutland under King Rorik of Denmark. Horwendil slays Koll, king of Norway, and marries Gerutha, the daughter of King Rorik ; their son is Amleth. Feng, jealous of his brother, slays Horwendil, and takes Gerutha to wife. Amleth feigns to be dull of wits and little better than a beast, while secretly planning vengeance. He baffles the courtiers by riddling words, which for them are nonsense, but are really significant. A girl, his foster-sister, is placed in his way, in the hope that his conduct may betray his true state of mind ; his foster-brother warns him of the snare, and he baffles his enemies. A friend of Feng, " more confident than wise," proposes to act as eavesdropper during an interview between Amleth and his mother. Amleth, crowing like a cock, flapping his arms like wings, and leaping hither and thither, discovers the eavesdropper hidden under straw, stabs him and brutally disposes of the body. He explains to his mother that his madness is feigned and that he plans revenge, and he gains her over to his side. His uncle sends Amleth to Britain, with two companions, who bear a letter graven on wood, requesting the king to slay Amleth. The letter is altered by Amleth, and his companions are put to death. His adventures in Britain do not affect Shakespeare's play. He returns, makes the courtiers drunk, nets them in hangings knitted by his mother, sets fire to the palace, and slays his uncle with the sword. He harangues the people, and is hailed as Feng's successor. After other adventures of crafty device and daring deed, Amleth dies in battle. Had he lived, favoured by nature and fortune, he would have surpassed Hercules.

Saxo's *History* was printed in 1514. In 1570 Belle-forest—freely rendering Saxo's Latin—told the story of Amleth in French in the fifth volume of his *Histoires tragiques*. The English translation of Belleforest's story, *The Historie of Hamblet*, is dated 1608, and may have been called forth by the popularity of Shakespeare's play.[1] Here the eavesdropper hides behind the hangings of Geruthe's chamber, and Hamblet cries, " A rat ! a rat ! " circumstances probably borrowed from Shakespeare.

As early as 1589 an English drama on the subject of Hamlet was in existence. It is referred to in that year by Thomas Nash in a printed letter accompanying Greene's *Menaphon*. We know from this passage, and other allusions, that it was a drama written under the influence of Seneca, and that a ghost appeared in it crying " Revenge ! " Henslowe's diary informs us that it was acted, not as a new play, at Newington Butts in June 1594. The suggestion that Thomas Kyd was the author—made long since—was supported with sub-stantial evidence by Mr. Fleay in his *Chronicle of the English Drama* (1891), and, in my opinion, was decisively

---

[1] It may be found in Furness's *Hamlet*, vol. ii., or in Collier's *Shake-speare's Library*, vol. i.

proved by Gregor Sarrazin in the section entitled " Der Ur-Hamlet " of his *Thomas Kyd und sein Kreis* (1892). It is not improbable that Nash, in the passage where he speaks of Hamlet, puns upon the name *Kyd*.[1] We may fairly assume that it was a companion piece to Kyd's *Spanish Tragedy*—itself a play of revenge (a father's revenge for a murdered son, inverting the Hamlet theme); of violent passion bordering on distraction; including among the *dramatis personæ* a ghost, and presenting, like *Hamlet*, a play within the play. Kyd translated Garnier's *Cornelia* from the French, and could read the story of Hamlet in Belleforest. English actors had visited Elsinore, and had lately returned to London, bringing their tidings of Denmark.

Mr. Corbin, in a very ingenius study, *The Elizabethan Hamlet* (1895), has conjectured that the lost play by Kyd exhibited a Hamlet resembling the Amleth of Saxo in his being rather a man of resolute action than a man of contemplation, and that his assumption of madness was the occasion of vulgar comedy; the affliction of insanity was, as we know, often regarded by Elizabethan dramatists from the comic point of view. The conjecture is well worthy of consideration. In developing his theory Mr. Corbin makes use, however, of one piece

[1 Nevertheless, after careful scrutiny of the various grounds for an allusion to Kyd here, McKerrow (*Works of T. Nashe*, iv. 449 *sqq.*) sums up as follows : " Nashe is, I think, speaking of not one writer, but of a group—probably, but not certainly, of dramatists. He did know of a Hamlet play, but the passage throws no light upon its authorship. There is no reason for supposing either Kyd or the *Spanish Tragedy* to be referred to." Professor J. Dover Wilson—in the New Cambridge Shakespeare (N. C. S. in later references), *Hamlet*, p. xvii. *et seq.*—supports the older view, and cites, especially, later discoveries, interesting if inconclusive, that Nash's " Kidde in Æsop " is not " a chance literary illustration," but one to the kid in Spenser's May eclogue, purposely used (for want of something more appropriate) to get a pun on Kyd ; and that in " enamored with the Foxes newfangles," he imitates the line " He was so enamored with the newell " (*Shep. Cal.*, May, 276). R. H. C.]

of evidence, which must be held as of doubtful value.
A rude German drama, *Der Bestrafte Brudermord*, found
in a manuscript dated 1710, is taken by Mr. Corbin and
others as based on Kyd's *Hamlet*. This is possible ;
but it seems to me far more probable that the German
play is a debased adaptation of Shakespeare's *Hamlet* in
its earliest form. Perhaps, as Tanger has suggested
(*Shakespeare Jahrbuch*, xxiii.), a few recollections of the
later form of Shakespeare's play were woven in by actors
who arrived in Germany at a later date.[1]

Under the date July 26, 1602, was entered in the
Stationers' Registers for the printer James Roberts, " A
booke called The Revenge of Hamlet Prince [of] Denmarke, as yt was latelie Acted by the Lord Chamberleyne
his servantes." There are no grounds for supposing that
Shakespeare wrote the play earlier than 1602.[2] In the
following year appeared in quarto, " The Tragicall
Historie of Hamlet Prince of Denmarke By William
Shake-speare. As it hath beene diverse times acted by
his Highnesse servants in the Cittie of London : as also in

---

[1] See Cohn's *Shakespeare in Germany* (1865) ; Latham's *Two Disserta-
tions on the Hamlet of Saxo Grammaticus and of Shakespear* (1872) ; and
Furness's *Hamlet*, vol. ii. A *Hamlet* was performed by English actors at
Dresden in 1626. Tanger's article, referred to above, is of great value.

[2] The note by Gabriel Harvey in a copy of Speght's *Chaucer* (1598),
mentioning *Hamlet*, was seen by Steevens, Bishop Percy, and Malone, but
its date was a matter of conjecture. Harvey lived for many years after the
publication of Shakespeare's *Hamlet*. [This note, happily recovered (see
Gabriel Harvey's Marginalia, ed. G. C. Moore Smith, 1913, Appendix II.
and Preface vii.-xii.) contains obstacles to dating it ; but certain words,
"The Earle of Essex much commendes Albion's England," induce the
editor, as Essex did not perish till February 1601, to place it between
sometime in 1598 and that event. Mr. W. J. Lawrence (*Times Literary
Supplement*, April 8 and May 20, 1926) argues for 1600 within these limits,
finding an allusion in " the humorous man shall end his part in peace "
(*Hamlet*, II. ii. 339, 340) to what happened at the production of Jonson's
Every Man Out of his Humour in 1599. The audience did not on this
occasion permit the humorous man to end his part in peace, resenting some
lines of " absurd and fulsome rant, bordering on profaneness," as Gifford
calls them, with which Macilente's concluding speech began his praise of,
and prayer for, the Queen. R. H. C.]

the two Vniversities of Cambridge and Oxford, and elsewhere. At London printed for N. L. and John Trundell.
1603." The Lord Chamberlain's servants of 1602—
Shakespeare's company—had, since the accession of
James I., become his Highness' servants. It is conjectured
that the play was acted at the Universities " at some entertainment in honour of the king's accession," the subject
being connected " with the native country of his queen."

In 1604 appeared a second Quarto : " The Tragicall
Historie of Hamlet, Prince of Denmarke. By William
Shakespeare. Newly imprinted and enlarged to almost
as much againe as it was, according to the true and
perfect Coppie. At London, Printed by I. R. for N. L.,
and are to be sold at his shoppe under Saint Dunstons
Church in Fleetstreet. 1604." I. R. stands, we may be
sure, for James Roberts.[1]

It is unquestionable that the copy for the Quarto of
1603 was surreptitiously obtained. Errors which seem
to be rather errors of hearing than of sight, or of a
compositor's memory in setting up a group of words,
indicate that, according to a practice of the time, a shorthand writer was employed to take notes of the speeches
during a theatrical performance. There are also errors
which look like errors of a copyist ; some of these may

[1 Professor A. W Pollard in *Shakespeare Folios and Quartos*, 1909,
p. 74, points out that this is proved " by the occurrence at the beginning
of the text' of Roberts's " headpiece of the Royal Arms," and identifies
Valentine Sims as printer of the 1603 Quarto by similar evidence. The
entry for Roberts in S. R. was, in his view (p. 73), " intended solely to place
an obstacle in the way of the book being licensed to anyone else," but
piracy dispensed with a licence. In his *Shakespeare's Fight with the Pirates*,
1920, he comments (p. 50) : " In this case the players seem to have con-
doned the attack, and Ling was allowed to publish a revised edition, which
was printed for him by Roberts, . . ," R. H. C.]

have occurred in writing out the shorthand notes for the printer. T. Bright's system of shorthand, moreover, gave scope for many errors in interpreting the characters of the stenographer.[1] But the conjecture of the editors of the *Cambridge Shakespeare* that the defects of the manuscript derived from shorthand " were supplemented by a reference to the authentic copy in the library of the theatre," seems to deserve consideration. The earlier portion of the Quarto is both fuller and less inaccurate as compared with the true text than the later ; perhaps the shorthand writer scamped his work ; perhaps the theatrical underling,[2] whom we may suppose as assisting him by reference to the copy in the theatre, was discovered, or had no opportunity of completing his dishonest labours. In some instances it looks as if only a hasty and partly incorrect note of the substance of a speech was made, and this was expanded into several feeble or incoherent lines.

The Quarto of 1603, containing 2143 lines, is shorter by some seventeen or eighteen hundred lines than the play as we construct it from the second Quarto and the Folio ; yet it gives substantially the whole action of the complete play. The names of two characters differ from those familiar to us — Polonius is here Corambis, and Reynaldo is Montano. Osric is here " a Bragart Gentleman " ; Francisco is known only as

[1] See on this subject a remarkable paper, " Shakespeare und die Stenographie," by Curt Dewischeit, in the *Shakespeare Jahrbuch*, xxxiv. (1898).

[2] It is now suggested, but perhaps first by Dr. Furnivall in his Introductions to Griggs's facsimile of Q 1, 1880, that this was a player whose memory partially recalled other parts besides his own. Dr. Furnivall noted that the parts of Horatio, Marcellus, and Voltemar are well done. Some passages from Q, which differ widely from the received text, or are absent from it, are given in Appendix II. R. H. C.]

first Centinel. The King and Queen of the " Mouse-trap " tragedy are a duke and duchess ; the duke's name is Albertus, not Gonzago ; the duke and duchess have been forty years married, not thirty. Yorick's skull has been twelve years in the ground, not three-and-twenty. Laertes has come from Paris to the late King's funeral, not to the coronation of King Claudius. Hamlet's in-dignant " 'Tis not alone my inky cloak " is addressed to Claudius, not to the Queen. The soliloquy " To be or not to be " and the " nunnery " dialogue with Ophelia occur in the same scene with the reading of Hamlet's love-letter, and before the " fishmonger " dialogue with Polonius ; lines spoken to Hamlet by the Ghost on the platform are here spoken by Hamlet to his mother in her closet ; Hamlet's comparison of Rosencrantz to a sponge appears here in another connection. It is the King, not Laertes, who proposes to anoint the rapier-point with venom. Gertrude, in the Closet scene, expressly declares that she was ignorant of her husband's murder, and she promises to assist her son in his revenge. There is a scene in which Horatio and the Queen confer about Hamlet's return to Denmark from shipboard, the Queen appearing as a confederate on Hamlet's side.

Such differences as these can be accounted for only in one of two ways — either, as the Clarendon Press editors maintain, a considerable portion of the old play is included in the Quarto of 1603, or that Quarto imper-fectly and often erroneously exhibits Shakespeare's work in a form which he subsequently revised and altered. When careful and judicious investigators fail to agree, the matter must be admitted to be doubtful. For my own part, repeated perusals have satisfied me that Shakespeare's hand can be discerned throughout the whole of the truncated and travestied play of 1603. The Shakespearian irony of many passages is unlike anything we find in plays of 1588–1589. With the exception of the following lines :—

> Look you now, here is your husband,
> With a face like Vulcan,
> A looke fit for a murder and a rape,
> A dull dead hanging looke, and a hell-bred eie,
> To affright children and amaze the world :

I see nothing that looks pre-Shakespearian, and I see much that is entirely unlike the work of Kyd. It is possible, indeed, that Kyd's work may have been revised before 1600, but we have no evidence to that effect. Here and there echoes of a phrase, or a line, or a rhyme in *Jeronimo*, or *The Spanish Tragedy*, or *Solyman and Perseda*, may be heard in the Quarto of 1603, as echoes of Marlowe and of Lyly may be heard elsewhere. But it has been aptly pointed out by Sarrazin that reminiscences of Shakespeare's own *Henry V.* are found in a passage which appears only in this first Quarto. Compare from the Quarto :—

> Well sonne *Hamlet* we in care of you : but specially
> In tender preservation of your health,
>   *   *   *   *   *
> The winde sits faire, you shall aboorde to-night,

with the following from *Henry V.*, II. ii. 12 and 58–59 :—

> Now sits the wind fair, and we will aboard.
>   *   *   *   *   *
> Though Cambridge, Scroop and Grey, in their dear care
> And tender preservation of our person.

c

The general style of the *Hamlet* of 1603 is much
more like that of an ill-reported play of that date than
like the style of a play of Kyd's and Marlowe's time ;
but the actor's speech about Hecuba and Priam, though
much reduced in length, stands out from the rest of the
play in this form as it does in the second Quarto and the
Folio, by virtue of its reproduction of a style which was
out of date at the opening of the seventeenth century.

The Quarto of 1604 is carelessly printed and ill
punctuated as compared with *Hamlet* of the Folio, yet
it represents more faithfully and fully what Shakespeare
wrote. The Folio, counting only passages of more than
one line, omits 218 lines ; the Quarto, 85. The most
considerable omissions in the Quarto are three—thirteen
lines immediately before the entrance of Osric in V. ii. ;
this seems to be due to accident ; secondly, the passage
about the boy actors in II. ii. ; the omission was probably
made, as Professor Hall Griffin suggests, because it would
be unbecoming in the King's servants to show hostility
to the children, who were servants of the Queen ;[1] thirdly,
part of the dialogue between Hamlet and Rosencrantz
and Guildenstern in an earlier passage of the same scene ;
the reason for the omission seems to me obvious—Denmark is spoken of as a prison, or as one of the worst
dungeons in the prison of the world, and Denmark was
the native country of the English Queen.

The Folio text was evidently cut for the purpose of
stage representation, and generally it may be described
as more theatrical, but less literary, than the text of
1604. The greater part of IV. iv., including Hamlet's

[¹ See note to Appendix I.]

very important soliloquy, is deleted ; so are his medita-
tions before the entrance of the Ghost in I. iv. ; Horatio's
description of the prodigies in Rome before the fall of
Cæsar, I. i. ; Claudius's remarkable words to Laertes, in
IV. vii., on the wearing effect of time on passion ; Hamlet's reflections on the monster Custom, III. iv. ; Hamlet's
lines about the courtiers and his resolve to hoist the
enginer with his own petar, III. iv. ; and much of his
mockery of Osric, V. ii.[1] Oaths and sacred words are
altered to avoid the legal offence of profanity. Some
actors' additions are introduced, such as the unhappy
" O, o, o, o " of the dying Hamlet, following his words
" The rest is silence." And there is a desire evident in
the editors of the Folio text to modernise certain words
which were regarded as old-fashioned.[2]

The duration of the action in the play presents
difficulties. It opens at midnight with the change of
sentinels. Next day Horatio and Marcellus, with Bernardo, inform Hamlet of the appearance of the Ghost ; it
cannot be the forenoon, for Hamlet salutes Bernardo
with " Good even, sir." On the night of this day Hamlet
watches and meets his father's ghost. The season of the
year is perhaps March ; the nights are bitter cold. The
second Act occupies part of one day ; Polonius despatches

---

[1] See Dr. Furnivall's Introduction to the second Quarto, prefixed to
Griggs's facsimile.

[2] The relation between Q 2 and F has been further elucidated by scientific
study of the texts and their bibliographical aspects (notably by Professor
J. Dover Wilson, in *Spellings and Misprints in Q 2 of Hamlet*, English
Association, *Essays and Studies*, 1924, x. 36; etc.). It is probable that
both ultimately derive from the same MS. source (Shakespeare's original
or near it), but that F was printed, without reference to Q2, from a transcript
which had been cut and adapted for stage purposes and used as a prompt
copy. See also Chambers, *William Shakespeare*, 1930, I. 408 *sqq.* R. H. C.]

Reynaldo to Paris, Ophelia enters alarmed by Hamlet's
visit, her father reads Hamlet's letter, the players arrive ;
and, when Hamlet parts from them, his words are, " I'll
leave you till to-night." But before this day arrives,
two months have elapsed since Hamlet was enjoined to
revenge the murder—it was two months since his father's
death when the play opened, and now it is " twice two
months." Next day Hamlet utters his soliloquy, " To
be or not to be," encounters Ophelia as arranged by
Polonius, gives his advice to the players, is present at
the performance of the play ; and, night having come, he
pleads with his mother, and again sees his father's spirit.
Here the third Act closes, but the action proceeds without interruption ; the King inquires for the body of
Polonius, and tells Hamlet that the bark is ready to bear
him to England. We must suppose that it is morning
when Hamlet meets the troops of Fortinbras. Two days
previously the ambassadors from Norway had returned,
with a request that Claudius would permit Fortinbras to
march through Denmark against the Poles ; Fortinbras
himself must have arrived almost as soon as the ambassadors, and obtained the Danish King's permission. In
IV. v. Ophelia appears distracted, and Laertes has returned from Paris to be revenged for Polonius's death.
An interval of time must have passed since Hamlet
sailed for England—an interval sufficient to permit
Laertes to receive tidings of the death of Polonius and
to reach Elsinore. In the next scene letters arrive
announcing that Hamlet is again in Denmark ; before
he was two days at sea, he became the pirates' prisoner.
On the day of the arrival of letters Ophelia is drowned.

Her flowers indicate that the time is early June. Ophelia's burial and Hamlet's death take place on the next day. Yet the time has been sufficient for Fortinbras to win his Polish victory and be again at Elsinore, and for ambassadors to return from England announcing the execution of Rosencrantz and Guildenstern. We might obligingly imagine that the pirate ship conveying Hamlet to Denmark was delayed by baffling winds; but his letters are written after he has landed, and they describe his companions as holding their course for England. The truth is, as stated by Professor Hall Griffin (whose record of the notes of time has aided me here), " Shakespeare is at fault "; he " did not trouble himself to reconcile . . . inconsistencies which practical experience as an actor would tell him do not trouble the spectator."

The division of the last three Acts of the play is made without the authority of any early edition. Act V. certainly opens aright. But the division between II. and III. is a matter of doubt, and the received division between III. and IV. is unfortunate. Mr. E. Rose proposed that III. should open with Hamlet's advice to the players (III. ii. of the received arrangement), and that IV. should open with the march of Fortinbras (our present IV. iv.). As regards IV., this is the division of Mr. Hudson in his *Harvard Shakespeare*; and but for the inconvenience of disturbing an accepted arrangement, to which references are made in lexicons and concordances, I should in this edition follow Mr. Hudson.

The names of the *dramatis personæ* incongruously mingle forms derived from the Hamlet tradition of the North with classical, Italian, and German forms. " Ger-

trude " is a modification of Saxo's "Gerutha." " Horatio,"
in the old play *Jeronimo*, is the name of Andrea's faithful
friend, who reappears in *The Spanish Tragedy*. Both
" Ofelia," the name of a shepherd, and " Montano " (the
name of Reynaldo in the Quarto of 1603) are found in
the *Arcadia* of Sannazaro. The autograph signatures—
dated 1577—of Jörgen Rossenkrantz and P. Guldenstern
appear on the same page of an old German album in
the Royal Public Library at Stuttgart, the original owner
of which had resided for some time at Copenhagen ; [1] it
does not follow that these individuals were in any sense
the originals of Shakespeare's courtiers ; an ambassador
named Rosencrantz was sent to England at the accession
of James the First, and there were other Guildensterns.
Shakespeare probably obtained the names from actors
who had returned from the Continent. " Fortinbras,"
wrote Mr. Elliot Browne (*Athenæum*, July 26, 1876),
" is evidently Fortebras, or Strongarm of the family of
Ferumbras of the romances, or may have come directly
from Niccolo Fortebraccio, the famous leader of the
condottieri."

It is not proposed here to notice the stage-history of
Hamlet, the interpretations by eminent actors, nor the
vast critical library that has grown around the play.
Critics, I think, have sometimes erred in not keeping
vividly before their imagination the nature of Shakespeare's task. They often speak as if the poet started
with some central idea of which Hamlet was to be the
exponent. " Shakespeare," wrote Goethe, " sought to

---

[1] See for facsimile *Shakespeare Jahrbuch*, xxv. ; and, for letters on the
subject, xxvi.

depict a great deed laid upon a soul unequal to the performance of it." "In Hamlet," wrote Coleridge, "Shakespeare seems to have wished to exemplify the moral necessity of a due balance between our attention to the objects of our senses and our meditation on the working of our minds—an equilibrium between the real and the imaginary worlds." I prefer to think of Shakespeare as setting to work with the intention of rehandling the subject of an old play, so as to give it fresh interest on the stage ; as following the subject given to him, and as following the instinctive leadings of his genius. The traditional Hamlet was distinguished by intellectual subtlety, by riddling speech, by a power of ingeniously baffling his pursuers, and, at the same time, by a love of truth. But the subtlety of Saxo's Amleth—and we may be sure the same is true of Kyd's Hamlet—was what Burke happily describes, in a different connection, as a " clumsy subtlety." If he would be taken to be mad, he affects unclean and brutal habits, or crows like a cock, or rides a horse with his head towards the tail. Shakespeare was attracted by the intellectual subtlety of Hamlet, and was inevitably led by his genius to refine this subtlety, and to diversify its manifestations. He was caught in the web of his own imaginings, and became so absorbed in his work that he forgot to keep it within the limits suitable for theatrical representation ; the tragedy has, perhaps, never been presented in its entirety on the English stage in consequence of its inordinate length. The swift and subtle wit that had its play at the Mermaid Tavern was now incarnated in one of the creatures of Shakespeare's imagination.

Hamlet is not the exponent of a philosophy ; he has, it is true, a remarkable power of reflection and a tendency to generalise, but he is not a philosophical thinker who seeks to co-ordinate his ideas in a coherent system. Perhaps Ulysses, perhaps Prospero approaches nearer to the philosopher, but neither Ulysses nor Prospero is a wit ; and Hamlet is a wit inspired by melancholy. He is swift, ingenious, versatile, penetrative ; and he is also sad. And when Shakespeare proceeded to follow the story in the main as he had probably received it from Kyd, it turned out that such subtlety overreached itself —which Shakespeare recognised as wholly right, and true to the facts of life. Hamlet's madness is not deliberately assumed ; an antic disposition is, as it were, imposed upon him by the almost hysterical excitement which follows his interview with the Ghost, and he ingeniously justifies it to himself by discovering that it may hereafter serve a purpose. But in truth his subtlety does not produce direct and effective action. Hamlet is neither a boisterous Laertes, who with small resources almost effects a rebellion in revenge for a murdered father, nor a resolute Fortinbras, who, mindful of his dead father's honour, can march through danger to victory. Hamlet's intellectual subtlety sees every side of every question, thinks too precisely on the event, considers all things too curiously, studies anew every conviction, doubts of the past, interrogates the future ; it delights in ironically adopting the mental attitudes of other minds ; it refines contempt into an ingenious art ; it puts on and puts off a disguise ; it assumes and lays aside the antic disposition ; it can even use frankness

as a veil,—for sometimes display is a concealment, as
happened with Edgar Poe's purloined letter. Hamlet
the subtle is pre-eminently a critic—a critic of art, a
critic of character, a critic of society, a critic of life, a
critic of himself.

The intellectual dexterity and versatility of Hamlet
are united with a moral nature essentially honest. He
will not hire a couple of assassins to despatch his father's
murderer. He will not himself take action until he has
evidence of the King's guilt. Like the Amleth of Saxo,
he is a lover of truth concealed in craft. His emotional
nature, though deeply disturbed by his mother's lapse
from loyalty, and liable to passionate fluctuations, is
sound at heart. He reverences the memory of his great
father, a man of action, whom Hamlet resembles as little
as he resembles Hercules. He is bound to Horatio by
ties of the deepest esteem and affection. He is kind to
the poor actors. He expends his utmost energy in an
effort to uplift and redeem his mother's faltering spirit.
He is over-generous in his estimate of Laertes. He has
loved Ophelia as a vision of beauty and innocence, and
is proportionately embittered when he supposes that he
has deceived himself and been deceived. But all his
inclinations are toward those who are unlike himself.
He is complex and self-tormenting ; Ophelia seems all
simplicity and innocence ; he is oppressed by melancholy
thought ; she is " something afar from the sphere of his
sorrow." Horatio is a man whose blood and judgment,
unlike Hamlet's own, are well commingled ; one who can
see the evil of the world, yet not grow world-weary ;
more of the antique Roman Stoic than a Dane. For

Fortinbras Hamlet has the admiration which the man of ideas feels for the man of resolute action. In Claudius he might have perceived some of his own intellectual subtlety and reflective habit, but conjoined with grosser senses and an evil moral nature ; and him Hamlet loathes with an impatient aversion.

Together with such an intellectual and such a moral nature, Hamlet has in him something dangerous—a will capable of being roused to sudden and desperate activity. It is a will which is determined to action by the flash and flame of an excitable temperament, or by those sudden impulses or inspirations, leaping forth from a sub-conscious self, which come almost like the revelation and the decree of Providence. It is thus that he suddenly conceives the possibility of unmasking the King's guilt, on the accidental arrival of the players, and proceeds without delay to put the matter to the test, suddenly overwhelms Ophelia with his reproaches of womanhood, suddenly stabs the eavesdropper behind the arras, suddenly, as if under some irresistible inspiration, sends his companions on shipboard to their death, suddenly boards the pirate, suddenly grapples with Laertes in the grave, suddenly does execution on the guilty King, plucks the poison from Horatio's hand, and gives his dying voice for a successor to the throne.

Hamlet's love for Ophelia is the wonder and delight in a celestial vision ; she is hardly a creature of earth, and he has poured into her ear almost all the holy vows of heaven. The ruin of an ideal leaves him cruelly unjust to the creature of flesh and blood. It is the strangest love-story on record. Never throughout the play is there one simple and sincere word uttered by lover to lover. The only true meeting of Hamlet and Ophelia is the speechless interview in which he reads her soul, despairs, and takes a silent and final farewell. Even in the letter, written prior to the terrible announcements of the Ghost, there is a conventional address and a baffling conclusion. After the silent parting, no true word, except when passion carries him away to undeserved reproach, is uttered by Hamlet to Ophelia. His love has for the first time its outbreak at her grave, when the pity of it for a moment restores his lost ideal. Never to Horatio, never to himself in soliloquy, does he utter the name of Ophelia.

Whether Shakespeare's choice and treatment of the Hamlet story was in any way connected with the history of Leicester, Essex, and the mother of Essex, or with the history of Mary Queen of Scots and Darnley, cannot be considered here. I do not think that a good case has been made out for either hypothesis.

The references to other plays of Shakespeare than Hamlet are to act, scene, and line as found in the *Globe Shakespeare*.

I have to thank two learned students of Elizabethan literature, Mr. W. J. Craig,[1] editor of *The Oxford Shakespeare*, and Mr. H. C. Hart, for aid kindly given to me in the preparation of this volume.

[1 Much additional comment and illustration of the text, mainly from this source, will be found in Appendix III, where also, at various points as elsewhere, advantage has been taken of the labours of Professor J. Dover Wilson, whose N. C. S. edition and *What Happens in Hamlet*, etc., have much furthered elucidation of the text and meaning of *Hamlet*. R. H. C.]

THE TRAGEDY

OF

HAMLET, PRINCE OF DENMARK

DRAMATIS PERSONÆ

CLAUDIUS, *King of Denmark.*
HAMLET, *Son to the late, and Nephew to the present King.*
FORTINBRAS, *Prince of Norway.*
HORATIO, *Friend to Hamlet.*
POLONIUS, *Lord Chamberlain.*
LAERTES, *his Son.*
VOLTIMAND,
CORNELIUS,
ROSENCRANTZ,
GUILDENSTERN, } *Courtiers.*
OSRIC,
A Gentleman,
A Priest.
MARCELLUS, } *Officers.*
BERNARDO,
FRANCISCO, *a Soldier.*
REYNALDO, *Servant to Polonius.*
A Captain.
English Ambassadors.
Players.
Two Clowns, Grave-diggers.

GERTRUDE, *Queen of Denmark, and Mother to Hamlet.*
OPHELIA, *Daughter to Polonius.*

Lords, Ladies, Officers, Soldiers, Sailors, Messengers, and Attendants.
Ghost of Hamlet's Father.

SCENE: *Elsinore.*

THE TRAGEDY

OF

HAMLET, PRINCE OF DENMARK

ACT I

SCENE I.—*Elsinore. A Platform before the Castle.*

FRANCISCO *at his post.* *Enter to him* BERNARDO.

Ber. Who's there?
Fran. Nay, answer me; stand, and unfold yourself.
Ber. Long live the king!
Fran. Bernardo?
Ber. He.   5
Fran. You come most carefully upon your hour.
Ber. 'Tis now struck twelve; get thee to bed, Francisco.

Act I. Scene I.] Acts and scenes are not marked in Q; in F only as far as II. ii.   1–5] Many editors follow Capell in printing as verse, the first line ending with *unfold.*   7. *now struck*] Steevens conj. *new-struck.*

2. *me*] *Me* emphatic, Francisco being the sentinel on guard.
3. *king*] Perhaps the watchword,
Horatio and Marcellus answer the challenge otherwise, but Francisco is not (line 15) at his post.

3

Fran. For this relief much thanks; 'tis bitter cold,
And I am sick at heart.
Ber. Have you had quiet guard?
Fran.   Not a mouse stirring.   10
Ber. Well, good night.
If you do meet Horatio and Marcellus,
The rivals of my watch, bid them make haste.
Fran. I think I hear them. Stand, ho! Who is there?

Enter HORATIO *and* MARCELLUS.

Hor. Friends to this ground.
Mar.   And liegemen to the Dane.   15
Fran. Give you good night.
Mar.   O, farewell, honest soldier:
Who hath relieved you?
Fran.   Bernardo has my place.
Give you good night.   [*Exit.*
Mar.   Holla! Bernardo!
Ber.   Say,—
What, is Horatio there?
Hor.   A piece of him.
Ber. Welcome, Horatio; welcome, good Marcellus.   20
Mar. What, has this thing appear'd again to-night?

14. *ho! Who is*] Q, *who's* F.   16. *soldier*] F, *souldiers* Q.   17. *has*] F, *hath* Q.   21. Mar.] Q 1, F ; Hora. Q.

13. *rivals*] *partners*, which is the reading of Q 1. Compare "rivality" in *Ant. and Cleop.* III. v. 8, meaning "partnership," and *The Tragedy of Hoffman* (1631):
"ile seat thee by my throne of state
And make thee rivall in those governments."
16. *Give*] Ellipsis for "God give."

Compare *Romeo and Juliet*, I. ii. 59.
19. *A piece of him*] Warburton supposed that Horatio gives his hand; it is night, adds Ingleby, and Horatio is hardly visible to Bernardo. Shakespeare's intention seems to be to show that Horatio, the sceptical, can answer jestingly.
21. *Mar.*] The agreement of Q 1

Ber. I have seen nothing.

Mar. Horatio says 'tis but our fantasy,
And will not let belief take hold of him
Touching this dreaded sight, twice seen of us :   25
Therefore I have entreated him along
With us to watch the minutes of this night,
That if again this apparition come,
He may approve our eyes and speak to it.

Hor. Tush, tush, 'twill not appear.

Ber.   Sit down awhile ;   30
And let us once again assail your ears,
That are so fortified against our story,
What we two nights have seen.

Hor.   Well, sit we down,
And let us hear Bernardo speak of this.

Ber. Last night of all,   35
When yond same star that's westward from the
    pole
Had made his course to illume that part of heaven
Where now it burns, Marcellus and myself,
The bell then beating one,—

Enter GHOST.

Mar. Peace! break thee off; look, where it comes
    again !   40

26, 27. *along With us to*] comma after *along* Q, after *us* F.   33. *two nights have*] F, *have two nights* Q.   39. *beating*] *towling* Q 1.   Enter *Ghost*] Q ; Enter the *Ghost* after *off*, line 40, F.

with Ff in assigning this speech to Marcellus is strong against the Quartos, which assign it to Horatio. "Thing" need not imply doubt or disrespect. Aufidius, *Cor.* IV. v. 122, addresses Coriolanus as "Thou noble thing ! " "This thing " may be ut-

tered with awe by Marcellus, or with an air of incredulity by Horatio. [See Appendix III.]

29. *approve*] corroborate, justify, as in *Ant. and Cleop.* I. i. 60 : "he approves the common liar."

Ber. In the same figure, like the king that's dead.

Mar. Thou art a scholar; speak to it, Horatio.

Ber. Looks it not like the king? mark it, Horatio.

Hor. Most like; it harrows me with fear and wonder.

Ber. It would be spoke to.

Mar.   Question it, Horatio.   45

Hor. What art thou that usurp'st this time of night,
Together with that fair and warlike form
In which the majesty of buried Denmark
Did sometimes march? by heaven I charge thee,
    speak!

Mar. It is offended.

Ber.   See, it stalks away.   50

Hor. Stay! speak, speak: I charge thee, speak!

                                            [*Exit Ghost.*

Mar. 'Tis gone, and will not answer.

Ber. How now, Horatio? you tremble and look pale;
Is not this something more than fantasy?
What think you on't?   55

Hor. Before my God, I might not this believe
Without the sensible and true avouch
Of mine own eyes.

Mar.   Is it not like the king?

---

41. *figure*,] F, no comma Q.   44. *harrows*] *horrors* Q 1.   45. *Question*] F, *Speake to* Q.

42. *scholar*] Latin was the language of exorcisms. Reed cites Beaumont and Fletcher, *Night Walker*, II. 1:
" Let's call the butler up, for he
    speaks Latin,
And that would daunt the devil."
44. *harrows*] Compare I. v. 16; and Milton, *Comus*, 565, " Amazed I stood, harrow'd with grief and fear."

45. Compare Boswell's *Life of Johnson* (ed. Birkbeck Hill, iii. 307): "Johnson once observed to me, 'Tom Tyers described me the best: "Sir (said he) you are like a ghost: you never speak till you are spoken to."'"

49. *sometimes*] sometime, formerly, as in *Henry VIII.* II. iv. 181.

Hor. As thou art to thyself:

    Such was the very armour he had on   60

    When he the ambitious Norway combated;

    So frown'd he once, when, in an angry parle,

    He smote the sledded Polacks on the ice.

    'Tis strange.

Mar. Thus twice before, and jump at this dead

    hour,   65

    With martial stalk hath he gone by our watch.

Hor. In what particular thought to work I know

    not;

    But, in the gross and scope of my opinion,

    This bodes some strange eruption to our state.

Mar. Good now, sit down, and tell me, he that

    knows,   70

    Why this same strict and most observant watch

    So nightly toils the subject of the land,

    And why such daily cast of brazen cannon,

    And foreign mart for implements of war;

---

61. *he*] omitted in F.   63. *sledded*] F, *sleaded* Q; *Polacks*] Mal., *pollax* Q 1, Qq 2, 3, 4; *Pollax* Ff 1, 2, Qq 5, 6; *Polax* F 3; *Pole-axe* F 4; *Polack* Pope and other editors (meaning the King of Poland).   65. *jump*] Q 1, Q; *just* F.   66. *hath he gone by*] *he passed through* Q 1.   68. *my*] F, *mine* Q.   73. *why*] F, *with* Q.

60. Furness asks, " Was this the very armour that he wore thirty years before, on the day Hamlet was born (see v. i. 155–176)? How old was Horatio?" But the armour would be remembered and be pointed out, when worn later.

62. *parle*] parley. *King John*, II. 205 : " this gentle parle."

63. *sledded Polacks*] Poles in sleds or sledges. See Polack in II. ii. 75, and IV. iv. 23. The Earl of Rochester, 1761, explained *sleaded* as loaded with lead, and *Polacks* as pole-axe. Boswell suggested that a person who carried the pole-axe was meant. " Sled " for sledge is found in Cotgrave's *French Dictionary*. Schmidt, reading " pollax (or pole-axe)," explains " sledded " as having a sled or sledge, *i.e.* a heavy hammer, to it.

65. *jump*] just, exactly. See v. ii. 386.

70. *Good now*] Please you, as in *Winter's Tale*, v. i. 19; Q 1 places a comma after " good," connecting " now " with " sit down."

72. *subject*] subjects, as in I. ii. 33.

Why such impress of shipwrights, whose sore
    task   75
Does not divide the Sunday from the week;
What might be toward, that this sweaty haste
Doth make the night joint - labourer with the
    day;
Who is't that can inform me?

Hor.   That can I;
At least the whisper goes so. Our last king,   80
Whose image even but now appear'd to us,
Was, as you know, by Fortinbras of Norway,
Thereto prick'd on by a most emulate pride,
Dared to the combat; in which our valiant
    Hamlet—
For so this side of our known world esteem'd
    him—   85
Did slay this Fortinbras; who, by a seal'd compact
Well ratified by law and heraldry,
Did forfeit, with his life, all those his lands
Which he stood seized of, to the conqueror;
Against the which, a moiety competent   90
Was gaged by our king; which had return'd
To the inheritance of Fortinbras,

88. *those*] F, *these* Q.   89. *of*] Q, *on* F.   91. *return'd*] F, *returne* Q.

75. *impress*] impressment, as in
Troilus and Cressida, II. i. 107.
77. *toward*] imminent, as in v. ii.
376.
83. *emulate*] emulous; not elsewhere in Shakespeare.
86. *compact*] Always accented by
Shakespeare on the last syllable, with
one exception : *1 Henry VI.* v. iv. 163
(Clar. Press).

87. *heraldry*] Part of a herald's
duty was to regulate the forms connected with a challenge and combat
of state importance.
89. *seized of*] possessed of—the
legal term still in use.
90. *moiety*] a portion, not necessarily a half. *1 Henry IV.* III. i. 96 :
"my moiety . . . equals not one of
yours."

Had he been vanquisher; as, by the same covenant
And carriage of the article design'd,
His fell to Hamlet.   Now, sir, young Fortin-
    bras,   95
Of unimproved mettle hot and full,
Hath in the skirts of Norway here and there
Shark'd up a list of lawless resolutes,
For food and diet, to some enterprise
That hath a stomach in 't; which is no other—   100
As it doth well appear unto our state—
But to recover of us, by strong hand
And terms compulsative, those foresaid lands
So by his father lost.   And this, I take it,
Is the main motive of our preparations,   105
The source of this our watch and the chief head
Of this post-haste and romage in the land.

93. *covenant*] *Cou'nant* F, *comart* Qq 2–5, *co-mart* Q 6 and many editors, Q of 1676 reads *compact*.   94. *article design'd*] Ff 2, 3, 4; *article desseigne* Qq 2, 3; *articles deseigne* Q 4; *Articles designe* Q 5; *Article designe* F 1. 96. *unimproved*] *inapproved* Q 1; Singer, ed. 2; Keightley.   98. *list*] *sight* Q 1; *lawless*] Q, *landlesse* F and many editors.   101. *As*] Q, *And* F. 103. *compulsative*] F, *compulsatorv* Q and many editors.

93. *covenant*] The "co-mart" of the Qq, if not a misprint, is of Shake-speare's coinage, meaning joint bar-gain.

94. *carriage*] process, or import.

96. *unimproved*] Clar. Press ex-plains as "untutored, not chastened by experience."   "Improve" is found in Chapman and Whitgift, meaning reprove (see Nares' *Glossary*), and "unimproved" may possibly mean unrebuked or unimpeached.

98. *Shark'd up*] Perhaps gathered as a sharker or swindler; or snatched indiscriminately as a shark swallows food.

98 *lawless*] The F "landless"

gives also an appropriate sense; but here Q 1 agrees with Q 2 in giving "lawless."

98. *resolutes*] braves.

99. *food and diet,*] Paid only by what they eat. Qq 1, 2 have no comma after "diet"; may the meaning be that the resolutes are to be the food and diet of a devouring enterprise, which has a stomach in it ("food for powder"), with a play on "stomach" in its second sense of stubborn resolu-tion?

107. *romage*] rummage, originally a nautical term for the stowage of a cargo (Skeat).

Ber. I think it be no other but e'en so:

Well may it sort that this portentous figure

Comes armed through our watch, so like the king 110

That was and is the question of these wars.

Hor. A mote it is to trouble the mind's eye.

In the most high and palmy state of Rome,

A little ere the mightiest Julius fell,

The graves stood tenantless and the sheeted
    dead 115

Did squeak and gibber in the Roman streets:

As stars with trains of fire and dews of blood,

Disasters in the sun; and the moist star,

Upon whose influence Neptune's empire stands,

Was sick almost to doomsday with eclipse: 120

And even the like precurse of fierce events,

As harbingers preceding still the fates

108-125. Ber. *I think . . . countrymen*] Q, omitted in **F.**   121. *fierce*]
Q 4 (*fearce*), *feare* Q, *fear'd* Collier's conjecture.

109. *sort*] suit, as in *Midsummer Night's Dream*, v. 55, "not sorting with a nuptial ceremony." Schmidt supposes it may mean "fall out," "have an issue," as in other passages of Shakespeare.

112. *mote*] The *moth* of Q is only an obsolete spelling of mote.

113. *state*] Wilson (Christopher North) pleads for "State" meaning Reigning City.

115-120.] Plutarch describes the prodigies preceding and following Cæsar's death—fires in the elements, spirits running up and down in the night, a pale sun, which gave little light or heat. Compare *Julius Cæsar*, I.iii. Such prodigies are very impressively described in Marlowe's *Lucan's First Booke translated*, published in 1600.

117, 118.] Perhaps a line following 116 has been lost; it may have mentioned prodigies in the heavens, or may have told of warriors fighting upon the clouds; in *Julius Cæsar*, II. ii. we read of such warriors who were "fiery," and from their encounters there "drizzled blood." Of many attempted emendations none is satisfactory. Malone conjectured " Astres with . . . Disastrous dimm'd the sun "; astre or aster is found in Florio's *Ital. Dict.* under " Stella " and in his translation of Montaigne. *New Eng. Dict.* explains "disasters" here as unfavourable aspects. The "moist star" is the moon—governess of floods; so in *Winter's Tale*, I. ii. 1: " Nine changes of the watery star." [By placing ll. 121-5 before l. 117, N. C. S. plausibly restores the sense without addition. R. H. C.]

122. *still*] constantly, as in *Tempest*, I. ii. 229; " the still vex'd Bermoothes."

And prologue to the omen coming on,
Have heaven and earth together demonstrated
Unto our climatures and countrymen. 125

Re-enter GHOST.

But, soft, behold! lo, where it comes again!
I 'll cross it, though it blast me. Stay, illusion!
If thou hast any sound, or use of voice,
Speak to me:
If there be any good thing to be done, 130
That may to thee do ease and grace to me,
Speak to me:
If thou art privy to thy country's fate,
Which, happily, foreknowing may avoid,
O, speak! 135
Or if thou hast uphoarded in thy life
Extorted treasure in the womb of earth,
For which, they say, you spirits oft walk in death,

[*The cock crows.*

Speak of it: stay, and speak! Stop it, Marcellus.

138. *you*] F, *your* Q. The cock crows] Q, omitted in F.

123. *omen*] the ominous event. Farmer cites from Heywood's *Life of Merlin* : "Merlin . . . His country's omen did long since foretell."

125. *climatures*] regions ; in which sense "climate" is commonly found. Dyce reads *climature*. Clar. Press suggests the inhabitants of our regions.

127. *I'll cross it, though it blast me*] Blakeway cites from Lodge's *Illustrations of British History*, iii. 48, a story of Ferdinando, Earl of Derby (who died 1594) : on Friday a tall man appeared, who twice crossed him swiftly ; and when the bewitched Earl came to the place where he saw this man, he first fell sick. Opposite this line Q has the stage direction : "It spreads his armes."

134. *happily*] haply. See II. ii. 408, and *Measure for Measure*, IV. ii. 98 (Clar. Press). Hudson explains it "fortunately." Furness writes : "The structure of this solemn appeal is almost identical with that of a very different strain in *As You Like It*, II. iv. 33-42."

Mar. Shall I strike at it with my partisan? 140
Hor. Do, if it will not stand.
Ber.   'Tis here!
Hor.   'Tis here!
Mar. 'Tis gone!   [*Exit Ghost.*
     We do it wrong, being so majestical,
     To offer it the show of violence;
     For it is, as the air, invulnerable, 145
     And our vain blows malicious mockery.
Ber. It was about to speak when the cock crew.
Hor. And then it started like a guilty thing
     Upon a fearful summons. I have heard,
     The cock, that is the trumpet to the morn, 150
     Doth with his lofty and shrill-sounding throat
     Awake the god of day; and, at his warning,
     Whether in sea or fire, in earth or air,
     The extravagant and erring spirit hies
     To his confine: and of the truth herein 155
     This present object made probation.
Mar. It faded on the crowing of the cock.
     Some say that ever 'gainst that season comes
     Wherein our Saviour's birth is celebrated,
     The bird of dawning singeth all night long; 160

140. *at*] F, omitted in Q.   150. *morn*] Q, *morning* Q 1, *day* F.   158. *say*] Q, *sayes* F.   160. *The*] Q 1, F; *This* Q.

140. *partisan*] a kind of halbert or pike.

150. *trumpet*] Malone quotes from England's *Parnassus*, 1600 (in a passage assigned to Drayton): "the cocke, the morning's trumpeter." "Trumpet" for "trumpeter" occurs in several passages of Shakespeare. *Henry V.* iv. ii. 61: "I will the banner from a trumpet take."

151. *lofty*] like "shrill," qualifies "sounding"; unless the uplifted throat of the crowing cock is meant.

154. *extravagant*] wandering out of bounds, vagrant. *Othello*, I. i. 137: "an extravagant and wheeling stranger." "Erring," straying.

156. *probation*] proof, as in *Measure for Measure*, v. 157.

And then, they say, no spirit can walk
  abroad;
The nights are wholesome; then no planets
  strike,
No fairy takes, nor witch hath power to
  charm,
So hallow'd and so gracious is the time.

Hor. So have I heard and do in part believe it. 165
But look, the Morn, in russet mantle clad,
Walks o'er the dew of yon high eastern
  hill;
Break we our watch up; and by my advice,
Let us impart what we have seen to-night
Unto young Hamlet; for, upon my life,   170
This spirit, dumb to us, will speak to him.
Do you consent we shall acquaint him
  with it,
As needful in our loves, fitting our duty?

Mar. Let's do 't, I pray; and I this morning
  know
Where we shall find him most conveniently. 175
                        [*Exeunt.*

---

161. *can walk*] F, *dare sturre* Q, *dare walke* Q 1.   163. *takes*] Q, *talkes* F.   164. *the*] F, *that* Q 1, Q.   167. *eastern*] F, *eastward* Q. 175. *conveniently*] Q 1, F; *convenient* Q.

161. *walk*] The Q "stir" has not the special ghostly significance of "walk," which is frequent in Shakespeare, *e.g. Winter's Tale*, v. i. 63: "Were I the ghost that walk'd."
162. *strike*] blast, especially of planetary influence. *Coriolanus*, II. ii. 117: "struck Corioli like a planet." Furness quotes Florio's *Dict.*: "As-

siderare: to blast or *strike* with a planet, to be *taken*."
163. *takes*] affects with malignant influence. *Merry Wives*, IV. iv. 32 (of Herne the Hunter):
  "And there he blasts the tree and
    takes the cattle."
So "taking airs" in *Lear*, II. iv. 166.

SCENE II.—*A Room of State in the Castle.*

Flourish.   Enter the KING, QUEEN, HAMLET, POLONIUS, LAERTES, VOLTIMAND, CORNELIUS, *Lords, and Attendants.*

King. Though yet of Hamlet our dear brother's death
The memory be green, and that it us befitted
To bear our hearts in grief and our whole king-
    dom
To be contracted in one brow of woe,
Yet so far hath discretion fought with nature   5
That we with wisest sorrow think on him,
Together with remembrance of ourselves.
Therefore our sometime sister, now our queen,
The imperial jointress of this warlike state,
Have we, as 'twere with a defeated joy,—   10
With one auspicious and one dropping eye,
With mirth in funeral and with dirge in marriage,
In equal scale weighing delight and dole,—
Taken to wife: nor have we herein barr'd
Your better wisdoms, which have freely gone   15
With this affair along: for all, our thanks.

Flourish] Q, omitted F; the stage direction here is Malone's. Q after
"Gertrad the Queene" has "Counsaile: as Polonius"; F names Ophelia as
present.   8. *sometime*] Q, *sometimes* F.   9. *of*] F, *to* Q.   11. *one*
. . . *one*] F, *an* . . . *a* Q.

9. *jointress*] Schmidt explains as dowager. Clar. Press: joint possessor. Hudson: heiress—"the Poet herein follows the history, which represents the former King to have come to his throne by marriage."

10. *defeated*] disfigured, marred, as in *Othello*, I. iii. 346; or destroyed, undone, as in *Othello*, IV. ii. 160: "his unkindness may defeat my life."

11.] Steevens notes the same thought in *Winter's Tale*, V. ii. 80, Grant White reads "drooping."

Now follows that you know: young Fortinbras,
Holding a weak supposal of our worth,
Or thinking by our late dear brother's death
Our state to be disjoint and out of frame, 20
Colleagued with the dream of his advantage,
He hath not fail'd to pester us with message,
Importing the surrender of those lands
Lost by his father, with all bonds of law,
To our most valiant brother. So much for him. 25
Now for ourself and for this time of meeting:
Thus much the business is; we have here writ
To Norway, uncle of young Fortinbras,—
Who, impotent and bed-rid, scarcely hears
Of this his nephew's purpose,—to suppress 30
His further gait herein; in that the levies,
The lists and full proportions, are all made
Out of his subject: and we here dispatch
You, good Cornelius, and you, Voltimand,
For bearers of this greeting to old Norway, 35
Giving to you no further personal power
To business with the king more than the scope

17. *know: young*] Walker; no comma after *know* Q, F; comma after
follows F.   21. *the*] F, *this* Q.   24. *bonds*] F, *bands* Q and many
editors.   25.] Enter Voltemand and Cornelius F.   26. *meeting:*] F 4,
meeting, Q, *meeting* F.   35. *For bearers*] Q 1, Q; *For bearing* F.

17. *that you know:*] that which
you know. The pointing is that
suggested by S. Walker; commonly
with commas after "follows" and
"know."

21. *Colleagued*] Theobald suggested
"Collogued," flattered, cajoled. The
"supposal," line 18, is colleagued,
united, with the "dream."

21. *his advantage*] his superiority
to us.

22. *pester*] annoy, and especially by
crowding, as in *Coriolanus*, IV. vi.
7: "Dissentious numbers pestering
streets."

23. *Importing*] having for import;
not, as Abbott explains, importuning.
See *Othello*, II. ii. 3.

32. *proportions*] number of troops,
as in *Henry V*. I. ii. 304: "let our
proportions for these wars Be soon
collected."

Of these delated articles allow.

Farewell, and let your haste commend your duty.

Cor., Vol. In that and all things will we show our
duty.   40

King. We doubt it nothing: heartily farewell.

                              [*Exeunt Voltimand and Cornelius.*

And now, Laertes, what's the news with you?

You told us of some suit; what is 't, Laertes?

You cannot speak of reason to the Dane,

And lose your voice: what would'st thou beg,
Laertes,   45

That shall not be my offer, not thy asking?

The head is not more native to the heart,

The hand more instrumental to the mouth,

Than is the throne of Denmark to thy father.

What would'st thou have, Laertes?

Laer.   Dread my lord,   50

Your leave and favour to return to France,

From whence though willingly I came to Denmark,

To show my duty in your coronation,

Yet now, I must confess, that duty done,

My thoughts and wishes bend again toward
France   55

38. *delated*] Q, *dilated* F, *related* Q 1.   40. Cor., Vol.] Q, Volt. F.   41.
Exeunt . . .] F 4, Exit: . . F, om. Q.   49. *is* . . . *to*] Q, F ; *to* . . .
is Warburton and other editors.   50. *Dread my*] F, *My dread* Q.   55.
toward] Q, *towards* F.

38. *delated*] Perhaps a different   47. *native*] cognate, connected by
spelling of the F "dilated," mean-   nature or birth, as in *All's Well*, I.
ing expressed at large. But it may   i. 238 : "To join like likes, and kiss
mean conveyed, carried, as in Bacon,   like native things."
Natural History: "the time wherein   53. *coronation*] In Q 1 Laertes asks
sound is delated . . . the delation   permission to leave "Now that the
of light is an instant."   funerall rites are all performed."

And bow them to your gracious leave and pardon.

King. Have you your father's leave? What says
    Polonius?

Pol. He hath, my lord, wrung from me my slow leave
    By laboursome petition, and at last
    Upon his will I seal'd my hard consent: 60
    I do beseech you, give him leave to go.

King. Take thy fair hour, Laertes; time be thine,
    And thy best graces spend it at thy will!
    But now, my cousin Hamlet, and my son,—

Ham. [*Aside.*] A little more than kin, and less than kind. 65

King. How is it that the clouds still hang on you?

Ham. Not so, my lord; I am too much i' the sun.

---

57. *Have . . . Polonius?*] Q, two lines F.   58. *He hath*] F, *Hath* Q.
58–60. *wrung . . . consent*] Q, omitted in F.   64.] Exit Q 1.   64.
son,—] *sonne.* Q, *sonne?* F, *son—* Rowe.   65. [*Aside*]] added by Theobald.
67. *so*] F, *so much* Q ; *i' the sun*] Capell, *i' th' Sun* F, *in the sonne* Q.

---

56. *pardon*] permission to depart, as
in III. ii. 332.

64. *cousin*] kinsman (exclusive of
parent, child, brother, and sister);
used elsewhere in Shakespeare for
uncle, niece, grandchild.

65.] It can hardly be doubted
that this — Hamlet's first word—is
spoken aside. Does it refer to the
King or to himself? If to himself, it
may mean a little more than a kinsman (for I am, incestuously, a step-
son), and less than kind, for I hate
the King. So Malone. Knight says
"little of the same *nature*" with
Claudius. More probably it refers
to the King, meaning : My step-father
(more than cousin), but in less than a
natural relation. Compare II. ii.
619: "lecherous, kindless (*i.e.* unnatural) villain." To "go" or
"grow out of kind" is found in
Baret's *Alvearie* and Cotgrave's
French Dict., meaning to degen-
erate or dishonour kindred. The
play upon kin or kindred and kind
or kindly is found in *Gorboduc*, in
Lyly's *Mother Bombie*, and in Rowley's
Search for Money. "Kind" for
"nature" occurs several times in
Shakespeare.

67. *i' the sun.*] Hamlet's delight in
ambiguous and double meanings
makes it probable that a play is intended on "sun" and "son." He
is too much in the sunshine of the
court, and too much in the relation
of son—son to a dead father, son to
an incestuous mother, son to an uncle-
father. It was suggested by Johnson
that there is an allusion to the
proverbial expression (see *Lear*, II.
ii. 168) : "Out of heaven's blessing
into the warm sun," which means to
be out of house and home ; Hamlet
is deprived of the throne. Schmidt
takes it to mean merely, "I am more
idle and careless than I ought to be."

2

Queen. Good Hamlet, cast thy nighted colour off,
And let thine eye look like a friend on Denmark.
Do not for ever with thy vailed lids   70
Seek for thy noble father in the dust:
Thou know'st 'tis common; all that lives must die,
Passing through nature to eternity.

Ham. Ay, madam, it is common.

Queen.   If it be,
Why seems it so particular with thee?   75

Ham. Seems, madam! nay, it is; I know not "seems."
'Tis not alone my inky cloak, good mother,
Nor customary suits of solemn black,
Nor windy suspiration of forced breath,
No, nor the fruitful river in the eye,   80
Nor the dejected haviour of the visage,
Together with all forms, modes, shows of grief,
That can denote me truly; these indeed "seem,"
For they are actions that a man might play;
But I have that within which passeth show;   85
These but the trappings and the suits of woe.

King. 'Tis sweet and commendable in your nature,
     Hamlet,

68. *nighted*] Q, *nightly* F. 70. *vailed*] Q; *veyled* Ff 1, 2; *veiled* Ff 3, 4. 72. *common;*] Theobald, *common,* F, *common* Q. *lives*] Q, F; *live* Ff 2, 3, 4 and many editors. 77. *good mother*] F; *coold mother* Qq 2, 3; *could smother* Qq 4–6. 82. *modes*] Q 1695, Capell; *moodes* Q; *Moods* F and many editors. *shows*] F; *chapes* Qq 2, 3; *shapes* Qq 4–6. 83. *denote*] F, Q 6; *deuote* Q. 85. *passeth*] F, *passes* Q. 87.] Q, two lines F.

68. *nighted*] black. So in *Lear*, IV. v. 13: "his nighted life" (of the blind Gloster).

69. *Denmark*] the King; so "Norway" in line 28.

70. *vailed*] cast down. *Merchant of Venice*, I. i. 28: "Vailing her high-top lower than her ribs."

82. *modes*] "Moods" may be right.

82. *shows*] The "show" of line 85, as Furness observes, is an intentional and emphatic repetition of the "shows" of this line.

To give these mourning duties to your father:
But, you must know, your father lost a father,
That father lost, lost his; and the survivor
    bound   90
In filial obligation for some term
To do obsequious sorrow; but to persever
In obstinate condolement is a course
Of impious stubbornness; 'tis unmanly grief;
It shows a will most incorrect to heaven,   95
A heart unfortified, a mind impatient,
An understanding simple and unschool'd:
For what we know must be and is as common
As any the most vulgar thing to sense,
Why should we in our peevish opposition   100
Take it to heart? Fie! 'tis a fault to heaven,
A fault against the dead, a fault to nature,
To reason most absurd, whose common theme
Is death of fathers, and who still hath cried,
From the first corse till he that died to-day,   105
" This must be so." We pray you, throw to earth
This unprevailing woe, and think of us
As of a father; for let the world take note,
You are the most immediate to our throne;
And with no less nobility of love   110

90. *lost, lost*] *dead, lost* Q 1.   96. *a mind*] F, *or minde* Q.   107. *un-prevailing*] *unavailing*, Hanmer.

92. *obsequious*] Suitable to obsequies, as in *Titus Andronicus*, v. iii. 152: "obsequious tears." See also *Sonnets*, xxxi. 5.

92. *persever*] Always accented by Shakespeare on the second syllable (Clar. Press).

107. *unprevailing*] unavailing. So " prevails " in *Romeo and Juliet*, III. iii. 60. Dryden, *Essay on Dramatic Poesy*: " He may often prevail himself of the same advantages."

109. *immediate*] The throne of Denmark was elective; see v. ii. 65; but Hamlet was the probable successor to Claudius.

Than that which dearest father bears his son
Do I impart toward you.   For your intent
In going back to school in Wittenberg,
It is most retrograde to our desire;
And we beseech you, bend you to remain   115
Here in the cheer and comfort of our eye,
Our chiefest courtier, cousin, and our son.

Queen. Let not thy mother lose her prayers, Hamlet:
I pray thee, stay with us; go not to Wittenberg.

Ham. I shall in all my best obey you, madam.   120

King. Why, 'tis a loving and a fair reply:
Be as ourself in Denmark.   Madam, come;
This gentle and unforced accord of Hamlet
Sits smiling to my heart; in grace whereof,
No jocund health that Denmark drinks to-day,   125
But the great cannon to the clouds shall tell,
And the king's rouse the heavens shall bruit again,

---

112. *toward*] Q, *towards* F.   113. *in Wittenberg*] *to Wittenberg*, Qq 4, 5.
119. *pray thee*] Q, *prythee* F.   120.] Q, two lines F.   127. *heavens*]
F, *heaven* Q.

112. *impart*] The verb has no object; perhaps it is a confused construction; possibly it is a case of the absorption of "it" by the "t" of "impart." To obtain an object Badham suggests the reading "nobility no less" in line 110. Johnson explains "impart" as impart myself.

113. *Wittenberg*] The university was founded in 1502; Luther had made it famous. In *The Tragedy of Hoffman* (1602), the foolish Ierom says, "I am no foole, I have bin at Wittenberg, where wit growes." Shakespeare may have heard of it in Marlowe's *Doctor Faustus*, and in Nash's *Life of Iacke Wilton*, 1594. It must be remembered that for Hamlet Wittenberg was a foreign university, to which he might go at any age, after his earlier education had been completed.

114. *retrograde*] Prof. Hales notes in Chapman's *May-Day* (vol. ii. p. 373, ed. 1873): "Be not retrograde to our desires." Originally an astrological term.   See *All's Well*, I. i. 212.

127. *rouse*] bumper, as in I. iv. 8, and *Othello*, II. iii. 66; Swedish *ras*, drunkenness.   Dekker, in *The Gul's Horn-Booke*, Proœmium, enumerating national drinking customs, mentions "the Danish Rowsa."

127. *bruit*] noise abroad, as in *Macbeth*, v. vii. 22.

Re-speaking earthly thunder.	Come away.

[*Flourish.	Exeunt all but Hamlet.*

Ham.	O! that this too too solid flesh would melt,

Thaw and resolve itself into a dew;	130

Or that the Everlasting had not fix'd

His canon 'gainst self-slaughter! O God! O God!

How weary, stale, flat, and unprofitable

Seem to me all the uses of this world!

Fie on 't! O fie! 'tis an unweeded garden	135

That grows to seed; things rank and gross in nature

Possess it merely.	That it should come to this!

But two months dead! nay, not so much, not two:

So excellent a king; that was, to this,

Hyperion to a satyr; so loving to my mother	140

That he might not beteem the winds of heaven

Flourish] Q, omitted F.	129. *solid*] F; *sallied* Q 1, Q; *sullied* Anon. conject.	132. *O God! O God!*] F, *ô God, God* Q.	134. *Seem*] Q, *Seemes* F.	135. *O fie!*] *ah fie* Q; *Oh fie, fie* F; *Oh fie* Ff 3, 4.	137. *come to this!*] F, *come thus* Q.

129. *too too*] Intensive reduplication; hyphened by some editors. Compare *Two Gentlemen of Verona*, II. iv. 205.

129. *solid*] *Solid* and *melt* are found in conjunction, as here, in *2 Henry IV.* III. i. 48. The *sallied* of Q and Q 1 is defended by Dr. Furnivall, who cites Cotgrave's *French Dict. saillie*, a sallie, eruption, violent issue; also *assaille*, assaulted, assayled. If we were to retain *sallied*, I should explain it as sullied, comparing II. i. 39, where F reads *sullyes* and Q *sallies*; and, seeing that Q 1 has here "this too much griev'd and sallied flesh," we have some reason to think that *sallied* may be right. See Appendix III. p. 238.

130. *resolve*] Caldecott cites Baret's *Alvearie*: "To thaw or resolve that

which is frozen, regelo." Compare *Timon*, IV. iii. 442.

132. *canon 'gainst self-slaughter*] So also *Cymbeline*, III. iv. 77–80. "Unless it be the sixth commandment, the 'canon' must be one of natural religion" (Wordsworth, *Shakespeare's Knowledge and Use of the Bible*, p. 149).

137. *merely*] completely. Compare *Tempest*, I. i. 59: "We are merely cheated of our lives."

140. *Hyperion*] Spenser, Gray, Keats, like Shakespeare, throw the accent on the second syllable.

141. *beteem*] permit; "beteene" in Ff 1, 2. So Golding, Ovid's *Metamorphoses* (published 1587):

"Yet could he not beteeme
The shape of any other bird then
eagle for to seeme."

Visit her face too roughly.   Heaven and earth!

Must I remember? why, she would hang on him,

As if increase of appetite had grown

By what it fed on ; and yet, within a month— 145

Let me not think on 't.—Frailty, thy name is woman!

A little month! or ere those shoes were old

With which she follow'd my poor father's body,

Like Niobe, all tears ; why she, even she—

O God ! a beast, that wants discourse of reason, 150

Would have mourn'd longer,—married with my uncle,

My father's brother, but no more like my father

Than I to Hercules.   Within a month?

Ere yet the salt of most unrighteous tears

Had left the flushing in her galled eyes,   155

She married.   O, most wicked speed, to post

With such dexterity to incestuous sheets!

It is not nor it cannot come to good ;

But break my heart, for I must hold my tongue!

143. *would*] F, *should* Q.   145. *month—*] *month,* Q, *month?* F.
147. *shoes*] Q, F ; *shows* Ingleby conj.   149. *even she*] F, omitted in Q.
150. *O God!*] Q, *O Heaven* F.   151. *my*]Q, *mine* F.   153. *month?*] F,
month, Q.   155. *the*] *their* Q 1 ; *in*] Q, *of* F.

147. *or ere*] "Or," an old form of
"ere"; so in line 183 of this scene, "Or
ever." The reduplication is found in
several other passages.

150. *discourse of reason*] discursive
power of reason. Found several
times in Florio's *Montaigne*, 1603.
Johnson's *Dictionary* defines *discourse*:
"the act of the understanding by which
it passes from premises to consequences." See IV. iv. 36, and *Troilus
and Cressida*, II. ii. 116.

153. *Hercules*] Perhaps a relic of the
history of Amlethus in Saxo Grammaticus, whose Hamlet is in some respects the opposite of Shakespeare's

Hamlet.   The closing words are:
"Hic Amlethi exitus fuit, qui si parem
naturæ atq. fortunæ indulgentiam
expertus fuisset, æquasset fulgore su-
peros, Herculea virtutibus opera
transcendisset."

155. *flushing*] Hudson and Rolfe
explain this as redness.   Clar. Press:
"The verb 'flush' is still used transi-
tively, meaning, to fill with water."

157. *dexterity*] adroitness.   Clar.
Press compares *1 Henry IV.* II. iv.
286.

159. *break*] "A subjunctive, not an
imperative, and 'heart' is a subject,
not a vocative" (Corson).

Enter HORATIO, MARCELLUS, *and* BERNARDO.

Hor. Hail to your lordship!

Ham.   I am glad to see you well: 160
  Horatio,—or I do forget myself.

Hor. The same, my lord, and your poor servant ever.

Ham. Sir, my good friend; I'll change that name with you:
  And what make you from Wittenberg, Horatio?
  Marcellus?   165

Mar. My good lord,—

Ham. I am very glad to see you.—[*To Bernardo.*]
  Good even, sir.—
  But what, in faith, make you from Wittenberg?

Hor. A truant disposition, good my lord.

Ham. I would not hear your enemy say so,   170
  Nor shall you do mine ear that violence,
  To make it truster of your own report
  Against yourself; I know you are no truant.
  But what is your affair in Elsinore?
  We'll teach you to drink deep ere you depart.   175

Hor. My lord, I came to see your father's funeral.

Ham. I pray thee, do not mock me, fellow-student;
  I think it was to see my mother's wedding.

---

165. *Marcellus?*] Capell, *Marcellus.* Q, F.   166. *lord,—*] Rowe; *lord.* Q,
F; *lord?* Cambridge.   167. *sir*] *sirs* Q 1.   170. *hear*] Q, *have* F.   171.
mine] F, *my* Q.   172. *make*] *take* Ff 2-4.   175. *to drink deep*] Q 1, F;
for to drinke Q.   177. *pray thee*] F, *pre thee* Q.   178. *see*] Q 1, F;
omitted Q.

160, 161.] Sir H. Irving, as Hamlet, delivers "I . . . well" as a conventional greeting to unrecognised
intruders; Hamlet then looks up and
perceives his friend.
    163. *change that name*] exchange
the name "friend." Johnson explains: "I'll be your servant, you
shall be my friend."
    164. *make you*] do you, as in II.
ii. 280.

Hor. Indeed, my lord, it follow'd hard upon.

Ham. Thrift, thrift, Horatio! the funeral baked-meats 180
Did coldly furnish forth the marriage tables.
Would I had met my dearest foe in heaven
Or ever I had seen that day, Horatio!
My father,—methinks I see my father.

Hor. O where, my lord?

Ham.   In my mind's eye, Horatio. 185

Hor. I saw him once; he was a goodly king.

Ham. He was a man, take him for all in all,
I shall not look upon his like again.

Hor. My lord, I think I saw him yesternight.

Ham. Saw? who?   190

Hor. My lord, the king your father.

Ham.   The king my father!

Hor. Season your admiration for a while
With an attent ear, till I may deliver,
Upon the witness of these gentlemen,
This marvel to you.

Ham.   For God's love, let me hear. 195

---

183. *Or ever I had*] Q, *Ere I had ever* F, *Ere ever I had* Q 1.   184. *My
father,*—] Rowe, *My father!* Cambridge, *O my father, my father,* Q 1.
185. *O where*] F, *Where* Q.   187. *in all,*] *in all* Q, *in all:* F.   190.
Saw? who?] F ; *Saw, who* Q 1, Q.   193. *attent*] Q, F; *attentive* Q 1, Qq
4–6, Ff 3, 4.   195. *God's*] *Gods* Q, *Heavens* F.

180. *baked-meats*] pastry. Collins:
"It was anciently the general custom
to give a cold entertainment to
mourners at a funeral. In distant
counties this practice is continued
among the yeomanry."

182. *dearest foe*] Clar. Press: "*Dear*
is used of whatever touches us nearly
either in love or hate, joy or sorrow."
In *1 Henry IV.* III. ii. 123, we find
"near'st and dearest enemy."

187. *a man,*] Edwin Booth, in
delivering this speech, paused after
"man," giving it as if something
higher than "king."

192. *Season your admiration*] Temper your astonishment. Compare, for
"season," II. i. 28, and for "admiration," III. ii. 342. So in Massinger's *The Renegado,* III. iii.
"Season your admiration."

Hor. Two nights together had these gentlemen,
    Marcellus and Bernardo, on their watch,
    In the dead vast and middle of the night,
    Been thus encounter'd : a figure like your father,
    Armed at point exactly, cap-a-pe,   200
    Appears before them, and with solemn march
    Goes slow and stately by them ; thrice he walk'd
    By their oppress'd and fear-surprised eyes,
    Within his truncheon's length ; whilst they, distill'd
    Almost to jelly with the act of fear,   205
    Stand dumb, and speak not to him.   This to me
    In dreadful secrecy impart they did ;
    And I with them the third night kept the watch ;
    Where, as they had deliver'd, both in time,
    Form of the thing, each word made true and
        good,   210
    The apparition comes.   I knew your father ;
    These hands are not more like.

Ham.   But where was this ?
Mar. My lord, upon the platform where we watch'd.

198. *vast*] Q 1, Qq 5, 6 ; *wast* Qq 2-4, F ; *waste* Ff 2-4 and many editors ;
waist Malone, Steevens, Variorum.   200. *Armed at point*] Q, *Armed to
poynt* Q 1, *Arm'd at all points* F.   202. *stately by them ; thrice*] Q,
stately : By them thrice F.   204. *his*] F, *this* Qq 4-6.   *distill'd*] Q, Q 1 ;
bestill'd F 1 ; *bestill'd* F 2 ; *be still'd* Ff 3, 4 ; *bechill'd* Collier (MS.).   205.
the act of] *th' effect of* Warburton.   213. *watch'd*] F, *watch* Q.

198. *vast*] vacancy, void, empti-
ness, as in *Tempest*, I. ii. 327, "vast
of night."   "Waste" of Ff has the
same sense.   Malone, supporting
"waist," quotes from Marston's *Malcontent* : "the immodest waist of
night."
    200. *at point exactly*] Clar. Press
explains "at all points," and quotes
Richard II. I. iii. 2 :

"*Mar.* Is Harry Hereford arm'd ?
    Aum. Yea, at all points."
    204. *distill'd*] melted. Dyce quotes
from Sylvester's *Du Bartas* : "Melt
thee, distill thee, turn to wax or snow."
Jelly is probably named because of
its quivering, like the quivering of
fear.
    205. *act*] action, operation, as in
Othello, III. iii. 328.

Ham. Did you not speak to it?

Hor.   My lord, I did;
But answer made it none; yet once methought 215
It lifted up it head and did address
Itself to motion, like as it would speak;
But even then the morning cock crew loud,
And at the sound it shrunk in haste away
And vanish'd from our sight.

Ham.   'Tis very strange. 220

Hor. As I do live, my honour'd lord, 'tis true;
And we did think it writ down in our duty
To let you know of it.

Ham. Indeed, indeed, sirs, but this troubles me.
Hold you the watch to-night?

Mar., Ber.   We do, my lord. 225

Ham. Arm'd, say you?

Mar., Ber.   Arm'd, my lord.

Ham.   From top to toe?

Mar., Ber. My lord, from head to foot.

Ham. Then saw you not his face?

Hor. O, yes, my lord; he wore his beaver up.

Ham. What, look'd he frowningly?   230

216. *it*] *its* Qq 5, 6, Ff 3, 4; *his* Q 1.   221. *honour'd*] *honourable* F1
2-4.   224. *Indeed, indeed*] Q 1, F; *Indeede* Q.   228. *face?*] F, *face*. Q.
230. *What, look'd he*] *How look't he*, Q 1.

214. *Did you*] Actors commonly emphasise "you"; Marcellus and Bernardo had been silent. Steevens argues for emphasis on "speak."

216. *it head*] "The possessive *it* occurs fourteen times in the Folio (not counting a doubtful case in *Two Gentlemen of Verona*, v. ii. 21), *it's* nine times, and *its* only once" (Rolfe). The usual form of the possessive of *it* in Elizabethan writers is *his*.

226. *Arm'd*] Refers, of course, to the Ghost.

228. *face?*] The Q *face*. may be right, uttered with a tone of disappointed expectation.

229. *beaver*] "In the 16th century the beaver became confounded with the visor, and could be pushed up entirely over the top of the helmet, and drawn down at pleasure" (Planché).

Hor. A countenance more in sorrow than in anger.

Ham. Pale, or red?

Hor. Nay, very pale.

Ham.   And fix'd his eyes upon you?

Hor. Most constantly.

Ham.   I would I had been there.

Hor. It would have much amazed you.   235

Ham. Very like, very like. Stay'd it long?

Hor. While one with moderate haste might tell a
hundred.

Mar., Ber. Longer, longer.

Hor. Not when I saw 't.

Ham.   His beard was grizzled? no?

Hor. It was, as I have seen it in his life,   240
A sable silver'd.

Ham.   I will watch to-night;
Perchance 'twill walk again.

Hor.   I warrant it will.

Ham. If it assume my noble father's person,
I 'll speak to it, though hell itself should gape
And bid me hold my peace. I pray you all,   245
If you have hitherto conceal'd this sight,
Let it be tenable in your silence still;
And whatsoever else shall hap to-night

---

232. *Pale, or*] Q, F ; *Pale or* Qq 4–6.   236. *Very like, very like*] Q 1,
F ; *Very like* Q.   239. *grizzled? no?*] *grissl'd, no.* Q, *grisly? no.* F,
grisly? Ff 2–4, *grizzled,—no?* Dyce.   241. *I will*] Q, *Ile* F.   242. *walk*] Q,
wake F; *warrant*] Q 1, Q ; *warrant you* F.   247. *tenable*] Q 1, Q ; *treble* F.

236. *like*] likely.
244. *gape*] Staunton suggests that
perhaps "gape" signifies *yell, howl,
roar*, rather than *yawn* or *open*, citing
Henry VIII. v. iv. 3.
247. *tenable*] The "treble" of F is

defended by Caldecott, meaning a
threefold obligation of silence. **G.**
Macdonald says, "The actor, in utter-
ing it, must point to each of the
three" witnesses. Clar. Press, "*treble*,
a mere misprint."

Give it an understanding, but no tongue:
I will requite your loves.   So fare you well: 250
Upon the platform, 'twixt eleven and twelve,
I 'll visit you.

All.   Our duty to your honour.

Ham. Your loves, as mine to you: farewell,

> [*Exeunt Horatio, Marcellus, and Bernardo.*

My father's spirit in arms! all is not well;
I doubt some foul play: would the night were
    come!   255
Till then sit still, my soul: foul deeds will rise,
Though all the earth o'erwhelm them, to men's eyes.

> [*Exit.*

SCENE III.—*A Room in Polonius's House.*

Enter LAERTES *and* OPHELIA.

Laer. My necessaries are embark'd; farewell:
And, sister, as the winds give benefit
And convoy is assistant, do not sleep,
But let me hear from you.

Oph.   Do you doubt that?

Laer. For Hamlet, and the trifling of his favour,   5

---

250. *you*] Q, *ye* F.   252. *duty*] *duties* Q 1.   253. *loves*] Q, *love* F.
254. *arms!*] F 4, *armes?* Ff 1–3, (*in armes*) in parenthesis Q.   256. *foul*] F.
fonde Q.   257. *them, to*] Pope included *Tho'* . . . *them* in parenthesis;
no comma after *them* in Q, F.

Scene III.

3. *convoy is assistant*] F (semicolon after *assistant*), *convay, in assistant* Q.
5. *favour*] Q, *favours* F and many editors.

---

255. *doubt*] suspect, fear.

Scene III.

3. *convoy*] means of **conveyance**.

Compare *All's Well*, IV. iv. 10 (Clar.
Press).   Perhaps it means an escort
of ships of war.

Hold it a fashion, and a toy in blood,
A violet in the youth of primy nature,
Forward, not permanent, sweet, not lasting,
The perfume and suppliance of a minute;
No more.

Oph.   No more but so?

Laer.   Think it no more: 10
For nature crescent does not grow alone
In thews and bulk; but, as this temple waxes,
The inward service of the mind and soul
Grows wide withal.   Perhaps he loves you
    now;
And now no soil nor cautel doth besmirch   15
The virtue of his will; but you must fear,
His greatness weigh'd, his will is not his own;
For he himself is subject to his birth;
He may not, as unvalued persons do,
Carve for himself, for on his choice depends   20

---

8. *Forward*] Q, Ff 3, 4; *Froward* F; *sweet, not*] *tho' sweet, not* Rowe, *sweet, but not* Capell.   9. *perfume and*] Q, omitted F.   10. *so?*] Rowe, *so.* Q, F.   12. *bulk*] F, *bulkes* Q; *this*] Q, *his* F.   16. *will*] Q, *feare* F. 18.] Omitted in Q.   20. *Carve*] *Crave* Qq 4-6.

6. *fashion, and a toy in blood*] a mode of youth, that he should serve a mistress, and a play of amorous temperament.

7. *primy*] of the spring-time.

8. No metrical emendation is necessary; the speaker dwells on "sweet," as if to draw out its meaning, and pauses slightly.

9. *suppliance*] Mason explains "an amusement to fill up a vacant moment."

10. *so?*] Corson prefers the "so." of Q, F; Ophelia does not question but submits.

13. *service*] Suggested, in the sense of religious service, by "temple."

15. *cautel*] craft, deceit. Used by Shakespeare only here and in *A Lover's Complaint*, 303. Cotgrave's *French Dict.* gives "Cautelle, a wile, cautell, deceit."

20. *Carve for himself*] Rushton quotes from Swinburn's *Treatise on Wills*, 1590: "it is not lawful for legataries to carve for themselves, taking their legacies at their own pleasure."

The safety and health of this whole state;
And therefore must his choice be circumscribed
Unto the voice and yielding of that body
Whereof he is the head.   Then if he says he loves you,
If fits your wisdom so far to believe it   25
As he in his particular act and place
May give his saying deed; which is no further
Than the main voice of Denmark goes withal.
Then weigh what loss your honour may sustain,
If with too credent ear you list his songs,   30
Or lose your heart, or your chaste treasure open
To his unmaster'd importunity.
Fear it, Ophelia, fear it, my dear sister,
And keep you in the rear of your affection,
Out of the shot and danger of desire.   35
The chariest maid is prodigal enough
If she unmask her beauty to the moon;
Virtue itself 'scapes not calumnious strokes;
The canker galls the infants of the spring
Too oft before their buttons be disclosed,   40
And in the morn and liquid dew of youth

21. *safety*] Q, *sanctity* F and many editors, *sanity* Hanmer (Theobald conj.); *health*] *the health* Warburton and many editors; *this*] Q, *the* F. 26. *particular act and place*] Q, *peculiar Sect and force* F.   34. *keep you in*] Q, *keepe within* F.   39. *infants*] Qq 2, 3, F; *infant* Qq 4–6, Ff 2–4. 40. *their*] Q, *the* F.

21. *safety*] "Sanity," as conjectured by Theobald, may be right. Safety is a trisyllable in Spenser's *Faerie Queene*, v. 4, 46 : "Where he himself did rest in safety"; but in line 43 of this scene it has the usual pronunciation, and so elsewhere in Shakespeare.

26. *particular act and place*] Editors make new readings by various combinations from Q and F. White reads "peculiar sect and place," understanding "sect" as class, rank.

36. *chariest*] Hudson reads "Th' unchariest," that is, the least reserved. "Chariest" means entirely modest.

39. *canker*] the canker-worm.

40. *buttons*] buds (Fr. *bouton*), as in *Two Noble Kinsmen*, III. i. 6.

Contagious blastments are most imminent.
Be wary then; best safety lies in fear:
Youth to itself rebels, though none else near.

Oph. I shall the effect of this good lesson keep, 45
As watchman to my heart. But, good my brother,
Do not, as some ungracious pastors do,
Show me the steep and thorny way to heaven,
Whilst, like a puff'd and reckless libertine,
Himself the primrose path of dalliance treads 50
And recks not his own rede.

Laer. O, fear me not.
I stay too long; but here my father comes.

Enter POLONIUS.

A double blessing is a double grace;
Occasion smiles upon a second leave.

Pol. Yet here, Laertes! Aboard, aboard, for shame! 55
The wind sits in the shoulder of your sail,
And you are stay'd for. There; my blessing with thee!
And these few precepts in thy memory
Look thou character. Give thy thoughts no tongue,

46. *watchman*] Q; *watchmen* Qq 4–6, F. 49. *Whilst*] F, *Whiles* Q, which omits *like*. 51. *rede*] Singer (ed. 2), *reed* Q, *reade* F. Enter *Polonius*] Capell, after *reed* Q, after *not* F. 57. *for. There;*] Theobald; *for, there* Q 1, Q; *for there:* F. *thee*] Q 1, Q; *you* F. 59. *Look*] Q, *See* F and many editors.

47. *ungracious*] graceless. "Swearest thou, ungracious boy?" *1 Henry IV.* ii. iv. 490.
49. *puff'd*] bloated. See *Merry Wives*, v. v. 160.
50. *primrose path*] Compare *Macbeth*, ii. iii. 21.
51. *recks . . . rede*] cares not for his own counsel. Clar. Press cites Burns, *Epistle to a Young Friend*: " And may ye better reck the rede."

59. Parallels for several of these precepts have been pointed out by Rushton (*Shakespeare's Euphuism*, p. 46) in Lyly's *Euphues*, and by Hunter in Lord Burghley's ten precepts for his son Robert.
59. *character*] Shakespeare accents the verb either, as here, on the second syllable, or on the first, as in *Sonnets*, cxxii. 2.

Nor any unproportion'd thought his act.   60
Be thou familiar, but by no means vulgar;
The friends thou hast, and their adoption tried,
Grapple them to thy soul with hoops of steel,
But do not dull thy palm with entertainment
Of each new-hatch'd, unfledged comrade.   Be-
     ware   65
Of entrance to a quarrel; but, being in,
Bear 't that the opposed may beware of thee.
Give every man thine ear, but few thy voice;
Take each man's censure, but reserve thy judgment.
Costly thy habit as thy purse can buy,   70
But not express'd in fancy; rich, not gaudy;
For the apparel oft proclaims the man;
And they in France of the best rank and station
Are most select and generous, chief in that.

62. *The*] F; *Those* Q 1, Q.   63. *them to*] Q 1, F; *them unto* Q; *hoops*] *hooks*, Pope and several editors.   65. *new-hatch'd*] Q, *unhatch't* F; *comrade*] F; *courage* Q 1, Q.   67. *opposed*] Q, F; *opposer* Qq 4–6.   68. *thine*] F, *thy* Q.   74. *Are . . . that*] Rowe, followed by many editors; *Are of a most select and generall chiefe in that:* Q 1; *Or of a most select and generous, chiefe in that:* Qq 2, 3; *Ar of a most select and generous, cheefe in that:* Q 4; *Are of a most select and generous, chiefe in that:* Qq 5, 6; *Are of a most select and generous cheff in that,* Ff.   See note below.

61. *vulgar*] common; be easy in your manners but do not make yourself cheap.

63. *hoops*] Clar. Press remarks in opposition to Pope's *hooks*: "grappling with hooks is the act of an enemy and not of a friend."

65. *comrade*] Accented on the second syllable, as in *1 Henry IV*. IV. i. 96. If the *courage* of Q be right, it must be understood as *bravery*, frequent in our old drama in the sense of a gallant. Examples of *courage* used of a person are cited in *New Eng. Dict.* from Hoby (1561) and W. Browne (1647).

69. *censure*] opinion, as in *Macbeth*, v. iv. 14: "our just censures."

74. *Are . . . that*] If we read "Are of a most select and generous chief in that," *chief* may be taken to mean *eminence*, as in Horman (quoted in *New Eng. Dict.*), "He wanne the chieffe at every game." If we read as here, *chief* means chiefly. The Cambridge editors suggest that "chiefe" and "of" in the margin of the MS. were meant as alternatives for "best" and "in," line 73, and got by mistake into line 74. They, therefore, favour White's "Are most select and gener-

Neither a borrower nor a lender be;   75
For loan oft loses both itself and friend,
And borrowing dulls the edge of husbandry.
This above all: to thine own self be true,
And it must follow, as the night the day,
Thou canst not then be false to any man.   80
Farewell: my blessing season this in thee!

Laer. Most humbly do I take my leave, my lord.

Pol. The time invites you; go, your servants tend.

Laer. Farewell, Ophelia, and remember well
What I have said to you.

Oph.   'Tis in my memory lock'd,   85
And you yourself shall keep the key of it.

Laer. Farewell.   [*Exit*

Pol. What is 't, Ophelia, he hath said to you?

Oph. So please you, something touching the Lord
Hamlet.

Pol. Marry, well bethought: 90
'Tis told me, he hath very oft of late

---

75. *lender be*] F, *lender boy* Q.   77. *dulls the edge*] F, *dulleth edge* Q, *dulleth the edge* Qq 4, 5.   83. *invites*] F, *inuests* Q.

ous in that." Staunton, reading "of a most," suggests *sheaf*, meaning class or set, for which he quotes examples from Jonson's plays. Malone, noting the heraldic meaning of *chef*, the upper third part of the shield, explains "approve themselves to be of a most select and generous escutcheon by their dress." Steevens conjectures "Select and generous, are most choice in that." Spence (*Notes and Queries*, 1875) proposes "Are, of a most, select and generous, chief in that" (*of a most* meaning mostly). Collier (MS.) reads: "Are of a most select and generous choice in that." I throw out the suggestion that we may retain *Or* from

Q, and emend *and*, reading "Or of a most select, are generous chief in that"—Polonius adding to "best rank and station" those who, though not of the "best," are yet of a select rank.

77. *husbandry*] thrift, as in *Macbeth*, II. i. 4.

81. *season*] Singer quotes Baret's *Alvearie*: "*To season* . . . to temper wisely, to make more pleasant and acceptable." Schmidt explains it "mature, ripen." Clar. Press compares *Merchant of Venice*, v. i. 107.

83. *invites*] Theobald follows Q *invests*, explaining it "besieges, presses upon you on every side."

3

Given private time to you, and you yourself
Have of your audience been most free and boun-
   teous :
If it be so—as so 'tis put on me,
And that in way of caution—I must tell you,   95
You do not understand yourself so clearly
As it behoves my daughter and your honour.
What is between you? give me up the truth.

Oph. He hath, my lord, of late made many tenders
   Of his affection to me.   100

Pol. Affection! pooh! you speak like a green girl,
Unsifted in such perilous circumstance.
Do you believe his tenders, as you call them?

Oph. I do not know, my lord, what I should think.

Pol. Marry, I'll teach you: think yourself a baby,   105
That you have ta'en these tenders for true pay,
Which are not sterling. Tender yourself more
   dearly;
Or—not to crack the wind of the poor phrase,
Running it thus—you'll tender me a fool.

Oph. My lord, he hath importuned me with love   110
In honourable fashion.

---

105. *I'll*] F, *I will* Q.   106. *these*] Q, *his* F.   109. *Running*]
Collier conj., Dyce, Cambridge, Furness ; *Wrong* Q; *Roaming* F ; *Wronging*
Pope and several editors ; *Wringing*, Warburton, Theobald and others ;
tender] render F 4.

94. *put on*] communicated to, as in
As You Like It, I. ii. 99.
  102. *Unsifted*] untried.
  103. *tenders*] Compare Middleton,
Women Beware Women, I. ii. : "If
now this daughter so tender'd—let
me come to your own phrase, sir."
  107. *Tender*] regard, take care of,
hold dear—frequent in Shakespeare.
  109. *Running*] Clar. Press, accepting this reading proposed by Collier,
observes its accordance with the figure
in the previous line.
  109. *fool*] Does this mean, You will
present yourself to me as a fool? or,
present me (to the public) as a fool?
or, can "fool" mean an innocent, a
baby?—for Polonius is not over-deli-
cate in his warnings. See *Romeo and
Juliet*, I. iii. 31 and 48.

Pol. Ay, fashion you may call it; go to, go to.

Oph. And hath given countenance to his speech, my
　　　lord,

　　　With almost all the holy vows of heaven.

Pol. Ay, springes to catch woodcocks. I do know,　115
　　　When the blood burns, how prodigal the soul
　　　Lends the tongue vows: these blazes, daughter,
　　　Giving more light than heat, extinct in both,
　　　Even in their promise, as it is a-making,
　　　You must not take for fire. From this time　120
　　　Be somewhat scanter of your maiden presence;
　　　Set your entreatments at a higher rate
　　　Than a command to parley. For Lord Hamlet,
　　　Believe so much in him, that he is young,
　　　And with a larger tether may he walk　125
　　　Than may be given you: in few, Ophelia,
　　　Do not believe his vows; for they are brokers,
　　　Not of that dye which their investments show,
　　　But mere implorators of unholy suits,

---

114. *almost . . . holy*] Q, *all the* F.　117. *Lends*] Q 1, Q; *Gives* F.
118. *both*] *birth* Badham conj.　120. *From this time*] Q, *For this time
Daughter,* F.　121. *somewhat*] F, *something* Q.　123. *parley*] F, *parle* Q.
128. *that dye*] Q, *the eye* F.

115. *woodcocks*] birds supposed to be witless, easily taken in springes or snares. Clar. Press quotes from Gosson's *Apologie for the Schoole of Abuse*: "Cupid sets up a springe for woodcocks."

117.] To amend the verse Pope read "Oh, my daughter"; Capell, "gentle daughter"; Nicholson conj. "bavin blazes"; S. T. Coleridge, "Go to, these," or "daughter, mark you."

122. *entreatments*] Johnson explains as company, conversation, French *entrétien*; Clar. Press, solicitations; Schmidt, invitations received; *New Eng. Dict.*, conversation, interview, from the commoner meaning of negotiation, discussion.

127. *brokers*] middlemen in making bargains; used specially of panders, procurers. Furness quotes Cotgrave: "*Maquinonner*, To play the Broker, also to play the bawd."

128. *dye . . . show*] colour shown by their vesture or garb. F "the eye" may mean tint or hue, as in *Tempest*, II. i. 55.

Breathing like sanctified and pious bawds,   130
The better to beguile. This is for all:
I would not, in plain terms, from this time forth,
Have you so slander any moment's leisure,
As to give words or talk with the Lord Hamlet.
Look to 't, I charge you; come your ways.   135
Oph. I shall obey, my lord.   [*Exeunt*

SCENE IV.—*The Platform.*

Enter HAMLET, HORATIO, *and* MARCELLUS.

Ham. The air bites shrewdly; it is very cold.
Hor. It is a nipping and an eager air.
Ham. What hour now?
Hor.   I think it lacks of twelve.
Mar. No, it is struck.
Hor. Indeed? I heard it not: it then draws near the
     season   5
Wherein the spirit held his wont to walk.
          [*A flourish of trumpets, and ordnance
                              shot off, within.*
What does this mean, my lord?

130. *bawds*] Theobald, Pope (ed. 2), Hanmer, Cambridge, Furness, Hudson; *bonds* Q, F and many editors.   133. *slander*] *squander*, Collier (MS.); *moment's*] Pope; *moments* Qq 4–6; *moment*, Qq 2, 3, F.   135. *ways*] *way* Ff 2–4.

Scene IV.
Scene IV.] Capell, omitted F.   1. *it is very cold*] Q, *is it very cold?* F.
5. *Indeed? I*] Capell; *Indeed; I* Q; *Indeed I* Q 1, F; *it then*] Q, *then it* F.
6. A flourish, etc.] Malone after Capell, A florish of trumpets and 2 peeces goes of Q, omitted F.

130. *bawds*] "Bonds" of Q, F is explained as vows or (Moberly) as law papers headed with religious formulæ.
133. *moment's*] Clar. Press, reading "moment," regards it as an adjective.   *Scene IV.*
2. *eager*] sharp (Fr. *aigre*), as in I. v. 69.

Ham. The king doth wake to-night and takes his rouse,
 Keeps wassail, and the swaggering up-spring reels;
 And as he drains his draughts of Rhenish down, 10
 The kettle-drum and trumpet thus bray out
 The triumph of his pledge.
Hor.   Is it a custom?
Ham. Ay, marry, is't;
 But to my mind, though I am native here
 And to the manner born, it is a custom   15
 More honour'd in the breach than the observance.
 This heavy-headed revel east and west
 Makes us traduced and tax'd of other nations;
 They clepe us drunkards, and with swinish phrase
 Soil our addition; and indeed it takes   20
 From our achievements, though perform'd at height,
 The pith and marrow of our attribute.
 So, oft it chances in particular men,

---

9. *wassail*] Q 1, Q; *wassels,* F.   12. *Is it*] *It is* F 2.   14. *But*] Q,
And F.   17-38. *This . . . scandal*] Q; omitted Q 1, F.

8. *wake*] hold a late revel; "so, in poets of a much earlier date, we find the words *watch* and *watching* employed as equivalent to 'debauch at night'" (Dyce, *Glossary*).

8. *rouse*] see I. ii. 127.

9. *up-spring*] Pope read "upstart," meaning the King. In Chapman's *Alphonsus* up-spring is named as a German dance. Elze shows that it was the *Hüpfauf,* "the last and consequently wildest dance at the old German merrymakings." The verb "reels" is taken by Staunton as a plural noun.

11. *kettle-drum*] Cleveland in *Fuscara, or The Bee Errant,* has the line "As Danes carowse by kettle-drums."

12. *triumph of his pledge*] his glorious achievement as drinker. Howell in his *Letters* tells of the Danish King Christian IV. (1588-1649) beginning thirty-five healths during a feast—"the King was taken away at last in his chair."

18. *tax'd*] censured; frequent in Shakespeare.

19. *clepe*] call, as in *Macbeth,* III. i. 94.

20. *addition*] something added by way of distinction, style of address, as in *Lear,* I. i. 138 : "The name and all the additions to a King."

22. *attribute*] what is attributed; hence reputation, as in *Troilus and Cressida,* II. iii. 125 : "Much attribute he hath."

That for some vicious mole of nature in them,
As, in their birth,— wherein they are not
   guilty,   25
Since nature cannot choose his origin,—
By the o'ergrowth of some complexion,
Oft breaking down the pales and forts of reason,
Or by some habit that too much o'er-leavens
The form of plausive manners; that these
   men,—   30
Carrying, I say, the stamp of one defect,
Being nature's livery, or fortune's star,—
Their virtues else—be they as pure as grace,
As infinite as man may undergo—
Shall in the general censure take corruption   35
From that particular fault : the dram of evil
Doth all the noble substance of a doubt
To his own scandal.

27. *the*] Pope, *their* Q.   32. *star*] Q, *scar* Theobald, Pope (ed. 2).
33. *Their*] Theobald, Pope (ed. 2) ; *His* Q.   36, 37.] See note below.

24. *mole of nature*] natural blemish. Theobald suggested "mould." Prof. Hales notes in Greene's *Pandosto* : "One mole staineth the whole face."

26. *his*] its.

27. *complexion*] temperament, resulting from the supposed combination of the four "humours" in the body in various proportions ; the complexions were sanguine, melancholic, choleric, and phlegmatic.

30. *plausive*] pleasing, popular. *All's Well*, I. ii. 53 : "plausive words."

32. *star*] perhaps a mark like a star. *Cymbeline*, v. v. 364 : "Upon his neck a mole, a sanguine star."

33. *Their*] *His* of Q may be Shakespeare's word, though grammatically incorrect.

34. *undergo*] support. *Measure for Measure*, I. i. 24 : "To undergo such ample grace and honour."

35. *censure*] opinion, judgment, as in I. iii. 69.

36–38. *the dram . . . scandal*] This difficult and perhaps corrupt passage is here printed as in Qq 2, 3, except that for *evil* these Qq read *eale*. The later Qq read *ease*. In II. ii. 638 : "May be a devil; and the devil hath power," Qq 2, 3 have *deale*; *evil* is frequently a monosyllable in Elizabethan poetry. I can hardly regard *evil* as an emendation open to reasonable doubt. The letters *vi* of a MS. might easily be mistaken for an Elizabethan manuscript *a*; the second *l* in "evill," "devill" might be taken for an *e*, or the

Enter GHOST.

Hor.   Look, my lord, it comes!

Ham. Angels and ministers of grace defend us!—

Be thou a spirit of health or goblin damn'd,   40

Bring with thee airs from heaven or blasts from hell,

Be thy intents wicked or charitable,

Thou comest in such a questionable shape

That I will speak to thee: I 'll call thee Hamlet,

King, father; Royal Dane, O, answer me!   45

Let me not burst in ignorance; but tell

Why thy canoniz'd bones, hearsed in death,

---

42. *intents*] Q, *events* F.   45. *father; Royal Dane, O*] Anon. conj. *St. James's Chronicle*, 15th Oct. 1761; *father, royal Dane, ô* Q; *Father, Royal Dane: Oh, oh* F.

MS. may have had *evile, devile*. It is possible, as Keightley suggests, that the sentence is interrupted before its completion by the Ghost's entrance. Most commentators regard it as complete, and attempt to emend "of a doubt." About eighty proposals are recorded in the *Cambridge Shakespeare*. Perhaps "often dout," meaning do out, efface, is the best of these. "Oft devote" (consign to evil) seems not to have been proposed. I would suggest what I suppose to be a new line of consideration. "Scandal" is commonly regarded as a noun; although "doth" is separated from "scandal" by one of those suspensions, by qualifying clauses, characteristic of this speech, may not "doth scandal" be the verb? We have in *Cymbeline*, III. iv. 62: "Sinon's weeping Did scandal many a holy tear." Here "the dram of evil doth scandal all the noble substance." The idea is that required; the language is Shakespearean. *To* in Shakespeare often means *as far as*; if we met "I am scandal'd to ignominy," we should understand it, like "sick to doomsday" (I. i. 120). The dram of evil scandals all the noble substance to its own (substance); "his" being here used for the modern "its." "Of" is frequent in the sense of *out of, by virtue of, e.g. Love's Labour's Lost*, II. 28: "Bold of your worthiness," and we still say "of your charity." Out of a mere doubt or suspicion the dram of evil degrades in reputation all the noble substance to its own. "Scandal" may have been meant to precede "to his own."

40. *spirit of health*] Clar. Press explains: "a healed or saved spirit."

43. *questionable*] inviting question. In *As You Like It*, III. ii. 393, "unquestionable," averse to conversation, occurs.

45. *father; Royal Dane, O,*] The pointing leads to "father" as the completion of the climax. This reading is adopted by Furness.

47. *canoniz'd*] The accent, as always in Shakespeare, is on the second syllable.

Have burst their cerements; why the sepulchre,
Wherein we saw thee quietly inurn'd,
Hath oped his ponderous and marble jaws,   50
To cast thee up again.   What may this mean,
That thou, dead corse, again, in complete steel,
Revisit'st thus the glimpses of the moon,
Making night hideous; and we fools of nature
So horridly to shake our disposition   55
With thoughts beyond the reaches of our souls?
Say, why is this? wherefore? what should we do?
                              [*Ghost beckons Hamlet.*

Hor. It beckons you to go away with it,
    As if it some impartment did desire
    To you alone.

Mar.   Look, with what courteous action   60
    It waves you to a more removed ground:
    But do not go with it.

Hor.   No, by no means.

Ham. It will not speak; then I will follow it.

Hor. Do not, my lord.

Ham.   Why, what should be the fear?
    I do not set my life at a pin's fee;   65
    And for my soul, what can it do to that,
    Being a thing immortal as itself?
    It waves me forth again; I 'll follow it.

49. *inurn'd*] F, *interr'd* Q 1, Q.   53. *Reuisit'st*] F 4, *Reuisites* Q,
Reuisits F.   56. *the reaches*] Q, *thee; reaches* F.   61. *waves*] Q 1, Q;
wafts F.   63. *I will*] Q, *will I* F.

52. *complete*] Accented here on the   54. *fools of nature*] The presence
first syllable. So in Massinger, *The*   of the supernatural shows how the
Emperor of the East, IV. iv. : "To   limitations of nature cheat and befool
march ten leagues a day in complete   us.
armour."

Hor. What if it tempt you toward the flood, my
    lord,
    Or to the dreadful summit of the cliff   70
    That beetles o'er his base into the sea,
    And there assume some other horrible form,
    Which might deprive your sovereignty of reason
    And draw you into madness? think of it;
    The very place puts toys of desperation,   75
    Without more motive, into every brain
    That looks so many fathoms to the sea
    And hears it roar beneath.

Ham.   It waves me still.—
    Go on; I 'll follow thee.

Mar. You shall not go, my lord.

Ham.   Hold off your hands!   80

Hor. Be ruled; you shall not go.

Ham.   My fate cries out,
    And makes each petty artery in this body
    As hardy as the Nemean lion's nerve.

                       [*Ghost beckons.*

    Still am I call'd? Unhand me, gentlemen;
                 [*Breaking from them.*

---

72. *assume*] Q, *assumes* F.   74. *draw*] *drive* Q 1.   75-78. *The very . . . beneath*] Q, omitted F.   78. *waves*] Q, *wafts* F.   80. *hands*] Q, *hand* F.   84. *call'd?*] F, *cald*, Q.

73. *deprive your sovereignty of reason*] Warburton, followed by Hanmer, reads *deprave*. For deprive see *Rape of Lucrece*, 1186 and 1752. Caldecott explains: "Dispossess the sovereignty of your reason." In the *Historie of Hamblet*, IV., "deprive himself" means lose the right to the throne.

75-78.] Delius suggests that these lines were omitted from the F because their substance, enlarged and elaborated, had been introduced into *King Lear.*

75. *toys*] freaks. See *Romeo and Juliet*, IV. i. 119: "inconstant toy."

83. *Nemean*] So accented also in *Love's Labour's Lost*, IV. i. 90.

83. *nerve*] muscle or sinew; so "nervy arm," *Coriolanus*, II. i. 177.

By heaven, I'll make a ghost of him that lets

me: 85

I say, away!—Go on; I'll follow thee.

                    [Exeunt Ghost and Hamlet.

Hor. He waxes desperate with imagination.

Mar. Let's follow; 'tis not fit thus to obey him.

Hor. Have after.—To what issue will this come?

Mar. Something is rotten in the state of Denmark.   90

Hor. Heaven will direct it.

Mar.   Nay, let's follow him.

                         [Exeunt.

SCENE V.—*Another Part of the Platform.*

Enter GHOST *and* HAMLET.

Ham. Whither wilt thou lead me? speak; I'll go no

further.

Ghost. Mark me.

Ham.   I will.

Ghost.   My hour is almost come,

When I to sulphurous and tormenting flames

Must render up myself.

Ham.   Alas, poor ghost!

Ghost. Pity me not, but lend thy serious hearing   5

To what I shall unfold.

Ham.   Speak; I am bound to hear.

Ghost. So art thou to revenge, when thou shalt hear.

Ham. What?

Ghost. I am thy father's spirit;

Doom'd for a certain term to walk the night,   10
And for the day confined to fast in fires,
Till the foul crimes done in my days of nature
Are burnt and purged away. But that I am
  forbid   *although?*
To tell the secrets of my prison-house,
I could a tale unfold whose lightest word   15
Would harrow up thy soul, freeze thy young blood,
Make thy two eyes, like stars, start from their
  spheres,
Thy knotted and combined locks to part
And each particular hair to stand an end,
Like quills upon the fretful porpentine: 20
But this eternal blazon must not be
To ears of flesh and blood. List, list, O, list!
If thou didst ever thy dear father love—

Ham. O God!

18. *knotted*] Q 1, Q ; *knotty* F.   19. *an end*] *on end* Q 1 and many
editors.   20. *fretful*] Q 1, F ; *fearefull* Q.   22. *List, list,*] Q, *list
Hamlet*, F.   23. *love*—] Rowe ; *love.* Q, F.   24. *God*] Q, *Heauen* F.

11. *to fast in*] Chaucer, *Persones Tale*, writes : "And moreover the miseise of helle shal been in defaute of mete and drinke" (Skeat's ed. iv. 577). In *Dekker his Dreame* (1620) one of the souls burning in hell roars for "cookes to give him meate." Theobald conjectured "confined fast"; Warburton read "too fast in"; Heath proposed "to lasting"; Steevens "to waste in."

19. *an end*] So in *2 Henry VI.*

III. ii. 318 : "Mine hair be fix'd an end" F ("on end" Qq).

20. *porpentine*] porcupine, as in *Comedy of Errors* III. i. 116. "Porcupine," given here by many editors, first appeared in Q 1676.

21. *eternal blazon*] promulgation of eternity. But "eternal" was used by Shakespeare as an adjective expressing abhorrence—"eternal devil," *Julius Cæsar*, I. ii. 160; "eternal villain," *Othello*, IV. ii. 130; possibly it has a like sense here.

Ghost. Revenge his foul and most unnatural murder. 25

Ham. Murder?

Ghost. Murder most foul, as in the best it is,
But this most foul, strange, and unnatural.

Ham. Haste me to know 't, that I, with wings as swift
As meditation or the thoughts of love, 30
May sweep to my revenge.

Ghost.   I find thee apt;
And duller shouldst thou be than the fat weed
That roots itself in ease on Lethe wharf,
Wouldst thou not stir in this.   Now, Hamlet, hear:
'Tis given out that, sleeping in mine orchard, 35
A serpent stung me; so the whole ear of Denmark
Is by a forged process of my death
Rankly abused; but know, thou noble youth,
The serpent that did sting thy father's life
Now wears his crown.

Ham.   O my prophetic soul! 40
My uncle?

Ghost. Ay, that incestuous, that adulterate beast,
With witchcraft of his wit, with traitorous gifts,—

26. *Murder?*] F, *Murther*. Q, *Murder!* Q6 and many editors.   27. *best*] *least* Q 1.   29. *Haste me*] Q, *Hast, hast me* F.   33. *roots*] Q 1, Q; *rots* F and many editors.   35. *'Tis*] Q, *It's* F; *mine*] F, *my* Q.   41. *My*] Q, *Mine* F.   *uncle?*] Q, F; *Uncle:* Q 4; *Uncle.* Q 5; *Uncle!* Q 6 and many editors.   43. *wit*] Pope; *wits* Q, F; *with*] Q, *hath* F, *and* F 4.

30. *meditation . . . love*] Hamlet's comparisons are appropriate to him—those of a thinker and a lover.

33. *roots*] The F *rots* receives some support from *Ant. and Cleop.* I. iv. 47: "rot itself."

33. *wharf*] seems used for bank of a river. See *Ant. and Cleop.* II. ii. 218.

37. *forged process*] falsified account.

Clar. Press suggests "official narrative," comparing the French *procès verbal*.

40. *O . . . soul*] This occurs also in Fletcher's *The Double Marriage*, II. iv. (vol. vi. 351, ed. Dyce); in Massinger's *The Bondman*, IV. i., and his *Emperor of the East* (near end of Act I.).

O wicked wit and gifts, that have the power
So to seduce!—won to his shameful lust   45
The will of my most seeming-virtuous queen: *she was guilty before his death.*
O Hamlet, what a falling-off was there!
From me, whose love was of that dignity
That it went hand in hand even with the vow
I made to her in marriage; and to decline   50
Upon a wretch, whose natural gifts were poor | *conceit!.*
To those of mine!
But virtue, as it never will be moved,
Though lewdness court it in a shape of heaven,
So lust, though to a radiant angel link'd,   55
Will sate itself in a celestial bed,
And prey on garbage.
But, soft! methinks I scent the morning air;
nical? Brief let me be. Sleeping within mine orchard,
My custom always in the afternoon,   60
Upon my secure hour thy uncle stole,
With juice of cursed hebenon in a vial,
And in the porches of mine ears did pour

---

45. *to his*] Q, Ff 3, 4; *to to this* F; *to this* F 2.   47. *a*] omitted in Qq
except Q 6.   56. *sate*] F, *sort* Q, *seat* Ff 3, 4 (Q 1 *fate*, a misprint).
58. *morning*] Q, *mornings* F.   59. *mine*] F, *my* Q.   60. *in*] Q 1, F;
of Q.   62. *hebenon*] F; *Hebona* Q 1, Q.   63. *mine*] F, *my* Q.

61. *secure*] careless, unsuspecting,
accented as in *Othello*, IV. i. 72: "To
lip a wanton in a secure couch."
Compare *Merry Wives*, II. i. 241:
"a secure fool."
62. *hebenon*] Grey conjectured
henebon, meaning henbane. Douce,
having found an example of *Ebeno*,
ebony, suggested that this was meant.
Elze conjectured *hemlock*; Beisly,
enoron, one of the names for deadly
nightshade. Nicholson (*N. Sh. Soc.*

Transactions, 1880–82) shows that
the yew was considered a most deadly
poison; that Ebenus was mediævally
applied to different trees, including
the yew; that Marlowe, Spenser, and
Reynolds use Heben for the yew;
and he maintains that in the words
"cursed" and "an enmity with
blood of man" Shakespeare was
adopting the description of the yew
found in Holland's *Pliny*, 1600.

The leperous distilment; whose effect
Holds such an enmity with blood of man   65
That swift as quicksilver it courses through
The natural gates and alleys of the body;
And with a sudden vigour it doth posset
And curd, like eager droppings into milk,
The thin and wholesome blood: so did it mine;   70
And a most instant tetter bark'd about,
Most lazar-like, with vile and loathsome crust,
All my smooth body.
Thus was I, sleeping, by a brother's hand
Of life, of crown, of queen, at once dispatch'd;   75
Cut off even in the blossoms of my sin, ✗
 ✗ Unhousel'd, disappointed, unaneled;
No reckoning made, but sent to my account
With all my imperfections on my head:
Oh, horrible! Oh, horrible! most horrible!   80
If thou hast nature in thee, bear it not;

67. *alleys*] Hanmer; *allies* Q 1, Q, F.   68. *posset*] F, *possesse* Q.
71. *bark'd*] Q 1, Q; *bak'd* F.   75. *of queen*] Q, *and Queene* F.

68. *vigour*] Staunton proposed *rigour*.
69. *eager*] Ff *aygre.* Cotgrave has "Aigre: Eagre, sharpe, tart, biting, sower."
71. *instant*] instantaneous, as in II. ii. 548.
75. *dispatch'd*] deprived, which is the reading of Q 1.
76. *blossoms*] White reads *blossom*, which Dyce had suggested; but compare *Winter's Tale*, v. ii. 135: "the blossoms of their fortune."
77. *Unhousel'd*] without receiving the eucharist (Old English *husel*). Tyrwhitt compares *Morte Darthur*, xxi. 12 (Lancelot dying): "So when he was howselyd and anelyd."

77. *disappointed*] Pope read *unanointed*; Theobald, *unappointed*, comparing *Measure for Measure*, III. i. 60. Boucher conjectures *unassoiled*, unabsolved. The meaning is, without equipment for the last journey.
77. *unaneled*] unanointed with extreme unction. See quotation from *Morte Darthur* above. Pope mistook it for having no knell rung.
80.] Given to Hamlet by several editors. Garrick, as Hamlet, pronounced this line; so does Sir H. Irving. Clarke observes that triple iteration is characteristic of the Ghost's diction.

Let not the royal bed of Denmark be

A couch for luxury and damned incest.

But, howsoever thou pursuest this act,

Taint not thy mind, nor let thy soul contrive 85

Against thy mother aught; leave her to heaven,

And to those thorns that in her bosom lodge,

To prick and sting her. Fare thee well at once!

The glow-worm shows the matin to be near,

And 'gins to pale his uneffectual fire; 90

Adieu, adieu, adieu! remember me. [*Exit.*

Ham. O all you host of heaven! O earth! what else?

And shall I couple hell? Oh, fie! Hold, hold, my
heart;

And you, my sinews, grow not instant old,

But bear me stiffly up. Remember thee? 95

Ay, thou poor ghost, while memory holds a seat

In this distracted globe. Remember thee?

Yea, from the table of my memory

I 'll wipe away all trivial fond records,

All saws of books, all forms, all pressures past, 100

91. *Adieu, adieu, adieu!*] Q, *Adue, adue, Hamlet :* F and many editors.
93. *Hold, hold,*] Q; *hold* Qq 4-6, F. 95. *stiffly*] F, *swiftly* Q.
95, 97. *thee?*] F, *thee,* Q. 96. *while*] F, *whiles* Q.

83. *luxury*] Dyce (*Gloss.*): lascivi-
ousness, its only sense in Shakespeare.

90. *uneffectual*] Warburton (approved by Dyce) explains : "shining
without heat." Steevens, "lost in the
morning light." See *Pericles,* II. iii.
43.

93. *Oh, fie*] Capell, Steevens, Mit-
ford, Dyce regard these words as
probably an interpolation.

97. *globe*] Hamlet's hand is upon
his forehead. See Appendix III.

98. *table*] tablet, as in *Two Gentle-*
men of Verona, II. vii. 3. In Massinger, *The Emperor of the East,* IV.
v., we find "Writ in the table of my
memory."

99. *fond*] foolish.

99. *records*] The accent in Shakespeare is variable, on the first, or
(as probably here) on the second
syllable.

100. *saws*] maxims, as in *As You*
Like It, II. vii. 156.

100. *pressures*] impressions. See
III. ii. 29. Elsewhere Shakespeare
uses *impressure* in the same sense.

That youth and observation copied there;
And thy commandment all alone shall live
Within the book and volume of my brain,
Unmix'd with baser matter: yes, by heaven!
O most pernicious woman!   105
O villain, villain, smiling, damned villain!
My tables,—meet it is I set it down,
That one may smile, and smile, and be a villain;
At least I 'm sure it may be so in Denmark.—

        [*Writing.*

So, uncle, there you are.—Now to my word;   110
It is " Adieu, adieu! remember me."
I have sworn 't.

Hor. [*Within.*] My Lord, my lord!

Mar. [*Within.*]   Lord Hamlet!

Hor. [*Within.*]   Heaven secure him!

Ham. So be it!

---

104. *yes*] Q, *yes, yes* F.   107. *My tables,*—] Pope, (*My tables*) Q 1, *My tables,* Q, *My Tables, My Tables ;* F.   109. *I 'm*] F, *I am* Q.   Writing.] Rowe ; omitted Q, F.   113. Hor. [Within.]] Hor. and Mar. within F, Hora. Q (see note below).   *Heaven*] F ; *Heavens* Q 1, Q.   114. Ham. *So be it*] Q, given to Marcellus in F.

107. *tables*] memorandum-book, as in *2 Henry IV.* II. iv. 289, and *Sonnets,* cxxii. 1. Hamlet's writing in his tables is a scholar's fantastic relief for over-wrought feelings, suggested to him by "table of my memory."

110. *word*] Steevens explains as "watch-word" ; perhaps order, word of command, as in *Julius Cæsar,* v. iii. 5 : "Brutus gave the word too early."

113. Within] Capell first marked thus the speech of Marcellus and that of Horatio which follows it. Wright (*Cambridge Sh.* vii. p. 600) thinks

the transference by Capell of the entrance of Horatio and Marcellus to follow line 116 unnecessary ; they may enter at " My lord, my lord ! " but, in the darkness, may be unseen by Hamlet.

114.] Many editors follow F in assigning "So be it !" to Marcellus. "There is something highly solemn and proper," observes Capell, "in making Hamlet say the Amen to a benediction pronounced on himself." Furness asks, " May it not refer to the conclusion of Hamlet's writing in his tables ? "

Hor. [*Within.*] Illo, ho, ho, my lord! 115
Ham. Hillo, ho, ho, boy! come, bird, come.

Enter HORATIO *and* MARCELLUS.

Mar. How is 't, my noble lord?

Hor. What news, my lord?

Ham. O, wonderful!

Hor. Good my lord, tell it.

Ham. No; you will reveal it.

Hor. Not I, my lord, by heaven.

Mar. Nor I, my lord. 120

Ham. How say you, then; would heart of man once
  think it?

  But you 'll be secret?

Hor., Mar. Ay, by heaven, my lord.

Ham. There 's ne'er a villain dwelling in all Denmark
  But he 's an arrant knave.

Hor. There needs no ghost, my lord, come from the
  grave 125

---

115. Hor.] Q 1, F; Mar. Q. 116. *bird*] F, *and* Q, *boy* Q 1. Enter
Horatio and Marcellus] Capell; placed after Hamlet's *I have sworn 't* in
Q, after *My lord, my lord!* in F. 117. Hor. *What news, my lord?*]
omitted Qq 4-6. 118. Ham.] Hora. Qq 4, 5. 119. *you will*] Q,
you 'l F. 121. *it?*] Q 1, F; *it.* Q. 122. *secret?*] F, *secret.* Q; *my
lord.*] Q 1, F; omitted Q. 123. *ne'er*] F, *never* Q.

---

115. *Illo*] Capell considered this
speech "too light for Horatio," and
assigned it with Q to Marcellus.
The call, answered by Hamlet in
falconer's fashion, is not meant as
such by the speaker, whether he be
Marcellus or Horatio. In *The Birth
of Merlin*, Prince Uter's "So ho,
boy, so, ho, illo ho!" is a mere
halloo.

116. *Hillo . . . come*] The cry of a
falconer to his birds. Steevens quotes

from Tyro's *Roaring Megge*, 1598:
"Ile go see the kyte: Come, come
bird, come."

121. *once*] ever, as in *Ant. and
Cleop.* v. ii. 50.

123. *Denmark*] Seymour suggests
that Hamlet at this word breaks off
his intended disclosure, pauses, and
gives it a jesting turn. Sir H. Irving
adopts this rendering, glancing at
Marcellus, as if his presence rendered
the confidence unwise.

To tell us this.

Ham.   Why, right; you are i' the right;
And so, without more circumstance at all,
I hold it fit that we shake hands and part;
You, as your business and desire shall point you;
For every man hath business and desire,   130
Such as it is; and, for mine own poor part,
Look you, I 'll go pray.

Hor. These are but wild and whirling words, my lord.

Ham. I 'm sorry they offend you, heartily;
Yes, faith, heartily.

Hor.   There 's no offence, my lord. 135

Ham. Yes, by Saint Patrick, but there is, Horatio,
And much offence too. Touching this vision here,
It is an honest ghost, that let me tell you;
For your desire to know what is between us,

126. *us*] *you* Q 1; *i' the*] Capell, *in the* Q, *i' th'* F.   129. *desire*] Q;
desires Q 1, F.   130. *hath*] Q, *ha's* F.   131. *mine*] F, *my* Q.   132. *Look
you, I 'll*] F, *I will* Q.   133. *whirling*] Theobald, *wherling* Q 1, *whurling*
Q, *hurling* F.   134. *I 'm*] F, *I am* Q.   136. *Horatio*] Q 1, Q; *my
Lord* F.   137. *too. Touching*] Rowe, *too, touching* Q 1, F ; *to, touching* Q;
too : touching Q 6.

127. *circumstance*] beating about
the bush, circumlocution, as in *Merchant of Venice*, I. i. 154.

136. *Saint Patrick*] In connection
with "the offence" there is special
propriety in the oath. It was given
out that a serpent stung Hamlet's
father; the serpent now wears his
crown. St. Patrick was the proper
saint to take cognisance of such an
offence, having banished serpents from
Ireland. In *Richard II.* II. i. 157,
Shakespeare alludes to the freedom
of Ireland from venomous creatures.
Campion in his *History of Ireland*,
written in 1571, mentions the legend.

In Shirley's *Saint Patrick for Ireland*,
serpents come on the stage, are
banned by the saint, and creep away.
Tschischwitz supposes that the oath
alludes to St. Patrick's Purgatory, and
I find mention of this place of tor-
ment in Dekker's *Olde Fortunatus*
(Pearson's *Dekker*, vol. i. p. 155).

136. *Horatio*] Corson defends the F
"my lord," as a retort to Horatio's
"my lord," line 135.

138. *honest*] Hudson supposes that
this means a real ghost, just what it
appears to be, not "the Devil" in
"a pleasing shape."

O'ermaster't as you may.   And   now,   good
  friends,   140
As you are friends, scholars and soldiers,
Give me one poor request.

Hor. What is 't, my lord? we will.

Ham. Never make known what you have seen to-night.

Hor., Mar. My lord, we will not.

Ham.   Nay, but swear 't.

Hor.   In faith, 145
My lord, not I.

Mar.   Nor I, my lord, in faith.

Ham. Upon my sword.

Mar.   We have sworn, my lord, already.

Ham. Indeed, upon my sword, indeed.

Ghost. [*Beneath.*] Swear.

Ham. Ah, ha, boy! say'st thou so? art thou there, true-
  penny?—   150
Come on; you hear this fellow in the cellarage;
Consent to swear.

Hor.   Propose the oath, my lord.

149. Beneath] Capell; Ghost cries under the Stage Q, F.   150. *Ah*] F
Ha Q.

147. *sword.*] The hilt, having the
form of a cross, is sworn on. See *1
Henry IV.* ii. iv. 371. Dyce quotes
from Mallet's *Northern Antiquities*
(i. 216, ed. 1770) to show that "the
custom of swearing on a sword pre-
vailed even among the barbarous
worshippers of Odin."

150. *true-penny*] Forby (*Vocab. of
East Anglia*): Hearty old fellow.
Collier says he has learnt, from
Sheffield authorities, that it is a mining term, signifying an indication in
the soil of the direction in which ore
is to be found. Marston, *The Malcontent*, 1604, III. iii., has an echo of
this scene: "Illo, ho, ho ho! arte
there, old true-penny." Middleton,
in *Blurt, Master-Constable*, names a
page Truepenny. Hamlet's recoil
from horror to half-hysterical jesting
is justified to his own consciousness
as intended to divert the conjectures
of his companions from the dreadful
nature of the Ghost's disclosure, which
he cannot reveal to Horatio in the
presence of Marcellus.

Ham. Never to speak of this that you have seen.
    Swear by my sword.

Ghost. [*Beneath.*] Swear.   155

Ham. *Hic et ubique?* then we'll shift our ground.—
    Come hither, gentlemen,
    And lay your hands again upon my sword:
    Never to speak of this that you have heard;
    Swear by my sword.   160

Ghost. [*Beneath.*] Swear.

Ham. Well said, old mole! canst work i' the earth so
        fast?
    A worthy pioner!—Once more remove, good friends.

Hor. O day and night, but this is wondrous strange!

Ham. And therefore as a stranger give it welcome. 165
    There are more things in heaven and earth,
        Horatio,
    Than are dreamt of in your philosophy.
    But come;
    Here, as before, never, so help you mercy,
    How strange or odd soe'er I bear myself,   170
    As I perchance hereafter shall think meet
    To put an antic disposition on,

---

153. *seen.*] F, *seene* Q, *seene*, Qq 4–6.   156. *our*] Q, *for* F.   157–160.]
Q has a comma after *sword*, line 158, and transposes lines 159, 160, with
no point between *sword* and *never*; F. as here, but with comma after *sword*,
line 158, and colon after *heard*, line 159; later Ff put full stop after *sword*,
line 158.   159. *heard*] *seene* Q 1.   161. *Swear*] Q 1, F; *Sweare by
his sword.* Q.   162. *earth*] Q 1, Q; *ground* F.   167. *your*] Q 1, Q; *our* F.

163. *pioner*] pioneer, and accented,
as in *Othello*, III. iii. 346.
165. *as . . . welcome*] Being a
stranger, take it in. Mason needlessly
suggests seem not to know it. Middleton, *Women Beware Women*, II. ii. :
"She's a stranger, madam. The
more should be her welcome."

167. *your*] Several editors prefer
our Ff. In either case, the emphasis
is probably on *philosophy*. Compare
for this use of *your* IV. iii. 22 : "Your
worm is your only emperor for diet."
172. *antic*] bizarre, fantastic; *Romeo
and Juliet*, II. iv. 29, "antic . . .
fantasticoes."

That you, at such times seeing me, never shall,
With arms encumber'd thus, or this head-shake,
Or by pronouncing of some doubtful phrase,   175
As " Well, well, we know," or " We could, an if we
    would,"
Or " If we list to speak," or " There be, an if they
    might,"
Or such ambiguous giving out, to note
That you know aught of me : this not to do,
So grace and mercy at your most need help you, 180
Swear.

Ghost. [Beneath.] Swear.

Ham. Rest, rest, perturbed spirit !

                                                [They swear.
                    So, gentlemen,
With all my love I do commend me to you;
And what so poor a man as Hamlet is   185
May do, to express his love and friending to you,
God willing, shall not lack.   Let us go in together;
And still your fingers on your lips, I pray.
The time is out of joint;—O cursed spite,
That ever I was born to set it right !—   190
Nay, come, let's go together.   *[Exeunt.*

173. *times*] Q 1, Q; *time* F.   174. *this head-shake*] Q 1, Q, (without hyphen), *thus, head shake* F.   176. *Well, well,*] Q, *well,* F.   176, 177. *an if . . an if*] Hanmer ; *and if . . . and if* Q, F.   177. *they*] Q 1, Q; *there* F.   179–181. *this . . . Swear*] Knight's punctuation of F text, *this doe sweare, So . . . you.* Q.   184. *I do*] omitted Ff 2–4.

174. *encumber'd*] commonly explained as "folded." Perhaps intertwined, Hamlet taking the arm of Horatio or Marcellus as he speaks. In Fenton's *Monophylo*, B. ii. 12, I find " encumbred laborinth."

178. *giving out*] intimation, as in *Measure for Measure,* I. iv. 54, *Othello,* IV. i. 131.

178. *to note*] Theobald and other editors correct the grammatical irregularity by reading *denote.*

ACT II

SCENE I.—*A Room in Polonius's House.*

Enter POLONIUS *and* REYNALDO.

Pol. Give him this money and these notes, Reynaldo.

Rey. I will, my lord.

Pol. You shall do marvellous wisely, good Reynaldo,
Before you visit him, to make inquire
Of his behaviour.

Rey.   My lord, I did intend it.   5

Pol. Marry, well said, very well said. Look you, sir,
Inquire me first what Danskers are in Paris;
And how, and who, what means, and where they
keep,
What company, at what expense; and finding
By this encompassment and drift of question   10
That they do know my son, come you more nearer
Than your particular demands will touch it;
Take you, as 'twere, some distant knowledge of him,
As thus, "I know his father and his friends,
And in part him." Do you mark this, Rey-
naldo?   15

Enter *Polonius* and *Reynaldo*] Enter old *Polonius* with his man or two Q.
1. *this*] Q, *his* F; *these*] Q, *these two* Qq 4–6, *those* Ff 2–4.   3. *marvel-lous*] Qq 4–6, *meruiles* Qq 2, 3, *marvels* F.   4. *to make inquire*] Q, *you make inquiry* F.   11, 12. *nearer Than*] Q, F (spelling *Then*); *neere Than* F 2; *near Then* F 3; *near, Then* F 4.   14. *As*] Q, *And* F.

4. *inquire*] so "strange inquire": *Pericles*, III. Prologue 22.
7. *Danskers*] Danes.
11–13.] The opposition is not be-tween particular (which perhaps means *personal*) demands and any other inquiries, but between demands or questions and the profession of ac-quaintance: leave questioning, and come nearer by throwing out a bait of imperfect knowledge. Jennens and Keightley read "nearer; Then"; but in what follows there are no "particular demands."

Rey. Ay, very well, my lord.

Pol. "And in part him; but," you may say, "not well;
But if 't be he I mean, he 's very wild,
Addicted " so and so; and there put on him
What forgeries you please; marry, none so
   rank   20
As may dishonour him; take heed of that;
But, sir, such wanton, wild and usual slips
As are companions noted and most known
To youth and liberty.

Rey.   As gaming, my lord.

Pol. Ay, or drinking, fencing, swearing, quarrelling,   25
Drabbing; you may go so far.

Rey. My lord, that would dishonour him.

Pol. Faith, no; as you may season it in the charge.
You must not put another scandal on him,
That he is open to incontinency;   30
That 's not my meaning; but breathe his faults so
   quaintly

26. *Drabbing*] *Or drabbing* Q 1.   28. *no*] F, omitted Q.

25. *fencing*] Perhaps named to show how Polonius regards the other supposed outbreaks of his son—as to be classed with addiction to the fencing-school. Fencers, however, had a like legal disrepute with players. In Middleton's *Spanish Gipsy*, II. ii. Sancho comes in "from playing with fencers," having lost cloak, band, and rapier at dice. The ill repute of fencers appears from other passages in Elizabethan drama. In Dekker's *Gul's Horn-Booke* he speaks of the danger to a rich young man of being "set upon" by fencers and cony-catchers (Dekker, ed. Grosart, vol. ii. p. 213).

28. *season*] qualify; see I. ii. 192.

29. *another*] Theobald conjectured *an utter*, which was adopted by Hanmer and some other editors; but Theobald himself withdrew the suggestion. Malone explains: "a very different and more scandalous failing: habitual incontinency." Hudson reads "open of incontinency," that he indulges his passions openly. Perhaps Malone is right; Polonius, who loves nice distinctions, sees a difference between occasional "drabbing" and lying wide open to the access of vice.

31. *quaintly*] delicately, ingeniously, as in *Merchant of Venice*, II. iv. 6.

That they may seem the taints of liberty,
The flash and outbreak of a fiery mind,
A savageness in unreclaimed blood,
Of general assault.

Rey.   But, my good lord,—   35
Pol. Wherefore should you do this?
Rey.   Ay, my lord,
I would know that.

Pol.   Marry, sir, here's my drift,
And, I believe, it is a fetch of warrant;
You laying these slight sullies on my son,
As 'twere a thing a little soil'd i' the work-
    ing,   40
Mark you,
Your party in converse, him you would sound,
Having ever seen in the prenominate crimes
The youth you breathe of guilty, be assured
He closes with you in this consequence;   45
" Good   sir,"   or   so,   or   " friend,"   or   " gentle-
    man,"
According to the phrase or the addition
Of man and country.

Rey.   Very good, my lord.

---

38. *warrant*] F, *wit* Q.   39. *sullies*] F, Qq 4, 5, 6; *sallies* Qq **2, 3.**
40. *i' the*] F, *with* Q.   42. *converse,*] Q, *converse;* F.   47. *or*] Q,
and F.

34. *unreclaimed*] untamed. Clar.
Press quotes Cotgrave, " Adomes-
tiquer : To tame, reclaim, make
gentle."
35. *Of general assault*] which assails
youth almost universally.
38. *fetch of warrant*] a warranted
device.

42. *converse*] " Shakespeare uses
the noun only three times, and with
the accent as here " (Rolfe).
45. *He . . . consequence*] " He falls
in with you into this conclusion "
(Caldecott); " in thus following up
your remark " (Schmidt).
47. *addition*] title, as in I. iv. 20.

Pol. And then, sir, does he this,—he does—what
    was I about to say? By the mass, I was   50
    about to say something; where did I leave?
Rey. At "closes in the consequence," at "friend or
    so," and "gentleman."
Pol. At "closes in the consequence," ay, marry;
    He closes with you thus: "I know the gentle-
      man;   55
    I saw him yesterday, or t' other day,
    Or then, or then, with such, or such, and, as you say,
    There was he gaming, there o'ertook in 's rouse,
    There falling out at tennis;" or perchance,
    "I saw him enter such a house of sale,"   60
    Videlicet, a brothel, or so forth.
    See you now;
    Your bait of falsehood takes this carp of truth;
    And thus do we of wisdom and of reach,
    With windlasses and with assays of bias,   65

49. *does he this,—he does—*] *does he this? He does :* F, *doos at this, a doos,* Q.
50. *By the mass*] Q, omitted in F.   51. *something*] *nothing* Ff 2-4.
52, 53. *at "friend . . . gentleman"*] omitted Q.   55. *closes with you thus*]
F, *closes thus* Q, *closeth with him thus* Q 1.   57. *or such*] Q, *and such* F.
58. *he,*] F, *a* Q.   60. *such*] Q, F ; *such or such* Qq 4, 5 ; *such and such* Q 6.
63. *takes*] F, *take* Q.

49–51.] *And then . . . leave?*]
Prose first by Malone. The attempts
to justify Q and F by constructing
verse miss the point that Polonius's
wits have failed him, and he topples
from verse to incoherency in prose.
Three lines, ending *say? . . . something . . . leave?* Q; ending *this?
. . . say? . . . leave?* F.

    52, 53.] Prose first in *Globe Shake-
speare.* Reynaldo steps down from
verse to enable Polonius to recover
his train of ideas. Two lines ending
consequence" . . . "gentleman" F.

58. *o'ertook*] Clar. Press : a " eu-
phemism for drunk "; perhaps it
means only surprised, caught. For
rouse, see I. ii. 127.

    64. *of reach*] Clar. Press: we who are
far-sighted ; compare "we of taste and
feeling," *Love's Labour's Lost*, IV. ii.
30. Q 1 has " being men of reach."
    65. *windlasses*] winding turns. So
in Golding's *Ovid*, B. vii. :
    "like a wily fox he
  runs not forth directly out,
Nor makes a windlasse over all the
    champion fields about ";

By indirections find directions out:
So, by my former lecture and advice,
Shall you my son.   You have me, have you not?
Rey. My lord, I have.
Pol.   God be wi' you ; fare ye well.
Rey. Good my lord !   70
Pol. Observe his inclination in yourself.
Rey. I shall, my lord.
Pol. And let him ply his music.
Rey.   Well, my lord.
Pol. Farewell !   [*Exit Reynaldo.*

Enter OPHELIA.

                How now, Ophelia ! what 's the matter?
Oph. Oh, my lord, my lord, I have been so affrighted ! 75
Pol. With what, i' the name of God ?
Oph. My lord, as I was sewing in my closet,

69. *ye well*] Q, *you well* F.   75. *Oh, my lord*] Q, *Alas* F.   76. *i' the*] Capell, *i' th* Q, *in the* F ; *God*] Q, *Heaven* F.   77. *closet*] Q, *chamber* F.

and in *Apollo Shroving*: "See how fortune came with a windlace about again."

65. *assays of bias*] a metaphor from bowls, the player sending his bowl towards the jack in a curve, knowing that the bias—the oblique line of motion—will bring it right.

66. *By . . . out*] By indirect means find out direct indications.

71. *Observe . . . yourself*] Johnson : "Perhaps this means in your own person, not by spies." Clar. Press : "Possibly it means conform your own conduct to his inclinations." Hanmer and Warburton read "e'en yourself." "In yourself" may possibly mean in regard to yourself.

73. *music*] Vischer explains : "His son may gamble, drink, swear, quarrel, drab, . . . only—let him ply his music : true cavalier - breeding !" Clarke : "Let him go on to what tune he pleases," which would agree well with the explanation of line 71 suggested by Clar. Press.

77. *closet*] a private chamber, as in III. ii. 346.   This is the only entirely sincere meeting of Hamlet with Ophelia in the play ; and it is entirely silent—the hopeless farewell of Hamlet.   Can her love discover him through his disguise of distraction?   He reads nothing in her face but fright ; he cannot utter a word, and feels that the estranging sea has flowed between them.   In no true sense do they ever meet again.

Lord Hamlet, with his doublet all unbraced;
No hat upon his head; his stockings foul'd,
Ungarter'd, and down-gyved to his ancle;　　80
Pale as his shirt; his knees knocking each other;
And with a look so piteous in purport
As if he had been loosed out of hell
To speak of horrors, he comes before me.

Pol. Mad for thy love?

Oph.　　　　　　My lord, I do not know,　85
But truly I do fear it.

Pol.　　　　　　What said he?

Oph. He took me by the wrist and held me hard;
Then goes he to the length of all his arm,
And, with his other hand thus o'er his brow,
He falls to such perusal of my face　　90
As he would draw it. Long stay'd he so;
At last, a little shaking of mine arm,
And thrice his head thus waving up and down,
He raised a sigh so piteous and profound
That it did seem to shatter all his bulk　95
And end his being; that done, he lets me go,
And with his head over his shoulder turn'd
He seem'd to find his way without his eyes;

---

87. *and . . . hard*] omitted Ff 2–4.　94. *piteous*] Q, F; *hideous* Ff 2–4.
95. *That*] F, *As* Q.　97. *shoulder*] Q, *shoulders* F.

78. *unbraced*] unfastened, as in *Julius Cæsar*, I. iii. 48.
80. *Ungarter'd*] See the conventional lover described in *As You Like It*, III. ii. 398.
80. *down-gyved*] fallen to the ancle, like gyves or fetters. Theobald read, with Qq 4, 5, *down-gyred*, explaining it "rolled down to the ancle."
82. *purport*] Clar. Press says ac-
cented on last syllable. But no other example of the word occurs in Shakespeare.
90. *perusal*] study. See *peruse*, IV. vii. 137.
91. *Long*] Pope read *Long time*.
95. *bulk*] frame. Florio (1611) has "Pettorata, a shock against the breast or bulk." See *Rape of Lucrece*, 467: "her heart . . . Beating her bulk."

For out o' doors he went without their help,
And to the last bended their light on me.   100
Pol. Come, go with me; I will go seek the king.
This is the very ecstasy of love;
Whose violent property fordoes itself
And leads the will to desperate undertakings,
As oft as any passion under heaven   105
That does afflict our natures. I am sorry,—
What, have you given him any hard words of late?
Oph. No, my good lord, but, as you did command,
I did repel his letters and denied
His access to me.

Pol.   That hath made him mad. 110
I am sorry that with better heed and judgement
I had not quoted him: I fear'd he did but trifle
And meant to wreck thee; but beshrew my jealousy!
By heaven, it is as proper to our age
To cast beyond ourselves in our opinions   115
As it is common for the younger sort
To lack discretion. Come, go we to the king:

99. *o' doors*] Theobald, *adoors* (with various spellings) Q, F ; *help*] Q 1, F ;
helps Q.   101. *Come,*] Q ; omitted F.   103. *fordoes*] *forgoes* Qq 4–6.
105. *passion*] F, *passions* Q.   106. *sorry,—*] Capell ; *sorry,* Q, F (Q 6
sorrie ;); *sorry.* Globe.   111. *heed*] Q, *speed* F.   112. *quoted*] F, *coted* Q;
fear'd] Q, *feare* F.   114. *By heaven*] Q 1, Q ; *It seemes* F.

102. *ecstasy*] madness, as in III.
i. 168, and elsewhere in this play.
103. *fordoes*] destroys; the *for* is
here negative, as in v. i. 243 : it is
intensive in "fordone," *Midsummer
Night's Dream*, v. 381.
106. *I am sorry,—*] Capell's pointing indicates a broken sentence.
Polonius takes it up again in line 111.
111. *heed*] Theobald preferred the
F *speed*, meaning success.
112. *quoted*] noted, observed, as in

Romeo and Juliet, I. iv. 31 : "What
curious eye doth quote deformities?"
113. *jealousy*] suspicion, as frequently in Shakespeare.
114. *is as proper*] belongs as much,
as in *Julius Cæsar*, I. ii. 41 : "Con-
ceptions only proper to myself."
115. *cast beyond*] overshoot. Clar.
Press explains *cast*: to contrive, design, plan, quoting Spenser, *Faerie
Queene*, I. v. 12, "he cast avenged
to be."

This must be known; which, being kept close, might move
More grief to hide than hate to utter love.
Come.   [*Exeunt.* 120

SCENE II.—*A Room in the Castle.*

Flourish. *Enter* KING, QUEEN, ROSENCRANTZ,
GUILDENSTERN, *and Attendants.*

King. Welcome, dear Rosencrantz and Guildenstern!
Moreover that we much did long to see you,
The need we have to use you did provoke
Our hasty sending.   Something have you heard
Of Hamlet's transformation; so call it,   5
Since not the exterior nor the inward man
Resembles that it was.   What it should be,
More than his father's death, that thus hath put him
So much from the understanding of himself,
I cannot dream of : I entreat you both,   10
That, being of so young days brought up with him,
And since so neighbour'd to his youth and humour,
That you vouchsafe your rest here in our court
Some little time; so by your companies
To draw him on to pleasures, and to gather   15

120. *Come.*] Q, omitted F.
                    Scene II.
   5. *call*] Q, *I call* F.   6. *Since not*] F, *Sith nor* Q.   10. *dream*] Q,
deeme F.   12. *since*] F, *sith* Q ; *humour*] F, *havior* Q.

118, 119. *which . . . love*] "The
king may be angry at my telling of   *Scene II.*
Hamlet's love ; but more grief would
come from hiding it " (Moberly).   2. *Moreover that*] Over and above
Hanmer read " to hide hate, than."   that.

So much as from occasion you may glean,
Whether aught to us unknown afflicts him thus,
That, open'd, lies within our remedy.

Queen. Good gentlemen, he hath much talk'd of you,
And sure I am two men there are not living   20
To whom he more adheres.   If it will please you
To show us so much gentry and good will
As to expend your time with us awhile
For the supply and profit of our hope,
Your visitation shall receive such thanks   25
As fits a king's remembrance.

Ros.   Both your majesties
Might, by the sovereign power you have of us,
Put your dread pleasures more into command
Than to entreaty.

Guil.   But we both obey,
And here give up ourselves, in the full bent   30
To lay our service freely at your feet,
To be commanded.

King. Thanks, Rosencrantz and gentle Guildenstern.

Queen. Thanks, Guildenstern and gentle Rosencrantz;
And I beseech you instantly to visit   35
My too much changed son.—Go, some of you,
And bring these gentlemen where Hamlet is.

16. *occasion*] Q, *occasions* F.   17. *Whether . . . thus*] Q, omitted F.
20. *are*] F, *is* Q.   23. *expend*] *extend* Qq 4, 5.   29. *But we*] Q, *We* F.
31. *service*] Q, *services* F.   32. *To be commanded*] omitted Qq 4–6.
36. *you*] Q, *ye* F.   37. *these*] Q, *the* F.

17. *Whether*] To be pronounced
as a monosyllable, as often elsewhere.
22. *gentry*] courtesy. Singer quotes
Baret's *Alvearie*: "Gentlemanlinesse
or gentry, kindlinesse, naturall good-
nesse. Generositas."
30. *bent*] limit of capacity; metaphor from the extent to which a bow
may be drawn.

Guil. Heavens make our presence and our practices
　Pleasant and helpful to him!
Queen. 　　　　　　　　　Ay, amen!
　　　　　[*Exeunt Rosencrantz, Guildenstern, and
　　　　　　　　　　　　　　some Attendants.*

Enter POLONIUS.

Pol. The ambassadors from Norway, my good lord,　40
　Are joyfully return'd.
King. Thou still hast been the father of good news.
Pol. Have I, my lord?　Assure you, my good liege,
　I hold my duty as I hold my soul,
　Both to my God and to my gracious king;　45
　And I do think, or else this brain of mine
　Hunts not the trail of policy so sure
　As it hath used to do, that I have found
　The very cause of Hamlet's lunacy.
King. Oh, speak of that; that do I long to hear.　50
Pol. Give first admittance to the ambassadors;
　My news shall be the fruit to that great feast.
King. Thyself do grace to them, and bring them in.
　　　　　　　　　　　　　　[*Exit Polonius.*
　He tells me, my dear Gertrude, he hath found
　The head and source of all your son's distemper.　55
Queen. I doubt it is no other but the main,—

39. *Ay*] Q, omitted F.　43. *Assure you*] F, *I assure* Q.　45. *and*] Q,
one F, Caldecott, Knight, Collier.　47. *sure*] be sure Ff 3, 4.　48. *it
hath*] Q, *I have* F.　50. *do I*] Q, *I do* F.　52. *fruit*] Q, *newes* F.
Exit Polonius] omitted Q, F.　54. *my dear Gertrude*] Q, *my sweet Queen,
that* F and many editors.

42. *still*] constantly; see I. i. 122.　*2 Henry VI.* I. i. 208: "look unto
52. *fruit*] dessert.　　　　　　　the main."
56. *the main*] the main cause, as in

His father's death, and our o'erhasty marriage.
King. Well, we shall sift him.——

Re-enter POLONIUS, *with* VOLTIMAND *and* CORNELIUS.

                  Welcome, my good friends!
Say, Voltimand, what from our brother Norway?
Volt. Most fair return of greetings and desires.   60
    Upon our first, he sent out to suppress
His nephew's levies, which to him appear'd
To be a preparation 'gainst the Polack,
But, better look'd into, he truly found
It was against your highness; whereat grieved   65
That so his sickness, age, and impotence
Was falsely borne in hand, sends out arrests
On Fortinbras; which he, in brief, obeys,
Receives rebuke from Norway, and, in fine,
Makes vow before his uncle never more   70
To give the assay of arms against your majesty.
Whereon old Norway, overcome with joy,
Gives him three thousand crowns in annual fee,
And his commission to employ those soldiers,
So levied as before, against the Polack;   75
With an entreaty, herein further shown,
                     [*Giving a paper.*
That it might please you to give quiet pass
Through your dominions for this enterprise,

57. *o'erhasty*] F, *hastie* Q.   Re-enter] Theobald, after line 57 F; Enter Embassadors Q, after line 57.   58. *my*] Q, omitted F.   73. *three*] Q 1, F; *threescore* Q.   78. *this*] Q, *that* Q 1, *his* F.

61. *first*] Caldecott: "Audience or opening of our business"; Clar. Press, "*i.e.* greeting and desire."
67. *borne in hand*] deluded, as in

Macbeth, III. i. 81; like French *maintenir.*
71. *assay*] trial.   But perhaps *assault*; see III. iii. 69.

On such regards of safety and allowance
As therein are set down.

King.   It likes us well,   80
And at our more consider'd time we 'll read,
Answer, and think upon this business.
Meantime we thank you for your well-took labour ;
Go to your rest ; at night we 'll feast together :
Most welcome home !

> [*Exeunt Voltimand and Cornelius.*

Pol.   This business is well ended.—   85
My liege, and madam, to expostulate
What majesty should be, what duty is,
Why day is day, night night, and time is time,
Were nothing but to waste night, day, and time.
Therefore, since brevity is the soul of wit,   90
And tediousness the limbs and outward flourishes,
I will be brief.   Your noble son is mad :
Mad call I it ; for, to define true madness,
What is 't but to be nothing else but mad ?
But let that go.

Queen.   More matter, with less art.   95

---

83. *well-took*] *well-look't* Ff 2–4.   85. *well*] Q, *very well* F.   90. *since*] F,
omitted Q.   94. *mad ?*] Qq 4–6, *mad,* Q, *mad.* F.

79. *regards . . . allowance*] safe and allowable conditions.   Clar. Press : "terms securing the safety of the country, and regulating the passage of the troops through it."

81. *consider'd time*] time for consideration.

86. *expostulate*] discuss, as in *Two Gentlemen of Verona*, III. i. 251. Hunter quotes from *A Brief Relation of the Shipwreck of Henry May*, 1593: "How these isles came by the name

of the Bermudas . . . I will not expostulate."

90. *wit*] understanding. Staunton explains it as wisdom ; Clar. Press, knowledge, as in *Merchant of Venice*, II. i. 18.

93, 94. *for . . . mad*] to attempt a definition of madness were to be mad oneself.   Or does Polonius give "to be mad" as his definition of madness ?

Pol. Madam, I swear I use no art at all.

That he is mad, 'tis true; 'tis true 'tis pity;

And pity 'tis 'tis true: a foolish figure;

But farewell it, for I will use no art.

Mad let us grant him then; and now remains   100

That we find out the cause of this effect,

Or rather say, the cause of this defect,

For this effect defective comes by cause:

Thus it remains, and the remainder thus.

Perpend: 105

I have a daughter,—have, while she is mine,—

Who, in her duty and obedience, mark,

Hath given me this; now gather and surmise. [*Reads.*

To the celestial, and my soul's idol, the most

beautified Ophelia,—   110

That's an ill phrase, a vile phrase; "beautified" is

a vile phrase; but you shall hear. Thus:

[*Reads.*] *In her excellent white bosom, these, &c.*

97. *he is*] F, *hee's* Q.   98. *'tis 'tis*] Q, *it is* F.   99. *farewell it*] *farewell, wit.*
Anon. conj.   104. *thus.*] F, *thus* Q.   106. *while*] Q 1, Q; *whil'st* F.   108. Reads]
Q 1676, The Letter F, omitted Q.   112, 113. *hear. Thus:* In] Malone (follow-
ing Jennens); *heare: thus in* Q; *heare these in* F; *hear—These to* Rowe; *hear
—These in* Capell; *hear. These. In* Knight.   113. &c.] omitted F.

96. *art*] Delius suggests that Polonius in replying to the Queen understands "art" as opposed to truth
and nature.
98. *figure*] a figure in rhetoric.
105. *Perpend*] ponder, consider.
Schmidt observes: "a word only used
by Pistol, Polonius, and the clowns."
110. beautified] used by Shakespeare in *Two Gentlemen of Verona*,
IV. i. 55.   Theobald read *beatified*,
which Capell approved as agreeing
with "celestial" and "idol." Dyce
takes "beautified" as meaning *beautiful* and not *accomplished.*   Nash

dedicated *Christ's Tears over Jerusalem*, 1594, "To the most beautified
lady, the lady Elizabeth Carey"; and
H. Olney dedicated R. L.'s *Diella*,
1596, "To the most worthily Honoured and vertuous beautified Ladie."
Greene described Shakespeare in a
vile phrase as an upstart crow "beautified with our feathers."   In Henry
Wotton's tale (1578), on which *Solyman and Perseda* is founded, I find:
"Persida, seeing a stranger beautified
in his feathers."
113. In . . . bosom] Clar. Press
compares *Two Gentlemen of Verona,*

Queen. Came this from Hamlet to her?

Pol. Good madam, stay awhile; I will be faithful.　115

[*Reads.*] *Doubt thou the stars are fire;*

Doubt that the sun doth move;

Doubt truth to be a liar;

But never doubt I love.

O dear Ophelia, I am ill at these numbers; 120
I have not art to reckon my groans; but that I
love thee best, O most best, believe it.　Adieu.

Thine evermore, most dear lady, whilst this
machine is to him,　　HAMLET.

This in obedience hath my daughter shown me; 125
And more above, hath his solicitings,
As they fell out by time, by means, and place,
All given to mine ear.

King.　　　　　　But how hath she
Received his love?

Pol.　　　　　　What do you think of me?

116. Reads] Letter Q, omitted F.　125. *shown*] Q, *shew'd* F.　126. *above*]
F, *about* Q ; *solicitings*] Q, *soliciting* F.

III. i. 250: letters delivered "Even in
the milk-white bosom of thy love."
There was a pocket in the breast of a
lady's dress, but there may be no
reference to it here.

116–124. Doubt] In the first two
lines and the fourth "doubt" means
be doubtful that; in the third it means
suspect. Hamlet's letter begins in the
conventional lover's style, which perhaps was what Ophelia would expect
from a courtly admirer; then there is
a real outbreak of passion and self-
pity; finally, in the word "machine,"
Hamlet indulges, after his manner,
his own intellectuality, though it may
baffle the reader; the letter is no more
simple or homogeneous than the

writer.　T. Bright, in *A Treatise of
Melancholy* (1586), explains the nature
of the body as that of a machine, connected with the "soul" by the inter-
mediate "spirit." He compares (p.
66) its action to that of a clock.

121. reckon] Delius suggests that
this may mean "to number metri-
cally."

124. machine is to him] whilst this
body is attached to him. See *Cymbeline,* v. v. 383, for use of "to."

126. *solicitings*] Solicit was sometimes—but perhaps not here—used of
immoral proposals.　Heywood, *The
Wise Woman of Hogsden,* I. i.: "I'll
visit my little rascall and soli-
cite."

King, As of a man faithful and honourable.   130
Pol. I would fain prove so. But what might you think,
　　When I had seen this hot love on the wing,——
　　As I perceived it, I must tell you that,
　　Before my daughter told me,——what might you,
　　Or my dear majesty, your queen here, think,   135
　　If I had play'd the desk or table-book,
　　Or given my heart a winking, mute and dumb,
　　Or look'd upon this love with idle sight ;
　　What might you think?   No, I went round to work,
　　And my young mistress thus I did bespeak ;   140
　　" Lord Hamlet is a prince, out of thy star ;
　　This must not be ; " and then I prescripts gave her,
　　That she should lock herself from his resort,
　　Admit no messengers, receive no tokens.
　　Which done, she took the fruits of my advice ;   145
　　And he, repulsed, a short tale to make,
　　Fell into a sadness, then into a fast,
　　Thence to a watch, thence into a weakness,
　　Thence to a lightness, and by this declension

132. *this*] *his* Ff 3, 4.   137. *a winking*] F, *a working* Q.   140. *thus*]
this Qq 4, 5.   141. *out of thy star*] Q, F ; *out of your starre* Q 1 ; *out of thy
sphere* Ff 2–4, Q 6.   142. *prescripts*] Q, *precepts* F.   143. *his*] F, *her* Q.
146. *repulsed*] F, *repell'd* Q.   149. *a*] omitted Q.

136. *desk or table-book*] silent reci-
pient.   Clar. Press explains : " If I
had been the agent of their corre-
spondence."   See *tables*, I. v. 107.
　137. *winking*] closed the eyes of
my heart.   " Wink " did not necessarily mean, as now, "a brief closure
of the eyes."   In *Sonnets*, xliii. I, it
is used for sleep.
　139. *round*] roundly, that is plainly.
See *round* in III. i. 191.
　141. *out of thy star*] above thee in
fortune.   See *Twelfth Night*, II. v.

156 : "In my stars I am above thee."
Nash, in *Pierce Pennilesse*, speaks of
the strict division of ranks in Denmark with reference to marriage :
" It is death there for anie but a husbandman to marry a husbandman's
daughter, or a gentleman's child to
joyne with any but the sonne of a
gentleman."
　148. *watch*] a sleepless state, as in
Cymbeline, III. iv. 43.
　149. *lightness*] lightheadedness.

Into the madness wherein now he raves   150
And all we mourn for.

King. Do you think 'tis this?

Queen.   It may be, very likely.

Pol. Hath there been such a time, I'd fain know that,
That I have positively said "'tis so,"
When it proved otherwise?

King.   Not that I know.   155

Pol. Take this from this, if this be otherwise.
If circumstances lead me, I will find
Where truth is hid, though it were hid indeed
Within the centre.

King.   How may we try it further?

Pol. You know, sometimes he walks four hours together   160
Here in the lobby.

Queen.   So he does, indeed.

Pol. At such a time I'll loose my daughter to him;
Be you and I behind an arras then;

---

150. *wherein*] Q, *whereon* F.   151. *mourn*] Q, *wail* F and many editors.
152. *'tis this*] F, *this* Q; *likely*] F, *like* Q.   153. *I'd*] F, *I would* Q.
160. *four*] Hanmer, followed by other editions, reads *for.*   161. *does*] Q,
has F.   163. *arras then;*] arras then, Q, F; *arras; then* Staunton.

156. *Take this from this*] Theobald
here added a stage direction, "Pointing to his head and shoulders"; he
has been followed by many editors.
Stage tradition may have guided
Theobald. But see lines 166, 167.
May not "this from this" mean the
chamberlain's staff or wand and the
hand which bears it?

159. *centre*] that is, of the earth,
and so, according to Ptolemaic as-
tronomy, of the universe. Compare
Midsummer Night's Dream, III. ii. 54.

160. *four*] Hanmer's emendation
for is specious. But Elze (*Shakespeare Jahrbuch*, B. xi.) has shown
the use by Elizabethan writers of four,
forty, forty thousand to express an in-
definite number. Malone cites Web-
ster, *Duchess of Malfi*: "She will
muse four hours together"; and Clar.
Press, Puttenham, *Arte of English
Poesie*: "laughing and gibing . . .
foure houres by the clocke."

162. *loose*] The word reminds the
King and Queen that he has restrained
Ophelia from communication with
Hamlet.

Mark the encounter; if he love her not,

And be not from his reason fall'n thereon,   165

Let me be no assistant for a state,

But keep a farm and carters.

King.   We will try it.

Queen. But look where sadly the poor wretch comes
reading.

Pol. Away, I do beseech you, both away;

I'll board him presently.——

> [*Exeunt King, Queen, and Attendants.*

Enter HAMLET [*reading*].

Oh, give me leave;   170

How does my good Lord Hamlet?

Ham. Well, God-a-mercy.

Pol. Do you know me, my lord?

Ham. Excellent well; you are a fishmonger.

167. *But*] Q, *And* F.   Enter *Hamlet*] placed after *We will try it*, line 167.
Q, F.   174. *Excellent*] Q, *Excellent, excellent* F.

170. *board*] accost, as in *Twelfth Night*, I. iii. 60.

170. *presently*] immediately, as in *Romeo and Juliet*, IV. i. 95.

170. *Oh, give me leave*] addressed to Hamlet. The *Exeunt* of King and Queen is indicated in Q after line 169; in F as here. Capell, supposing the words to be addressed to the King and Queen, placed *Exeunt* after "leave." [So N. C. S., rightly, comparing *King John*, I. i. 230. R. H. C.]

174. *fishmonger*] Malone : " Fish-monger was a cant term for wencher"; he cites B. Rich's *Irish Hubbub* : " him they call Senex fornicator and old fishmonger." Farmer and Henley's *Slang Dictionary* gives obscene meanings under " fish " and " fish-market," which suggest that fish-monger may have meant bawd, but I have found no example. There are Elizabethan references to the smell of fishmongers, which here could be easily indicated by an actor, as if Polonius had brought an ill air with him. Presently, however, Hamlet discourses on procreation, connecting Ophelia with his talk. Perhaps the following from Platt's *Jewell House*, 1594 (p. 97, ed. 1653), may be cited : " And some hold opinion that the females . . . do conceive only by licking of salt. And this maketh the Fishmongers' wives so wanton and beautiful." Whiter notices that in Jonson's *Masque of Christmas*, Venus, as a tire woman, says, " I am a fish-monger's daughter." Does Jonson only mean sea-born, or mean wanton and beautiful? Joubert (*Seconde*

Pol. Not I, my lord.   175

Ham. Then I would you were so honest a man.

Pol. Honest, my lord?

Ham. Ay, sir; to be honest, as this world goes, is
to be one man picked out of ten thousand.

Pol. That's very true, my lord.   180

Ham. For if the sun breed maggots in a dead dog,
being a good kissing carrion,—Have you a
daughter?

Pol. I have, my lord.

Ham. Let her not walk i' the sun: conception is a 185
blessing; but not as your daughter may conceive:—friend, look to 't.

Pol. [*Aside.*] How say you by that?   Still harping

177. *lord?*] F, *lord.* Q, *lord!* Dyce.   179. *man*] omitted in Ff 3, 4; *ten*] Q,
two F.   182. *good kissing carrion*] Q, F; *god kissing carrion* Warburton
and many editors; *god-kissing carrion* Malone.   186. *not*] F, omitted
in Q.   188. [*Aside*]] Capell, placed by Steevens before *Still*.

partie des erreurs populaires, 1600,
p. 169) considers the popular opinion
"que l'usage du poisson engendre
beaucoup de semence." See Apuleius'
curious defence against the charge
that he had made a magical use of
fish in his courtship of a widow.
    176. *honest*] Ben Jonson's "Town
gull," Master Mathew (*Every Man
in his Humour*, I. iii.) is a citizen's
son: "His father's an honest man, a
worshipful fishmonger, and so forth."
    181–183. *For . . . daughter*] Re-
taining the *good* of Q, F, *good kissing*
(which might be hyphened) must be
explained, with Caldecott, Corson,
Furness, good for kissing.   But much
might be said on behalf of Warburton's
emendation, which Johnson accepted
with an outbreak of admiration—*god
kissing*; compare "common-kissing
Titan," *Cymbeline*, III. iv. 166, and
see *1 Henry IV.* II. iv. 133.   In *King*

Edward III. (1596) we have: "The
freshest summer's day doth soonest
taint The loathed carrion that it seems
to kiss."   In support of *god-kissing*
Malone cites *Lear*, II. i. 9: "ear-
kissing arguments."   Hamlet ironically justifies the severance by
Polonius of Ophelia from himself:
all the world is evil, even the sun
has the basest propensities; if a dead
dog is corrupted by the sun, how
much more your daughter by me.
Staunton supposes that Hamlet reads,
or pretends to read, these words. See
a parallel from St. Augustine quoted
by Ingleby, *Shakespeare Hermeneu-
tics*, p. 159.
    185. *conception*] Steevens supposed
that there is a quibble, as in *Lear*, I. i.
12, between "conception," *understanding*, and "conceive," *to be pregnant*.
    188. *by*] concerning, as in *Merchant
of Venice*, I. ii. 58.

on my daughter: yet he knew me not at first;
he said I was a fishmonger: he is far gone, far   190
gone: and truly in my youth I suffered much
extremity for love; very near this.   I 'll
speak to him again.—What do you read,
my lord?

Ham. Words, words, words.   195

Pol. What is the matter, my lord?

Ham. Between who?

Pol. I mean the matter that you read, my lord.

Ham. Slanders, sir: for the satirical rogue says here
that old men have grey beards, that their faces 200
are wrinkled, their eyes purging thick amber
and plum-tree gum, and that they have a
plentiful lack of wit, together with most weak
hams; all which, sir, though I most powerfully
and potently believe, yet I hold it not honesty 205
to have it thus set down; for you yourself, sir,
should be old as I am, if like a crab you could
go backward.

Pol. [*Aside.*] Though this be madness, yet there is
method in 't.—Will you walk out of the air, 210
my lord?

Ham. Into my grave?

190, 191. *far gone, far gone*] F, *farre gone* Q.   197. *who*] Q, F; *whom* Ff
2-4.   198. *that you read*] Q, *you meane* F.   199. *rogue*] Q, *slave* F.
202. *and*] Q, *or* F.   203. *most*] Q, omitted F.   206. *you yourself*] F,
vour selfe Q.   207. *should be old*] F, *shall grow old* Q.   209. Aside]
Johnson.   212. *grave?*] F, *grave.* Q.

197. *Between who?*] Clar. Press: 199. *the satirical rogue*] War-
"Hamlet purposely misunderstands   burton refers to Juvenal, *Sat.* x. 188.
the word to mean 'cause of dispute,'   210-213.] Several editors prefer
as in *Twelfth Night*, III. iv. 172."   the Q *grave.* Compare Jonson's

Pol. Indeed, that is out o' the air. [*Aside.*] How
pregnant sometimes his replies are! a happi-
ness that often madness hits on, which reason 215
and sanity could not so prosperously be delivered of. I will leave him, and suddenly
contrive the means of meeting between him
and my daughter.—My honourable lord, I will
most humbly take my leave of you. 220

Ham. You cannot, sir, take from me any thing that
I will more willingly part withal; except my
life, except my life, except my life.

Pol. Fare you well, my lord.

Ham. These tedious old fools! 225

Enter ROSENCRANTZ *and* GUILDENSTERN.

Pol. You go to seek the Lord Hamlet; there he is.

Ros. [*To Polonius.*] God save you, sir!

[*Exit Polonius.*

Guil. My honoured lord!

Ros. My most dear lord!

Ham. My excellent good friends! How dost thou, 230
Guildenstern?—Ah, Rosencrantz? Good lads,
how do ye both?

213. *that is out o' the*] F, *that's out of the* Q; Aside] Capell.
216. *sanity*] F, *sanctity* Q. 217, 218. *and suddenly . . . him*] F,
omitted in Q. 219, 220. *My . . . humbly*] F, *My lord, I will* Q.
221. *sir*] F, omitted in Q. 222 *will*] F, *will not* Q; *except my life*] three
times as here, in Q; *except my life, my life.* F. Marked *aside* by White,
Hudson. 226. *the Lord*] Q, *my Lord* F. 227. To Polonius] Malone.
228. *My*] Q, *Mine* F. 231. *Ah,*] Q, *Oh,* F. 232. *ye*] F, *you* Q.

Every Man in His Humour, II. i.:
"*Dame Kitely*: For love's sake,
sweetheart, come in out of the
air. *Kitely*: How simple, and how
subtle are her answers!" This
curious parallel is found in Jonson's
Folio 1616, and in the Quarto 1601.
Shakespeare acted in Jonson's play;
perhaps this is an echo that lived in
his brain.

Ros. As the indifferent children of the earth.

Guil. Happy in that we are not over-happy;

On Fortune's cap we are not the very button. 235

Ham. Nor the soles of her shoe?

Ros. Neither, my lord.

Ham. Then you live about her waist, or in the
middle of her favours?

Guil. Faith, her privates we. 240

Ham. In the secret parts of Fortune? Oh, most
true; she is a strumpet. What's the news?

Ros. None, my lord, but that the world's grown
honest.

Ham. Then is doomsday near; but your news is 245
not true. Let me question more in particular:
what have you, my good friends, deserved at
the hands of Fortune, that she sends you to
prison hither?

Guil. Prison, my lord? 250

Ham. Denmark's a prison.

Ros. Then is the world one.

Ham. A goodly one; in which there are many
confines, wards, and dungeons; Denmark being
one o' the worst. 255

Ros. We think not so, my lord.

Ham. Why, then 'tis none to you; for there is

234, 235. *over-happy ; On Fortune's cap we*] F, *ever happy on Fortune's
lap, We* Q. 239. *favours ?*] Q, *favour ?* F. 242. *What's the*] F,
What Q. 243. *that*] F, omitted Q. 246–278. *Let me . . . attended*]
F, omitted in Q.

233. *indifferent*] average, as in *Two
Gentlemen of Verona*, III. ii. 44.
241. *In . . . Fortune*] Does Hamlet
already suspect them, and hint that

they are seeking fortune by dishonour-
able means?
254. *confines*] places of confine-
ment.

nothing either good or bad, but thinking makes
it so; to me it is a prison.

Ros. Why, then your ambition makes it one; 'tis 260
too narrow for your mind.

Ham. O God, I could be bounded in a nut-shell,
and count myself a king of infinite space, were
it not that I have bad dreams.

Guil. Which dreams indeed are ambition; for the 265
very substance of the ambitious is merely the
shadow of a dream.

Ham. A dream itself is but a shadow.

Ros. Truly, and I hold ambition of so airy and light
a quality that it is but a shadow's shadow.   270

Ham. Then are our beggars bodies, and our
monarchs and outstretched heroes the beggars'
shadows.   Shall we to the court? for, by my
fay, I cannot reason.

Ros., Guil. We'll wait upon you.   275

Ham. No such matter; I will not sort you with the
rest of my servants; for, to speak to you like
an honest man, I am most dreadfully attended.

264. *bad dreams*] Malone—perhaps
by a printer's error — read "had
dreams," a "noble emendation," as
Johnson might have called it, attained
probably by accident.

271. *beggars bodies*] The monarch
or hero is an outstretched shadow; a
shadow is thrown by a body; body is
the opposite of shadow; therefore the
opposite of monarch, and heroes,
namely, beggars, are bodies. Whether
at one or two removes—shadow, or
shadow's shadow—it is a beggar who
produces an ambitious monarch.
Hamlet's private meaning may possibly be that his uncle is a shadow
—a mockery king—with a beggar for
its substance.   He purposely loses
himself in his riddles, and, being incapable of reasoning, will to the
court, where just thinking is out of
place.

274. *fay*] faith.

278. *dreadfully attended*] Hamlet
speaks like an honest man, but knows
his meaning will not be understood;
he *is* dreadfully attended, by Memory
and Horror, and wronged Love, and
the duty of Revenge.   Let the
courtiers suppose he has a madman's
suspicions of dangerous followers.

But, in the beaten way of friendship, what
make you at Elsinore? 280

Ros. To visit you, my lord; no other occasion.

Ham. Beggar that I am, I am even poor in thanks;
but I thank you; and sure, dear friends, my
thanks are too dear a halfpenny. Were you
not sent for? Is it your own inclining? Is 285
it a free visitation? Come, deal justly with
me; come, come; nay, speak.

Guil. What should we say, my lord?

Ham. Why, any thing, but to the purpose. You
were sent for; and there is a kind of confession 290
in your looks, which your modesties have not
craft enough to colour: I know the good king
and queen have sent for you.

Ros. To what end, my lord?

Ham. That you must teach me. But let me con- 295
jure you, by the rights of our fellowship, by
the consonancy of our youth, by the obligation
of our ever-preserved love, and by what more
dear a better proposer could charge you withal,
be even and direct with me, whether you were 300
sent for, or no.

Ros. [*Aside to Guildenstern.*] What say you?

282. *even*] F, *ever* Q.   286. *Come*] F, *come, come,* Q.   289. *Why*]
omitted in Q; *any thing, but*] Q 6, *any thing but* Q, *any thing. But* F.
290. *of*] Q, omitted in F.   299. *could*] F, *can* Q.   302. Aside to
Guildenstern] Globe ed.; To Guilden. Theobald; To Hamlet Delius conject.

280 *make*] do, as in I. ii. 164.   299. *proposer*] speaker. So " Pro-
284. *a halfpenny*] at a halfpenny.   posing," speaking, in *Much Ado*, III.
289. *but*] only. Clarke thinks it   i. 3.
also includes the effect of " except "   300. *even*] plain, honest.
—a covert sarcasm.

Ham. [*Aside.*] Nay, then I have an eye of you.—
If you love me, hold not off.

Guil. My lord, we were sent for.   305

Ham. I will tell you why; so shall my anticipation
prevent your discovery, and your secrecy to
the king and queen moult no feather. I have
of late,—but wherefore I know not,—lost all
my mirth, forgone all custom of exercises; and 310
indeed it goes so heavily with my disposition
that this goodly frame, the earth, seems to me
a sterile promontory; this most excellent
canopy, the air, look you, this brave o'erhanging firmament, this majestical roof fretted 315
with golden fire, why, it appears no other thing
to me than a foul and pestilent congregation
of vapours. What a piece of work is a man!
how noble in reason! how infinite in faculty!

303. Aside] Steevens.   307. *discovery, and*] Q, *discovery of* F, with
colon after *queen*, line 308.   310. *exercises*] Q, *exercise* F.   311. *heavily*]
Q, *heavenly* F.   314, 315. *o'erhanging*] ore-hanged Qq 4-6.   315.
firmament] Q, omitted in F.   316. *appears*] F, *appeareth* Q, *appeared*
Ff 2-4.   316, 317. *no . . . than*] F, *nothing to me but* Q.   318. *a piece*]
F, *peece* Q; *a man*] man Q 6, Dyce (ed. 2), Furness.   319. *faculty*] F,
faculties Q.   319-322. Q points with commas after *faculties, moving,
action, apprehension,* and colon after *God.*

303. *of you*] on you. So " of " for
" on " in II. ii. 27.
  307. *prevent your discovery*] anti-
cipate your disclosure.
  310. *custom of exercises*] In T.
Bright's *A Treatise of Melancholy*
(1586), p. 126, occur the words
" custom of exercise." It is a passage
in which Bright describes melancholy
men as sometimes very witty; as
" exact and curious in pondering the
very moments of things "; as de-
liberating long " because of doubt and
distrust "; and as troubled with fear-

ful dreams. I can hardly doubt that
Shakespeare was acquainted with
Bright's Treatise.
  315. *fretted*] Clar. Press compares
Cymbeline, II. iv. 88 :
      " The roof o' the chamber
  With golden cherubins is fretted."
Fret is an architectural term, used
here loosely for emboss, or adorn.
  318. *a man*] Dyce (ed. 2) thinks
" a " in Qq. 2-5 was shuffled out of
its place before *piece*, and that Ff,
instead of transposing " a," added
another before *piece.*

in form and moving how express and admir- 320
able! in action how like an angel! in apprehension how like a god! the beauty of the
world! the paragon of animals! And yet, to
me, what is this quintessence of dust? man
delights not me; no, nor woman neither, though 325
by your smiling you seem to say so.

Ros. My lord, there was no such stuff in my
thoughts.

Ham. Why did you laugh then, when I said "man
delights not me"?   330

Ros. To think, my lord, if you delight not in man,
what lenten entertainment the players shall
receive from you; we coted them on the
way; and hither are they coming, to offer you
service.   335

Ham. He that plays the king shall be welcome; his
majesty shall have tribute of me; the adven-
turous knight shall use his foil and target; the
lover shall not sigh gratis; the humorous man
shall end his part in peace; the clown shall 340

325. *no*] omitted in Q; *woman*] F, *women* Q.   329. *you*] F, *yee* Q;
then] Q, omitted in F.   337. *of me*] F, *on me* Q.   340-342. *the clown . . .
sere*] omitted in Q.

320. *express*] exact. Clar. Press
quote Hebrews i. 3: "express
image." Schmidt, "expressive."
325, 326.] to follow such a confession with laughter, from any cause, is
a measure of the courtiers' intelligent
sympathy.
332. *lenten*] meagre, as in *Twelfth
Night*, I. v. 9.
333. *coted*] overtook and passed
beyond. Golding's *Ovid Met.* B. x.:
"With that Hippomenes coted her"

(Lat. *præterit*); used specially as a
term in coursing, and so explained by
Turbervile.
339. *humorous man*] "Not the
funny man or jester . . . but the
actor who personated the fantastic
characters . . . for the most part
represented as capricious and quarrel-
some" (Staunton). "Such characters
as Faulconbridge, Jaques, and Mer-
cutio" (Delius). The characters of the
stock company suit the present play

make those laugh whose lungs are tickle o' the
sere; and the lady shall say her mind freely,
or the blank verse shall halt for 't. What
players are they?

Ros. Even those you were wont to take such delight 345
in, the tragedians of the city.

Ham. How chances it they travel? their residence,
both in reputation and profit, was better both
ways.

Ros. I think their inhibition comes by the means of 350
the late innovation.

Ham. Do they hold the same estimation they did
when I was in the city? are they so followed?

Ros. No, indeed, they are not.

Ham. How comes it? do they grow rusty? 355

Ros. Nay, their endeavour keeps in the wonted
pace; but there is, sir, an eyrie of children,

341. *tickle*] Staunton conject., Clar. Press, *tickled* F. 343. *blank*] F,
black Q. 345. *such*] Q, omitted in F. 354. *they are*] F, *are they* Q.
355–383. *How . . . load too*] omitted in Q.

—King Claudius, who receives such
tribute as he deserves from Hamlet;
Laertes, the fencer; Hamlet, the lover,
who sighs gratis; Polonius, who ends
his part as "most secret and most
grave"; the grave-digger; and Ophelia,
who speaks her mind in madness
somewhat too freely. See App. III.
341, 342. *tickle o' the sere*] Explained
first by Nicholson, and independently
by Clar. Press: *sere*, the bar or
balance-lever of a gun-lock (from
"serre," a talon), a stop-catch; if
"tickle," ticklish, loose, unsteady,
the gun goes off at a touch; lungs
tickle o' the sere, lungs that move to
laughter at a touch.
342. *lady*] Hamlet is ironical; the
lady, of course, will have indecent

words to utter; if she omits them,
the halting blank verse will betray
her delicacy.
347. *residence*] *i.e.* in the city.
350, 351.] See Appendix, p. 229.
357, 358. *eyrie of children, little
eyases*] eyrie or aerie, brood of nest-
lings; eyases, unfledged hawks. "Cry
out" carries on the metaphor. In *The
Gentleman's Recreation*, Part II. p.
21 (ed. 1686), we find "the name
Eyrie lasts as long as she is in the
Eyrie. These are very troublesome
in their feeding, *do cry very much.*"
Middleton, in *Father Hubburd's
Tales*, 1604, speaks of "a nest of
boys" at the Blackfriars "able to
ravish a man" (noted by Prof.
Hales).

little eyases, that cry out on the top of question
and are most tyrannically clapped for 't; these
are now the fashion, and so berattle the 360
common stages—so they call them—that many
wearing rapiers are afraid of goose-quills, and
dare scarce come thither.

Ham. What, are they children? who maintains 'em?
how are they escoted? Will they pursue the 365
quality no longer than they can sing? will
they not say afterwards, if they should grow
themselves to common players,—as it is most
like if their means are no better,—their writers
do them wrong, to make them exclaim against 370
their own succession?

Ros. 'Faith, there has been much to-do on both
sides, and the nation holds it no sin to tarre

---

360. *berattle*] F 2, *be-ratled* F.   368, 369. *most like*] Pope, *like most* F.
369. *no*] *not* F 2.

358. *cry . . . question*] clamour
forth the height of controversy, utter
shrilly the extreme matter of debate.
"Cry out" may be regarded as a
verb; to "cry on" is frequent in
Shakespeare; "cry out on" may be a
combination of the two; "question"
is a matter in dispute; the "top of
question" is the matter in dispute
pushed to extremity. Other explanations have been proposed. Clar.
Press: "Probably, to speak in a
high key, dominating conversation."
For "question" in this sense, see
Merchant of Venice, IV. i. 70. In
Armin's *Nest of Ninnies*, p. 55 (Sh.
Soc. reprint) occurs: "Cry it up in
the top of question." Prof. Hales
notes from *Adam Bede*: "Mrs.
Poyser keeps at the top o' the talk
like a fife."

359. *tyrannically*] outrageously;

probably alluding to what Bottom
calls "a tyrant's vein," or "a part
to make all split" (Rolfe).

361. *common stages*] the public,
as distinguished from the private,
theatres.

362. *rapiers*] fashionable gallants
are afraid to visit the "common"
theatres, so unfashionable have the
writers for the children made them.

365. *escoted*] paid. Dyce quotes
Cotgrave, "*Escotter*, Every one to pay
his shot."

366. *quality*] profession, and speci-
ally of players; so Massinger, *The
Picture*, II. i.:
"How do you like the quality?
You had a foolish itch to be an
actor."

373. *tarre*] set on to fight, used
specially of dogs, as in *Troilus ana
Cressida*, I. iii. 392.

them to controversy; there was, for a while,
no money bid for argument, unless the poet 375
and the player went to cuffs in the question.

Ham. Is't possible?

Guil. Oh, there has been much throwing about of
brains.   380

Ham. Do the boys carry it away?

Ros. Ay, that they do, my lord; Hercules and his
load too.

Ham. It is not very strange; for my uncle is King
of Denmark, and those, that would make 385
mows at him while my father lived, give
twenty, forty, fifty, an hundred ducats a-piece,
for his picture in little. 'Sblood, there is something in this more than natural, if philosophy
could find it out.   390

[Flourish of trumpets within.

Guil. There are the players.

Ham. Gentlemen, you are welcome to Elsinore.
Your hands, come; the appurtenance of welcome is fashion and ceremony: let me comply

---

384. *my*] Q, *mine* F.   386. *mows*] F, *mouths* Q.   387. *fifty*] Q,
omitted F; *an*] F, *a* Q.   388. *'Sblood*] Q, omitted F.   393. *hands,
come ;*] F; *hands come then*, Qq 2, 3; *hands, come then* Qq 4, 5; *hands : come
then*, Q 6.

375. *argument*] plot of a play, as in
III. ii. 244.
376, 377. *question*] Perhaps means
dialogue; perhaps controversy, debate; the poet for the children attacks
the common players.
381. *carry it away*] win the day.
382. *Hercules*] An allusion to the
Globe Theatre, the sign of which was
Hercules carrying the globe.

386. *mows*] grimaces, Fr. *moue.*
388. *picture in little*] miniature.
The children—miniature actors—now
carry away Hercules; so too have
fashions changed with respect to
kings.
393. *appurtenance*] adjuncts.
394. *comply*] observe the formalities
of courtesy, as in v, ii. 192; *garb*,
fashion.

6

with you in this garb, lest my extent to the 395
players, which, I tell you, must show fairly
outwards, should more appear like entertainment than yours.   You are welcome; but my
uncle-father and aunt-mother are deceived.

Guil. In what, my dear lord?   400

Ham. I am but mad north-north-west; when the
wind is southerly, I know a hawk from a
handsaw.

Re-enter POLONIUS.

Pol. Well be with you, gentlemen!

Ham. Hark you, Guildenstern;—and you too;—at 405
each ear a hearer: that great baby you see
there is not yet out of his swaddling-clouts.

395. *this*] Q, *the* F; *lest my*] F, Q 6; *let me* Qq 2, 3; *let my* Qq 4, 5.
397. *outwards*] Q, *outward* F.   406, 407. *you see there is*] *as you see is* Qq
4–6.   407. *swaddling*] Q, *swathing* F.

395. *extent*] behaviour, deportment,
as in *Twelfth Night*, IV. i. 57. Collier
proposed ostent.

401–403. *I am . . . handsaw*] I
am mad only in one point of the
compass. T. Bright, in *A Treatise of
Melancholy* (1586), mentions the
south and south-east winds as the
most suitable for sufferers from melancholy (chap. xxxix.). Burton gives
other opinions. A southerly wind
would, according to Bright, favour
Hamlet's sanity. North and north-
west, we may infer, would be the most
unfavourable. The word *hawk* was
and is used for a plasterer's tool, but no
example has been found earlier than
1700. *Hack*, however, is an Elizabethan name for a tool for breaking
or chopping up, and for agricultural
tools of the mattock, hoe, and pick-
axe type (*New Eng. Dict.*). *Handsaw* might suggest *hack*, for we
find in *1 Henry IV.* II. iv. 187, "My
sword hackt like a hand-saw." It is,
however, generally assumed that
"handsaw" here is a corruption of
heronshaw or *hernsew*; "no other
instances of the phrase (except as
quotations from Shakespeare) have
been found" (*New Eng. Dict.*). J. C.
Heath (quoted in Clar. Press) explains: the heron flying down the
north wind is ill seen, the spectator
looking south towards the sun; flying
north, on a south wind, it can be
easily distinguished from the hawk.
Does Hamlet imagine the two courtiers
as hawks loosed to pursue him? Elsewhere he compares them to hunters
driving him unto the toils. *The
Gentleman's Recreation* gives directions for the pursuit of a hern by a
pair of hawks. The south wind is
generally represented by Shakespeare
as a wind of evil contagion. Does
Hamlet mean that he can recognise
the King's birds of chase flying on an
ill wind? See App. III.

Ros. Happily he's the second time come to them;
 for, they say, an old man is twice a
 child.   410

Ham. I will prophesy he comes to tell me of the
 players; mark it.—You say right, sir; o'
 Monday morning; 'twas so, indeed.

Pol. My lord, I have news to tell you.

Ham. My lord, I have news to tell you. When 415
 Roscius was an actor in Rome,—

Pol. The actors are come hither, my lord.

Ham. Buz, buz!

Pol. Upon my honour—

Ham. Then came each actor on his ass,—   420

Pol. The best actors in the world, either for tragedy,
 comedy, history, pastoral, pastoral-comical,
 historical-pastoral, tragical-historical, tragical-
 comical-historical-pastoral, scene individable,
 or poem unlimited; Seneca cannot be too 425

408. *he's*] F, *he is* Q.   411. *prophesy he*] *prophecy, he* Qq 2, 3, *prophecy
that he* Qq 4-6, *Prophesie. Hee* F, *Prophesie, He* Ff 2-4.   412. *o'*] Capell,
a Q, *for a* F.   413. *morning ;*] *morning,* Qq 2, 3, *morning* Qq 4-6, F; *so*]
Q 1, F; *then* Q.   416. *was*] omitted in F.   419. *my*] Q, *mine* F;
honour—] Rowe ; *honour.* Q, F.   420. *came*] Q, *can* F.   422, 423. *pastoral-comical,   historical-pastoral,*] *Pastoricall-Comicall-Historicall-Pastorall*
F, Q omits the classes of drama which follow *historical-pastoral.*

408. *Happily*] Haply, as in i. i. 134.
412. *You say*] Hamlet would mislead Polonius as to the subject of their
conversation.
418. *Buz*] Blackstone says, "It was
an interjection used at Oxford when
anyone began a story that was generally known before." Schmidt: "An
interjection to command silence."
420. *Then . . . ass*]Johnson: "This
seems to be the line of a ballad."
Elze supposes that Hamlet makes
"on his ass" equivalent to Polonius's
"upon my honour."

424. *scene individable*]a play which
observes unity of place ; "poem unlimited," a play which disregards the
unities.
425, 426. *Seneca . . . Plautus*]
Seneca's tragedies had been translated by Newton and others, and
influenced the English drama. See
Cunliffe, *The Influence of Seneca on
Elizabethan Tragedy* (1893). Shakespeare's *Comedy of Errors* is founded on
Warner's translation of the *Menæchmi*
of Plautus.

heavy, nor Plautus too light. For the law of
writ and the liberty, these are the only men.

Ham. O Jephthah, judge of Israel, what a treasure
hadst thou!

Pol. What a treasure had he, my lord?   430

Ham. Why,

> *One fair daughter, and no more,*
> *The which he loved passing well.*

Pol. [*Aside.*] Still on my daughter.

Ham. Am I not i' the right, old Jephthah?   435

Pol. If you call me Jephthah, my lord, I have a
daughter that I love passing well.

Ham. Nay, that follows not.

Pol. What follows then, my lord?

Ham. Why,   440

> *As by lot, God wot,*

and then, you know,

> *It came to pass, as most like it was,—*

426, 427. *light. For . . . liberty, these*] Theobald, *light for . . . liberty: these* Q, *light, for . . . Liberty. These* F.   430. *What a treasure*] *What treasure* S. Walker, conject. Dyce (ed. 2).   434. Aside] Capell.   436–438. *If . . . not*] omitted in Qq 4–6.

426, 427. *law of writ and the liberty*] Capell: "This means pieces written in rule and pieces out of rule." Corson suggests that Seneca exemplified the law and Plautus the liberty of writing. Probably, however, the reference is to written plays and extemporised parts. In Middleton's *The Spanish Gipsy*, the gipsy-actors can perform in "a way which the Italians and the Frenchmen use":

> "That is, on a word given, or some slight plot,
> The actors will extempore fashion out
> Scenes neat and witty."

Rowe and other editors read "law of wit."

428. *Jephthah*] Steevens communicated the "pious chanson" to Percy; a reprint from a blackletter copy will be found in Child's *English and Scottish Ballads*. Hamlet quotes from the first stanza. Jephthah sacrificed his daughter; before her death she went into the wilderness to bewail her virginity. So with Ophelia. In lines 444, 445 Hamlet says "the first row of the pious chanson will show you more,"—perhaps he refers to the line "Great wars there should be."

the first row of the pious chanson will show
you more; for look where my abridgement 445
comes.

Enter four or five Players.

You are welcome, masters; welcome, all. I
am glad to see thee well: welcome, good friends.
—O, my old friend! Why, thy face is
valanced since I saw thee last; comest thou 450
to beard me in Denmark?—What, my young
lady and mistress! By 'r lady, your ladyship
is nearer to heaven than when I saw you last,
by the altitude of a chopine. Pray God, your
voice, like a piece of uncurrent gold, be not 455
cracked within the ring.—Masters, you are all

---

444. *pious chanson*] Qq 2–5; *Pons Chanson* F; *Pans Chanson* Ff 2–4, Q 6;
godly Ballet Q 1. 445, 446. *abridgement comes*] Q 1, Q; *abridgements
come* F. 447. *You are*] Q, *Y'are* F. 448. *thee*] Q, F; *ye* Dyce (ed. 2).
449. *my*] F, omitted Q; *Why, thy*] Q, *Thy* F. 450. *valanced*] Q, *valiant*
F. 452. *By 'r lady*] F, Q 1; *by lady* Qq 2–4; *my Lady* Qq 5, 6; *ladyship*]
Lordship Ff 3, 4. 453. *to heaven*] Q, *heaven* F.

444. *pious chanson*] The "godly
Ballet" of Q 1 confirms the reading
of Q. Attempts have been made by
reference to the French "Chanson du
Pont Neuf" to justify the Folio misprint. The ballad is "pious" as
having a scriptural subject. "Row"
perhaps means stanza, or perhaps
column of a broadside ballad.
445. *abridgement*] See *Midsummer
Night's Dream*, v. i. 39, where *abridgement* means an entertainment, which
shortens the time. Here it has both
this meaning and that of cutting short
the talk.
450. *valanced*] fringed (with a
beard).
454. *chopine*] Italian *ciopinno*.
Minsheu defines Spanish *chapin* "a

high cork shoe. Coryat in *Crudities*,
1611, describes the Venetian "chapi-
neys" as worn by ladies under the
shoes, sometimes half a yard high.
The boy who plays the lady has grown
since Hamlet saw him last. See
App. III.
456. *cracked within the ring*]
coins cracked within the circle which
surrounded the sovereign's head
were unfit for currency. Usurers,
Lodge tells us in *Wits Miserie*, 1596,
bought up "crackt angels" at nine
shillings a piece. Is there a play
on "ring"—a voice that rings clear
and true? In Beaumont's *Remedy
of Love* (xi. 477, Dyce) we find the
same expression: "If her voice be
bad, crack'd in the ring."

welcome. We 'll e'en to 't like French falconers,
fly at any thing we see : we 'll have a speech
straight ; come, give us a taste of your quality;
come, a passionate speech.   460
First Play. What speech, my good lord ?
Ham. I heard thee speak me a speech once, but
it was never acted; or, if it was, not above
once; for the play, I remember, pleased not
the million; 'twas caviare to the general; but   465
it was,—as I received it, and others, whose
judgments in such matters cried in the top
of mine,—an excellent play, well digested in
the scenes, set down with as much modesty
as cunning. I remember, one said there were   470
no sallets in the lines to make the matter
savoury, nor no matter in the phrase that
might indict the author of affection; but called
it an honest method, as wholesome as sweet,
and by very much more handsome than fine.   475

457. *French*] Q 1, F ; *friendly* Q.   461. *good*] Q 1, Q ; omitted in F.
467. *judgments*] Q, *judgement* F.   470. *were*]Q ; *was* Q 1, F.   473. *indict*] Collier ; *indite* Q, F ; *affection*] Q, *affectation* F.   474, 475. *as wholesome . . . fine*] Q, omitted in F.

457. *French falconers*] "It was the
fashion of our ancestors to sneer at
the French as falconers. They did
not regard the rigour of the game,
but condescended to any quarry that
came in their way" (D. H. Madden,
The Diary of Master William Silence,
p. 146).
459. *quality*] see line 366.
465. *caviare*] The spelling of Q 1
"caviary" and of F 1 "caviarie"
indicates the pronunciation here.
465. *the general*] the multitude.
Malone notes that Lord Clarendon
uses the word in this sense.

467, 468. *cried in the top of mine*]
sounded with authority above mine.
Perhaps a metaphor from a dog's
"over-topping" (baying more loudly
than the rest of the cry).
471. *sallets*] salads, containing
savoury herbs ; here, spicy impro-
prieties. Pope read *salts* (ed. 1) and
salt (ed. 2).
473. *affection*] means the same as
F *affectation*. *Love's Labour's Lost*, v.
i. 4 : "witty without affection."
475. *more handsome than fine*] more
becoming and graceful than showy.

One speech in it I chiefly loved; 'twas Æneas'
tale to Dido; and thereabout of it especially,
where he speaks of Priam's slaughter. If it
live in your memory, begin at this line: let
me see, let me see;—   480
The rugged Pyrrhus, like th' Hyrcanian beast,—
'tis not so; it begins with Pyrrhus:—
The rugged Pyrrhus,—he whose sable arms,
Black as his purpose, did the night resemble
When he lay couched in the ominous horse,—   485
Hath   now   this   dread   and   black   complexion
    smear'd
With heraldry more dismal; head to foot
Now is he total gules; horridly trick'd
With blood of fathers, mothers, daughters, sons,
Baked and impasted with the parching streets,   490
That lend a tyrannous and a damned light
To their lords' murder; roasted in wrath and fire,
And thus o'er-sized with coagulate gore,

476. *speech*] Q, *cheefe speech* F.   477. *tale*] Q 1, F; *talke* Q.   478. *where*]
Q 1, F; *when* Q.   482. *'tis not so ;*] Qq 2, 3 (later Qq omit *so*); *It is not
so :* F.   486. this] his Q 1, Q 6.   487. dismal ; head to foot] F, dismall
head to foote, Q.   491. and a] Q, and F.   492. their lords' murder]
Capell, their Lords murther Q, their vilde murthers F, their lord's murder
Steevens.

481. The rugged Pyrrhus] This tale
of Æneas to Dido is made to stand
out from the general movement of the
play by being written in the tragic
style of Shakespeare's early contem-
poraries. *Dido, Queen of Carthage*,
says Fleay, was written by Marlowe
and Nash. The narrative of Priam's
death he ascribed to Nash (and afterwards to Marlowe). He supposed
that this scene was written by Shakespeare in 1594, in competition with
the scene in *Dido*, and was introduced

about 1601 into the first draught of
Hamlet. This is conjecture ; what is
certain is that Shakespeare reproduces,
without any intention of burlesque, a
style which he had left far behind
him.

481. Hyrcanian beast] the tiger ; see
Macbeth, III. iv. 101.

488. gules] heraldic for red, as in
Timon of Athens, IV. iii. 59. "Trick'd"
may also be the heraldic term, meaning to describe in drawing.

With eyes like carbuncles, the hellish Pyrrhus
Old grandsire Priam seeks.   495
So, proceed you.

Pol. 'Fore God, my lord, well spoken, with good
accent and good discretion.

First Play.   *Anon he finds him*
Striking too short at Greeks ; his antique sword, 500
Rebellious to his arm, lies where it falls,
Repugnant to command ; unequal match'd,
Pyrrhus at Priam drives ; in rage strikes wide ;
But with the whiff and wind of his fell sword
The unnerved father falls.   Then senseless Ilium, 505
Seeming to feel this blow, with flaming top
Stoops to his base, and with a hideous crash
Takes prisoner Pyrrhus' ear ; for, lo ! his sword,
Which was declining on the milky head
Of reverend Priam, seem'd i' the air to stick ;   510
So, as a painted tyrant, Pyrrhus stood,
And like a neutral to his will and matter,
Did nothing.
But, as we often see, against some storm,
A silence in the heavens, the rack stand still,   515
The bold winds speechless and the orb below

---

496. *So, proceed you*] Q, omitted F.
505. Then senseless Ilium] F, omitted Q.
like] F, Like Q.

502. match'd] Q, match F.
506. this] Q, his F.   512. And

504, 505. But . . . falls] Compare
Dido, Queen of Carthage :
   "Which he disdaining whiskt his
      sword about,
   And with the wind thereof the
      king fell down."
511. painted tyrant] Compare *Macbeth*, v. viii. 25–27.

512. a neutral] one indifferent to
his purpose and its object.
515. rack] Dyce (*Gloss.*) : "a mass
of vapoury clouds."   "The winds in
the upper region, which move the
clouds above (which we call the
rack)" (Bacon, *Sylva Sylvarum*, ii. §
115).

As hush as death, anon the dreadful thunder
Doth rend the region ; so, after Pyrrhus' pause,
Aroused vengeance sets him new a-work ;
And never did the Cyclops' hammers fall   520
On Mars's armour, forged for proof eterne,
With less remorse than Pyrrhus' bleeding sword
Now falls on Priam.
Out, out, thou strumpet, Fortune ! All you gods,
In general synod take away her power ;   525
Break all the spokes and fellies from her wheel,
And bowl the round nave down the hill of heaven
As low as to the fiends !

Pol. This is too long.

Ham. It shall to the barber's, with your beard.— 530
Prithee, say on ; he 's for a jig or a tale of
bawdry, or he sleeps : say on ; come to
Hecuba.

First Play. But who, O, who had seen the mobled
queen—   535

Ham. " The mobled queen ? "

Pol. That 's good ; " mobled queen " is good.

519. Aroused] Collier ; A rowsed Q, F.   521. Mars's armour] Capell,
Marses Armor Q, Mars his Armours F.   524. strumpet, Fortune] hyphened
in F.   534. who, O, who] F, who, a woe Q, who, ah woe Q 6.   534,
536. mobled] Q, Ff 2–4 ; inobled F ; ennobl'd Capell.   536. *queen ?*] F,
Queene. Q.   537. *mobled . . . good*] omitted in Q.

518. region] Clar. Press : "Originally a division of the sky marked out
by the Roman augurs. In later times
the atmosphere was divided into three
regions—upper, middle, and lower."
Used by Shakespeare for the space of
air, as in *Romeo and Juliet*, ii. ii. 21.
531. *jig*] a ludicrous metrical com-
position, sometimes given on stages
by the clown, sometimes, as Cotgrave
says, " at the end of an Enterlude,
wherein some pretie Knaverie is
acted."
534. mobled] muffled. Warburton
quotes from Sandys' *Travels* : "Their
[Turkish women's] heads and faces
are so mabled in fine linen." Farmer
quotes Shirley, *Gentleman of Venice* :
" The moon does mobble up herself.'

First Play. *Run barefoot up and down, threatening the*
flames

With bisson rheum ; a clout upon that head

Where late the diadem stood ; and for a robe,   540

About her lank and all o'er-teemed loins,

A blanket, in the alarm of fear caught up ;

Who this had seen, with tongue in venom steep'd,

'Gainst Fortune's state would treason have pro-
nounced :

But if the gods themselves did see her then,   545

When she saw Pyrrhus make malicious sport

In mincing with his sword her husband's limbs,

The instant burst of clamour that she made,—

Unless things mortal move them not at all,—

Would have made milch the burning eyes of
heaven   550

And passion in the gods.

Pol. Look, whether he has not turned his colour
and has tears in 's eyes.   Prithee, no more.

Ham. 'Tis well; I 'll have thee speak out the rest
of this soon.—Good my lord, will you see the   555
players well bestowed ? Do you hear, let
them be well used, for they are the abstracts
and brief chronicles of the time ; after your

538. flames] Q, flame F.   539. upon] Q, about F.   551. passion in]
passioned Hanmer, passionate Collier MS.   553. *Prithee*] Q, *Pray you* F.
555. *of this*] Q, omitted F.   556. *bestowed ?*] Theobald, bestowed ; Q,
bestow'd. F ; *you hear*] Q, *ye heare* F.   557. abstracts] F, abstract Q.

539. bisson] blinding. More commonly "blind" or "purblind," as
in *Coriolanus*, II. i. 70.
544. state] perhaps, as often, power,
majesty ; but possibly seat or chair of
dignity, as in *Macbeth*, III. iv. 5.
550. milch] moist, as in Drayton

Polyolbion, xiii. 171, "exhaling the
milch dew."
551] Marston, in *The Insatiate
Countess*, I. i., refers to "a player's
passion" weeping for "old Priam"—
evidently pointing to this scene.

death you were better have a bad epitaph than
their ill report while you live. 560

Pol. My lord, I will use them according to their
desert.

Ham. God's bodykins, man, much better! Use
every man after his desert, and who should
'scape whipping? Use them after your own 565
honour and dignity; the less they deserve,
the more merit is in your bounty. Take
them in.

Pol. Come, sirs.

Ham. Follow him, friends: we'll hear a play to- 570
morrow.

> [*Exit Polonius, with all the Players, but
> the First.*

Dost thou hear me, old friend; can you play
The Murder of Gonzago?

First Play. Ay, my lord.

Ham. We'll ha't to-morrow night. You could, 575
for a need, study a speech of some dozen or
sixteen lines, which I would set down and
insert in't, could you not?

First Play. Ay, my lord.

Ham. Very well. Follow that lord; and look you 580
mock him not.

> [*Exit First Player.*

560. *live*] Q, *lived* F.   563. *bodykins*] F, *bodkin* Q; *much*] Q, *farre* Q 1,
omitted F.   564. *should*] F, *shall* Q. Exit, &c.] Dyce, Exit Polon. F
after line 569; Exeunt Pol. and Players Q after "Elsinore," line 583.
576. *for a need*] Q 1, F; *for need* Q; *dozen*] Q 1, F; *dosen lines* Q.
578. *in't*,] Q, *in't?* F; *you*] Q, *ye* F. Exit First Player] Dyce, omitted Q, F.

563. *bodykins*] dear body—diminu-   576, 577. *dozen or sixteen lines*]
tive of endearment.   See III. ii. 200 (note).

—My good friends, I 'll leave you till night;
you are welcome to Elsinore.

Ros. Good my lord!

Ham. Ay, so, God be wi' ye!

     [*Exeunt Rosencrantz and Guildenstern.*
       —Now I am alone. 585

Oh, what a rogue and peasant slave am I!
Is it not monstrous that this player here,
But in a fiction, in a dream of passion,
Could force his soul so to his own conceit
That from her working all his visage wann'd; 590
Tears in his eyes, distraction in 's aspect,
A broken voice, and his whole function suiting
With forms to his conceit? And all for nothing!
For Hecuba?
What 's Hecuba to him, or he to Hecuba, 595
That he should weep for her? What would
  he do
Had he the motive and the cue for passion
That I have? He would drown the stage with tears,
And cleave the general ear with horrid speech,
Make mad the guilty and appal the free, 600

585. *God be wi' ye*] *God buy to you* Q, *God buy 'ye* F. Exeunt . . .]
Globe Sh.; Exeunt after line 584 Q, F. 589. *own*] Q, *whole* F. 590. *his
visage*] F, *the visage* Q; *wann'd*] *wand* Q, *warm'd* F. 591. *in 's*] F, *in
his* Q. 593. *nothing !*] Capell, *nothing*, Q, *nothing ?* F. 594. *Hecuba ?*]
F, *Hecuba.* Q, *Hecuba!* Capell. 595. *to Hecuba*] Q 1, F; *to her* Q.
597. *the cue for*] F, *that for* Q.

586. *peasant slave*] Furness: "It
is shown by Furnivall in *Notes and
Queries*, 12th April and 3rd May
1873, that it was possible for Shakespeare to have seen in the flesh some
of the bondmen or ' peasant slaves '
of England."

592. *function*] operation of the
faculties, as in *Macbeth*, I. iii. 140;
conceit, conception.
600. *free*] innocent, as in III. ii.
254.

Confound the ignorant, and amaze indeed
The very faculties of eyes and ears.
Yet I,
A dull and muddy-mettled rascal, peak,
Like John-a-dreams, unpregnant of my cause, 605
And can say nothing; no, not for a king,
Upon whose property and most dear life
A damn'd defeat was made.   Am I a coward?
Who calls me villain? breaks my pate across?
Plucks off my beard, and blows it in my face? 610
Tweaks me by the nose? gives me the lie i' the
  throat,
As deep as to the lungs? Who does me this?
Ha!
'Swounds, I should take it; for it cannot be
But I am pigeon-liver'd, and lack gall 615
To make oppression bitter; or ere this
I should have fatted all the region kites
With this slave's offal; bloody, bawdy villain!

---

602. *faculties*] Q, *faculty* F.   613. *Ha!*] separate line Steevens; begins
line 614 Q, F; *Ha?* F.   614. *'Swounds*] Q, *Why* F.   618. *offal;
bloody,*] *offall, bloody,* Q, *Offall, bloudy: a* F.

601. *amaze*] confound, as in *King
John*, IV. ii. 137.
604. *peak*] to dwindle, pine; hence
to play a mean part, as in *Merry
Wives*, III. v. 71.
605. *John-a-dreams*] found also in
Armin, *Nest of Ninnies*, 1608. "John-
a-droynes" is found in Nash, *Have
with you to Saffron Walden*, 1596.
605. *unpregnant*] unimpregnated,
unquickened by my cause. See *Measure for Measure*, IV. iv. 23.
607. *property*] proprietorship (of
crown and wife).
608. *defeat*] undoing, act of destruc-
tion, as in v. ii. 58. Chapman,
Revenge for Honour:
  "That he might meantime make a
    sure defeat
  On our good aged father's life."
615. *pigeon-liver'd*] The pigeon was
supposed to secrete no gall.   So
Dekker, *The Honest Whore* (Pearson's
Dekker, ii. p. 20), "Sure hee's a
pigeon, for he has no gall." Gall,
the physical cause of rancour, bitter-
ness.
617. *region kites*] kites of the air;
see line 518.

Remorseless, treacherous, lecherous, kindless villain !

O, vengeance !   620

Why, what an ass am I !   This is most brave,

That I, the son of a dear father murder'd,

Prompted to my revenge by heaven and hell,

Must, like a whore, unpack my heart with words,

And fall a-cursing, like a very drab,   625

A scullion !

Fie upon 't ! foh !   About, my brain !   I have
    heard

That guilty creatures, sitting at a play,

Have, by the very cunning of the scene,

Been struck so to the soul that presently   630

They have proclaim'd their malefactions ;

For murder, though it have no tongue, will
    speak

With most miraculous organ.   I 'll have these
    players

Play something like the murder of my father

Before mine uncle ; I 'll observe his looks ;   635

620. *O, vengeance !*] omitted in Q.
This] Q, *I* [*i.e. Ay*] *sure, this* F.
a deere murthered Q, *the Deere murthered* F.
Q, *cullion* Theobald.   627. *brain*] F, *braines* Q ;

621. *Why,*] *Why* Q, *Who ?* F ;
622. *a dear father murder'd*] Q 4,
    626. *scullion*] F, *stallyon*
    I] F, *hum, I* Q.

619. *kindless*] unnatural.
622. *dear father murder'd*] Halliwell supports the reading, "a dear
murdered " by comparing the phrase
"the dear departed."
627. *About, my brain !*] Wits, to
your work ! Steevens quotes from
Heywood, *The Iron Age*, Part
II. :
    "My brain about again ! for thou
        hast found
    New projects now to work on."
The *Hum* of Q is a meditative

interjection, retained by *Cambridge
Sh.* and by Furness.
628. *play*] Massinger had this passage probably in his mind in writing
The Roman Actor, II. i.   In *A Warn-
ing for Fair Women*, 1599, the tale is
told of a woman led by a play to
confess her husband's murder. Heywood, in his *Apology for Actors*, tells
of this case, and of another at
Amsterdam.
630. *presently*] immediately, as in
line 170.

I 'll tent him to the quick; if he but blench
I know my course. The spirit that I have seen
May be the devil; and the devil hath power
To assume a pleasing shape; yea, and perhaps
Out of my weakness and my melancholy,   640
As he is very potent with such spirits,
Abuses me to damn me. I 'll have grounds
More relative than this. The play 's the thing
Wherein I 'll catch the conscience of the king.

[*Exit.*

ACT III

SCENE I.—*A Room in the Castle.*

Enter KING, QUEEN, POLONIUS, OPHELIA, ROSEN-
CRANTZ, *and* GUILDENSTERN.

King. And can you, by no drift of circumstance,
Get from him why he puts on this confusion,

636. *he but*] F, *a doe* Q.   638. *be the devil*] F, *be a deale* Q (*deale*
repeated again in this line in Q).

Act III. Scene I.

1. *circumstance*] F, *conference* Q.

636. *tent*] probe, as in *Cymbeline*,
III. iv. 118.
636. *blench*] flinch, quail; used
specially of the eyes.
638. *devil*] Coleridge quotes from
Browne's *Religio Medici*, Part I. § 37,
to show that he held the belief that
ghosts are often devils abusing men to
damn them. See on this subject
Spalding's *Elizabethan Demonology*.
642. *Abuses*] deceives, deludes, as
in *Tempest*, v. i. 112.
643. *relative*] closely related, to

the purpose, conclusive; used only
here by Shakespeare.

Act III. Scene I.

1. *drift of circumstance*] Clar. Press
explain: "roundabout method," referring to "circumstance" in I. v. 127,
"drift" in II. i. 10, and both words
(but not in connection) in *Troilus
and Cressida*, III. iii. 113, 114. May
it mean tendency or significance of
incidental facts?

Grating so harshly all his days of quiet
With turbulent and dangerous lunacy?

He had confessed —this

Ros. He does confess he feels himself distracted,   5
But from what cause he will by no means speak.

Guil. Nor do we find him forward to be sounded,

behaviour to Polonius But, with a crafty madness, keeps aloof,
When we would bring him on to some confession
Of his true state.

Queen.   Did he receive you well?   10

Ros. Most like a gentleman.

Guil. But with much forcing of his disposition.

Ros. Niggard of question, but of our demands
Most free in his reply.

Queen.   Did you assay him
To any pastime?   15

Ros. Madam, it so fell out that certain players
We o'er-raught on the way; of these we told
him,
And there did seem in him a kind of joy
To hear of it; they are about the court
And, as I think, they have already order   20
This night to play before him.

19. *about*] F, *heere about* Q.

13, 14. *Niggard . . . reply*] Warburton transposed "Niggard" and
"Most free." Malone explains
"Niggard of question," slow to begin
conversation. Clarke — over-ingeni-
ously: "Sparing of speech when
questioned, but of demands respect-
ing ourselves he was very free in
return." Clar. Press: "Perhaps they
did not intend to give a correct account
of the interview." The courtiers between them try to piece out an account,
which will not discredit them, of an
unsuccessful interview; Rosencrantz
would suggest that they have not
wholly failed; Guildenstern that this
was in spite of much difficulty. They
wish to turn off any inquiry as to
Hamlet's sharp examination of them
and his discovery that they were sent
for.

17. *o'er-raught*]over-reached, overtook.

Pol.   'Tis most true;
  And he beseech'd me to entreat your majesties
  To hear and see the matter.
King. With all my heart; and it doth much con-
        tent me
    To hear him so inclined.—   25
    Good gentlemen, give him a further edge, *keenness*
    And drive his purpose on to these delights.
Ros. We shall, my lord.
              [*Exeunt Rosencrantz and Guildenstern.*
King.   Sweet Gertrude, leave us too:
  For we have closely sent for Hamlet hither,
  That he, as 'twere by accident, may here   30
  Affront Ophelia.
    Her father and myself, lawful espials,
    Will so bestow ourselves that, seeing unseen,
    We may of their encounter frankly judge,
    And gather by him, as he is behaved,   35
    If 't be the affliction of his love or no
    That thus he suffers for.
Queen.   I shall obey you.—
  And for your part, Ophelia, I do wish
  That your good beauties be the happy cause
  Of Hamlet's wildness; so shall I hope your
      virtues   40

---

27. *on to*] F, *into* Q.   28. *too*] F, *two* Q.   30. *here*] Q, *there* F.
32. *lawfal espials*] F, omitted in Q.   33. *Will*] F, *Wee 'le* Q.   38. *your*]
Q, F; *my* Qq 4–6, Pope and others.   Exit Queen] Theobald, omitted Q, F.

29. *closely*] secretly, as in *King*   32. *espials*] spies, as in *1 Henry*
John, IV. i. 133.   *VI.* I. iv. 8.
31. *Affront*] confront, encounter,   39, 40. *beauties . . . virtues*] S.
as in *Winter's Tale*, v. i. 75.   Walker proposed *beauty* and *virtue*,
                                              which Furness adopts.

7

Will bring him to his wonted way again,
To both your honours.

Oph.   Madam, I wish it may.

[*Exit Queen.*

Pol. Ophelia, walk you here.——Gracious, so please you,
We will bestow ourselves. [*To Ophelia.*] Read on
this book,   *give an excuse for*
That show of such an exercise may colour   45
Your loneliness.   We are oft to blame in this,——
'Tis too much proved,——that with devotion's visage
And pious action we do sugar o'er
The devil himself.

King. [*Aside.*]   Oh, 'tis too true!
How smart a lash that speech doth give my con-
science!   50
The harlot's cheek, beautied with plastering art,
Is not more ugly to the thing that helps it *(maid)*
Than is my deed to my most painted word.
O heavy burden!   *^deceptive*

Pol. I hear him coming; let's withdraw, my lord.   55

[*Exeunt King and Polonius.*

He has a conscience

Enter HAMLET.

Ham. To be, or not to be: that is the question:

43. *please you*] Q, *please ye* F.   46. *loneliness*] F, *lowlines* Q.   48. *sugar*]
Q, *surge* F.   49. Aside] Capell, at line 50 Pope; *'tis too*] Q, *'tis* F.
55. *let's*] F, omitted Q.   Enter *Hamlet*] F, after *burden*, line 54, Q.

43. *Gracious*] addressed to the
King.
45. *exercise*] act of devotion (the
book being one of prayers), as in
King Richard III. III. vii. 64: "his
holy exercise."
52. *to*] compared to, as in I. ii. 140.

56. *To be, or not to be :*] Explained
by Johnson as a future life, or non-
existence after death; by Malone, to
live, or to commit suicide. G. Macdonald regards the words as the close
of a preceding train of thought, not
to be connected with what follows

Whether 'tis nobler in the mind to suffer
The slings and arrows of outrageous fortune,
Or to take arms against a sea of troubles,   *violent change of metaphor*
And by opposing end them? To die, — to
    sleep,—   60
No more; and by a sleep to say we end
The heart-ache, and the thousand natural shocks
That flesh is heir to, 'tis a consummation   *- completing*
Devoutly to be wish'd. To die;—to sleep;—
To sleep! perchance to dream! ay, there's the
    rub;   65
For in that sleep of death what dreams may come,
When we have shuffled off this mortal coil,

60, 61. *To die,— . . . No*] Pope, *die to sleepe No* Q, *dye, to sleepe No* F. 63. *to,*] *too;* Q, *too?* F.   64, 65. *die ;—to sleep ;—To sleep !*] Capell, *die to sleepe, To sleepe,* Q, F.

Hunter, who would place the soliloquy, with Q I, in Act II. sc. ii. supposes it is suggested by the book which Hamlet is there represented as reading. Perhaps, the explanation lying in what immediately follows, it means, Is my present project of active resistance against wrong to be, or not to be? Hamlet anticipates his own death as a probable consequence.

57. *in the mind*] This is to be connected with "suffer," not with "nobler."

58. *slings and arrows*] Walker, with an anonymous writer of 1752, would read "stings." "Slings and arrows" is found in Fletcher's *Valentinian*, I. iii.

59. *sea*] Various emendations have been suggested: Theobald, "siege"; also, "th' assay" or "a 'say"; Hanmer, "assailing"; Warburton, "assail of"; Bailey, "the seat." It has been shown from Aristotle, Strabo, Ælian, and Nicolas of Damascus that the Kelts, Gauls, and Cimbri exhibited their intrepidity by armed combats with the sea, which Shakespeare might have found in Abraham Fleming's translation of *Ælian*, 1576. But elsewhere Shakespeare has "sea of joys," "sea of glory," "sea of care." Here the central metaphor is that of a battle ("slings and arrows"); the "sea of troubles," billows of the war, merely develops the metaphor of battle, as in Scott, *Marmion*, VI. xxvi. :

> "Then mark'd they, dashing
>   broad and far,
> The broken billows of the war,
> And plumed crests of chieftains
>   brave,
> Floating like foam upon the
>   wave."

63. *consummation*] Compare *Cymbeline*, IV. ii. 280 :

> "Quiet consummation have :
> And renowned be thy grave !"

65. *rub*] impediment, as in *King Henry V.* II. ii. 188.

67. *mortal coil*] trouble or turmoil of mortal life. In this sense *coil* occurs several times in Shakespeare,

Must give us pause: there's the respect
That makes calamity of so long life;
For who would bear the whips and scorns of
    time,   70
The oppressor's wrong, the proud man's con-
    tumely, _insult·_
The pangs of disprized love, the law's delay,
The insolence of office, and the spurns
That patient merit of the unworthy takes,
When he himself might his quietus make   75
With a bare bodkin? who would fardels bear,
To grunt and sweat under a weary life,
But that the dread of something after death,
The undiscover'd country from whose bourn
No traveller returns, puzzles the will,   80

imagery seemingly accidental.

71. _proud_] Q, _poore_ F.   72. _disprized_] F, _despiz'd_ Q and many editors.
76. _fardels_] Q, _these Fardles_ F.

as in _Tempest_, I. ii. 207. He nowhere uses it in the sense of concentric rings, nor does the _New English Dictionary_ give an example earlier than 1627. The notion that _mortal coil_ means the body, encircling the soul, may be set aside. [Hardly, at least as a secondary meaning. N. C. S. refers to N. E. D. _coil_, v. 3. R. H. C.]

68, 69. _there's . . . life_] There's the consideration that makes calamity so long-lived.

70. _time_] the times, the world, as in _King John_, v. ii. 12, "a sore of time." But perhaps it may mean time as opposed to eternity.

72. _disprized_] undervalued, misprised. _Troilus and Cressida_ (Folio text), IV. v. 74: "disprising The knight opposed." The Q _despised love_ is preferred by many editors.

75. _quietus_] acquittance; the law-term, "quietus est," for the settle-

ment of an account; as in _Sonnets_, cxxvi. 12.

76. _bare bodkin_] unsheathed dagger; or _bare_ may mean "mere." Sidney, _Arcadia_: "I . . . doe defie thee in a mortal affray from the bodkin to the pike upward."

76. _fardels_] packs, burdens, as in _Winter's Tale_, IV. iv. 728.

77. _grunt_] groan. Steevens quotes Turbervile, _Ovid Epist._ xiv.: "of dying men the grunts." Compare _Julius Cæsar_, IV. i. 22: "To groan and sweat under the business."

80. _returns_] The Ghost has not crossed the bourn or boundary of death, or returned to mortal life; cockcrow and day-dawn startle him away. Perhaps, however, Hamlet at the present time, doubtful as to whether the devil may not have been abusing him (close of Act II.), will not let the apparition enter into his calculations.

And makes us rather bear those ills we have
Than fly to others that we know not of?
Thus conscience does make cowards of us all,
And thus the native hue of resolution
Is sicklied o'er with the pale cast of thought,   85
And enterprises of great pitch and moment
With this regard their currents turn awry
And lose the name of action.   Soft you now!
The fair Ophelia?   Nymph, in thy orisons
Be all my sins remember'd.

Oph.   Good my lord,   90
How does your honour for this many a day?

83. *of us all*] Q 1, F ; omitted Q.   86. *pitch*] Q, *pith* F.   87. *awry*] Q,
away F.   89. *Ophelia?*] F, *Ophelia*, Q, *Ophelia!* Hanmer.

85. *thought*] often used of anxious or melancholy thought, as in *Julius Cæsar*, II. i. 187 : "take thought and die for Cæsar."   See IV. v. 187.
86. *pitch*] height, as in *King Richard III.* III. vii. 188; used of a falcon's soaring, *1 King Henry VI.* II. iv. 11.   The Folio *pith* is preferred by many editors, and appears in late Quartos from 1676 onwards.
88. *action*] With the thought of action this soliloquy opens and closes. The train of ideas is as follows :— Active resistance to evil or passive fortitude—which is more worthy of me?   To end troubles—perhaps by one's own death?   Well, the sleep of death will be most welcome ; but what if there be terrible dreams? The fear of the hereafter is universal, else men would not endure the ills of life ; and thus it is that, perplexed by calculating consequences, we drop away from heroic action.   Parallels, as possible sources for parts of this soliloquy, have been pointed out in Catullus (no traveller returns), Cardan (death a sleep), Seneca (no traveller returns, and fear of futurity), Mon-

taigne (sea of troubles, death a desirable "consummation," conscience makes cowards), Cornelius Agrippa (country of the dead irremeable), Marlowe's *Edward II.* (Mortimer goes as a traveller to discover countries yet unknown).   It seems probable, as Professor Skeat notices, that there are reminiscences here of the translation ascribed to Chaucer of *The Romaunt of the Rose*, lines 5637–5696; the word *fardels* is perhaps one of the echoes from this passage. It is worth noting that Mr. G. Macdonald eliminates the thought of suicide from the soliloquy, supposing that the bare bodkin is imagined as directed against an enemy.   Suicide, indeed, is not the theme of the soliloquy, but it incidentally enters into it.   "Clelia" in his *God in Shakespeare* construes the opening sentence thus : "Whether 'tis nobler to bear evil or to resist it the question is To be, or not to be, *i.e.* Is there a life after death?"   The note of interrogation after "end them," line 60, was first introduced by Pope.

Remembers to act (handwritten)

Ham. I humbly thank you; well, well, well.

Oph. My lord, I have remembrances of yours,
That I have longed long to re-deliver;
I pray you now, receive them.

Ham.   No, not I;   95
I never gave you aught.

Oph. My honour'd lord, you know right well you did;
And, with them, words of so sweet breath composed
As made the things more rich; their perfume
lost,
Take these again; for to the noble mind   100
Rich gifts wax poor when givers prove unkind.
There, my lord.

Might have heard a rustle. (handwritten)

Ham. Ha, ha! are you honest?

Oph. My lord?

Ham. Are you fair?   105

Oph. What means your lordship?

---

92. *you; well, well, well.*] F, *you well.* Q.   95. *you now,*] F, *you now*
Q, *you, now* Theobald and other editors; *No, not I*] Q, *No, no* F.
97. *you know*] Q, *I know* F and many editors.   99. *the things*] F, *these
things* Q; *rich; their perfume lost*] Q, *rich, then perfume left*: F, *rich, than
perfume left* F 4.

96. *aught*] For a moment Hamlet has been touched by the sight of Ophelia with her book of prayers. Yet there is estrangement in the word "Nymph." She inquires for his health (having seen him yesterday); he answers as to a stranger; formally, as he does to Osric, v. ii. 82; and with some impatience; he will tell her nothing. She produces his gifts; he has been sent for by the King; Ophelia, like Rosencrantz and Guildenstern, has doubtless also been sent for; he falls back on his accustomed method of baffling half-truths. These toys were the gift of another Hamlet to another Ophelia—not his.

99. *their perfume*] the perfume of the gifts, derived from the sweet words.

101. *unkind*] The sententious generalisation, couched in rhyme, has an air of having been prepared. And whence this false accusation of unkindness? Has she not rehearsed her part to Polonius?

103. *honest*] a word which covers both truthfulness and chastity. For the meaning "chaste" Staunton quotes an apt example from Shirley, *The Royal Master*, IV. i. Withals' *Dictionarie* (1608), p. 73: "She is faire, that is honest: est alma sancta."

Ham. That if you be honest and fair, your honesty
should admit no discourse to your beauty.

Oph. Could beauty, my lord, have better commerce
than with honesty?   110

Ham. Ay, truly; for the power of beauty will sooner
transform honesty from what it is to a bawd
than the force of honesty can translate beauty
into his likeness; this was sometime a paradox,
but now the time gives it proof. I did love 115
you once.

Oph. Indeed, my lord, you made me believe so.

Ham. You should not have believed me; for virtue
cannot so inoculate our old stock but we shall
nal sin relish of it; I loved you not. *He intends* 120 *to hunt her*

Oph. I was the more deceived.

Ham. Get thee to a nunnery; why wouldst thou be *Disgust of mankind*
a breeder of sinners? I am myself indifferent

---

107. *your honesty*] F, *you* Q. 110. *with*] Q, *your* F. 119. *inoculate*]
F, *euocutat* Q, *evacuate* Qq 4–6. 122. *to*] F, omitted Q.

107, 108.] Hamlet had ironically
baffled Polonius by commending his
wisdom in restraining and secluding
Ophelia; the same irony will serve
again. Your father and brother were
right; your virtue should permit no
one to hold converse with your beauty.
Ophelia replies as if Hamlet had said
that beauty and honesty should not
hold converse with each other, and
he accepts her reading of his words.

109. *commerce*] intercourse, as in
Twelfth Night, III. iv. 191.

111–116.] I loved you once—in the
days when it was a paradox—an ab-
surdity—to say that beauty could sooner
transform virtue into a procuress for
lust than virtue could translate beauty
to its own likeness. But now, the
world, the present time, proves the

paradox true; Hamlet thinks of his
mother; of his own honesty represented
as a wanton passion for beauty; of
Ophelia's virtue, which cannot be
trusted by Polonius to act as guardian
of her beauty, but will rather corrupt
his and her honesty.

119. *inoculate*] used in the botanical
sense, to graft by the insertion of a
bud; virtue cannot so graft love in our
old evil stock but that we shall have a
flavour of this evil stock. So Bishop
Hall: "That Palatine vine, late inocu-
lated with a precious bud of our royal
stem."

120. *I loved you not*] it was not true
love, for the taint of evil was in it; so
your father has told you, and you have
acted in accordance with his orders.

123. *indifferent*] fairly, as in v. ii. 97.

honest; but yet I could accuse me of such
things that it were better my mother had not 125
borne me. I am very proud, revengeful, ambitious; with more offences at my beck than
I have thoughts to put them in, imagination
to give them shape, or time to act them in.
What should such fellows as I do crawling 130
between heaven and earth? We are arrant
knaves all; believe none of us. Go thy ways
to a nunnery. Where's your father?

*She lies, probably
out of pure fright*

Oph. At home, my lord.

Ham. Let the doors be shut upon him, that he may 135
play the fool no where but in's own house.
Farewell.

Oph. Oh, help him, you sweet heavens!

Ham. If thou dost marry, I'll give thee this plague
for thy dowry: be thou as chaste as ice, as 140
pure as snow, thou shalt not escape calumny.
Get thee to a nunnery, go; farewell. Or, if

127. *beck*] Q, F; *backe* Q 1.   131. *heaven and earth*] Q 1, F; *earth and heaven* Q.   132. *all*] Q 1, F; omitted Q.   136. *no where*] Q, *no way* F.
138, 147.] marked Aside, Furness.   142. *go*] F, omitted Q.

126,127. *very proud, revengeful, ambitious*] Hamlet brings general accusa-
tions against manhood and womanhood; but these particular vices are
ironically named as those of which he
has been suspected or calumniously
accused: very proud, he who honours
the poor Horatio, and hails the actor
as a friend, yet he is suspected of
treating Ophelia lightly, as an inferior
who may be basely used; revengeful,
he who groans under the duty of
vengeance, yet who is doubtless
suspected of revenge by the King;
ambitious, he who would go back to
Wittenberg, and could be contented

in a nutshell, yet whose disappointed
ambition has been a subject for the
probing of Rosencrantz and Guildenstern.

133. *Where's your father*] Perhaps
an arrow shot at a venture; or perhaps
he has caught sight of the King and
Polonius as they retire. It is to be
considered as a possibility that Ophelia
may not have been aware of her
father's espionage.

141. *calumny*] Is this promise of
dowry half meant for Polonius's ear?
His calumnies of Hamlet will come
home to roost on his own house.

thou wilt needs marry, marry a fool; for wise
men know well enough what monsters you
make of them.   To a nunnery, go; and 145
quickly too.   Farewell.

Oph. O heavenly powers, restore him!

Ham. I have heard of your paintings too, well
enough; God has given you one face, and
you make yourselves another; you jig, you 150
amble, and you lisp, and nickname God's
creatures, and make your wantonness your
ignorance.   Go to, I'll no more on't; it hath
made me mad.   I say we will have no more
marriages; those that are married already, all 155
but one, shall live; the rest shall keep as they
are.   To a nunnery, go.   [*Exit.*

Oph. Oh, what a noble mind is here o'erthrown!
The courtier's, soldier's, scholar's, eye, tongue, sword;
The expectancy and rose of the fair state, 160

147. *O*] F, omitted Q.   148. *paintings*] Q 1, Q; *pratlings* F; *pratling*
Ff 2–4; *too*] F, omitted Q.   149. *has*] F, *hath* Q; *face*] Q 1, Q; *pace* F.
150. *yourselves*] Q, *your selfe* F; *jig*] Q 1676, *gig* Q, *gidge* F, *fig* Q 1.
150, 151. *you amble*] F, *and amble* Q.   151. *lisp*] F, *list* Q; *and nickname*]
F, *you nickname* Q.   152, 153. *your ignorance*] Q 1, F; *ignorance* Q.
154, 155. *no more marriages*] Q 1, F; *no mo marriage* Q.   159. *soldier's,*
scholar's] Q, F; *scholler, souldier* Q 1.   160. *expectancy*] F, *expectation* Q.

144. *monsters*] Delius refers to
Othello, IV. i. 63: "A horned man's
a monster." So Fletcher, *Rule a
Wife and have a Wife*, II. i.: "Though
he [a wronged husband] see himself
become a monster." Hamlet reproaches Ophelia only through the
general evil of womanhood.

148. *paintings*] The F "prattlings" and "pace" are possibly not
misprints; "pace" referring to "jig"
and "amble"; "prattlings" to
"lisp" and "nickname."

151. *nickname*] call things by
names of immodest suggestion, and
profess childish ignorance. Compare
Romeo and Juliet, II. i. 35: "that
kind of fruit As maids call medlars,
when they laugh alone."

155, 156. *all but one*] a shaft meant
to strike the eves-dropping King.

159. *soldier's, scholar's*] The order
"scholar's, soldier's" corresponding
to "tongue, sword" may be more
rhetorically, but not therefore dram-
atically, correct.

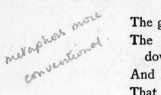

metaphor more conventional

The glass of fashion, and the mould of form,

The observed of all observers, quite, quite down!

And I, of ladies most deject and wretched,

That suck'd the honey of his music vows,

Now see that noble and most sovereign reason, 165

Like sweet bells jangled out of tune, and harsh;

blossomi...

That unmatch'd form and feature of blown youth

madness

Blasted with ecstasy; Oh, woe is me,

To have seen what I have seen, see what I see!

Re-enter KING *and* POLONIUS.

King. Love? his affections do not that way tend; 170

Nor what he spake, though it lack'd form a little,

He judges well. Madness not due to Ophelia.

Was not like madness. There's something in his soul

O'er which his melancholy sits on brood;

And I do doubt the hatch and the disclose

163. *And I*] Q, *Have I* F.   164. *music*] F, *musickt* Q.   165. *that noble*] F, *what noble* Q.   166. *jangled out of tune,*] F, *jangled out of time,* Q, *jangled, out of tune* Capell and many editors.   167. *feature*] F, *stature* Q.   169. *see I*] Q marks Exit here. So Elze.   170. *Love?*] F, *Love,* Q.

162. *observed of all observers*] Perhaps meaning honoured by all who pay the marks of honour, a common meaning of *observer*.
166. *tune*] The Q misprint *time* occurs in F, *Macbeth*, IV. iii. 235.
167. *feature*] the whole shape or cast of the body, as frequently in Shakespeare.
168. *ecstasy*] see II. i. 102.
169. *see I*] Elze supposes that

Ophelia withdraws to seek her father, returns at line 186, and is immediately sent away.
170. *affections*] emotions or passions.
174. *disclose*] Steevens quotes *The Booke of Huntynge, Hawkyng, Fishing*: "First they ben eges, and after they ben *disclosed* haukes." See v. i. 309.

Will be some danger; which for to prevent, 175
I have in quick determination
Thus set it down: he shall with speed to
    England,
For the demand of our neglected tribute:
Haply the seas and countries different
With variable objects shall expel 180
This something-settled matter in his heart,
Whereon his brains still beating puts him thus
From fashion of himself. What think you on 't?

Pol. It shall do well; but yet do I believe
The origin and commencement of his grief 185
Sprung from neglected love.——How now, Ophelia?
You need not tell us what Lord Hamlet said;
We heard it all.——My lord, do as you please;
But, if you hold it fit, after the play,
Let his queen mother all alone entreat him 190
To show his grief; let her be round with him;
And I 'll be placed, so please you, in the ear
Of all their conference. If she find him not,
To England send him, or confine him where
Your wisdom best shall think.

King.   It shall be so: 195
Madness in great ones must not unwatch'd go.
                              [*Exeunt.*

175. *for to*] Q, *to* F.   181. *something-settled*] hyphened by Warburton.
185. *his grief*] Q, *this greefe* F.   186. Elze marks Enter Ophelia.
188.] Theobald marks Exit Ophelia.   191. *grief*] Q, *Greefes* F.   192.
placed, so please you,] Q (*so . . . you*) in parentheses, *plac'd so, please you* F.
196. *unwatch'd*] F, *unmatcht* Q.

191. *round*] see II. ii. 139.   193. *find*] detect, as in *All's Well,*
                                        v. ii. 46.

SCENE II.—*A Hall in the Castle.*

Enter HAMLET *and two or three of the Players.*

Ham. Speak the speech, I pray you, as I pronounced it to you, trippingly on the tongue;
but if you mouth it, as many of your players
do, I had as lief the town-crier spoke my
lines. Nor do not saw the air too much with　5
your hand, thus; but use all gently; for in
the very torrent, tempest, and, as I may say,
the whirlwind of passion, you must acquire
and beget a temperance that may give it
smoothness. Oh, it offends me to the soul　10
to hear a robustious periwig-pated fellow tear
a passion to tatters, to very rags, to split the
ears of the groundlings, who, for the most
part, are capable of nothing but inexplicable
dumb-shows and noise; I would have such a　15
fellow whipped for o'er-doing Termagant; it
out-herods Herod; pray you, avoid it.

Topical allusion.
Criticizes
overacting.

3. *your players*] Q 1, F; *our players* Q.　4. *spoke*] Q, *had spoke* F.
5, 6. *much with your*] Q, *much your* F, *much, your* Caldecott.　8. *the*
whirlwind of passion] F, *whirlwind of your passion* Q.　11. *hear*] Q, *see* F.
15. *would*] Q 1, Q; *could* F.

8, 9. *acquire and beget*] acquire,
through training and practice; beget,
through a native artistic impulse.

11. *robustious*] sturdy, as in *King
Henry V.* III. vii. 159.

11. *periwig-pated*] Steevens quotes
from *Every Woman in her Humour*,
1609: "as none wear . . . periwigs
but players and pictures."

13. *groundlings*] spectators of the
play who stood in the pit, paying, as
we learn from Jonson, a penny for
admission; *capable,* receptive, appre-
hensive.

16. *Termagant*] the god of the
Saracens, as represented in old romances and mystery plays. Florio,
1611: "*Termigisto,* a great boaster,
quarreller, killer, tamer or ruler of
the universe; the child of the earth-
quake and of the thunder, the brother
of death."

17. *Herod*] the violent Herod of
old sacred plays. In the Coventry
play of the Nativity a braggart speech
is followed by the stage direction,
"Here Erode ragis in thys pagond
and in the strete also."

First Play. I warrant your honour.

Ham. Be not too tame neither, but let your own
discretion be your tutor; suit the action to the   20
word, the word to the action; with this special
observance, that you o'erstep not the modesty
of nature; for any thing so overdone is from
the purpose of playing, whose end, both at
the first and now, was and is, to hold, as   25
'twere, the mirror up to nature; to show
virtue her own feature, scorn her own image,
and the very age and body of the time his
form and pressure. Now this overdone, or
come tardy off, though it make the unskilful   30
laugh, cannot but make the judicious grieve;
the censure of the which one must in your
allowance o'erweigh a whole theatre of others.
Oh, there be players that I have seen play,
and heard others praise, and that highly, not   35
to speak it profanely, that neither having
the accent of Christians nor the gait of

18, 43. First Player] Capell; Player Q, F.   22. *o'erstep*] Q, *ore-stop* F.
23. *overdone*] F, *ore-doone* Q.   27. *her own feature*] F, *her feature* Q.
30. *off*] F, *of* Q 6, Theobald, Furness; *make*] F, *makes* Q.   32. *the
which one*] F, *which one* Q.   33. *o'erweigh*] Q, F; *ore-sway* Ff 2-4.
35. *praise*]F, *praysd* Q.

23. *from*] away from, contrary to, as in *Julius Cæsar*, I. iii. 35.
28. *very age*] actual generation. Bailey proposes "visage," comparing *2 Henry IV.* II. iii. 3: "visage of the times."
29. *pressure*] impress. Compare I. v. 100.
30. *come tardy off*] as we say "hanging fire"; coming to an issue slowly and ineffectively. Compare

Two Gentlemen of Verona, II. i. 116: "it came hardly off"; *Timon of Athens*, I. i. 29: "this comes off well and excellent."
32. *censure*] judgment, as in I. iii. 69.
36. *profanely*] refers to what follows about the creation of men, not by God, but by nature's journeymen.

Christian, pagan, nor man, have so strutted
and bellowed that I have thought some of
nature's journeymen had made men and not   40
made them well, they imitated humanity so
abominably.

First Play. I hope we have reformed that in- *fairly*
differently with us, sir.

Ham. Oh, reform it altogether.   And let those   45
that play your clowns speak no more than is
set down for them; for there be of them that
will themselves laugh, to set on some quantity
of barren *foolish* spectators to laugh too, though in
the mean time some necessary question of   50
the play be then to be considered; that's
villanous, and shows a most pitiful ambition
in the fool that uses it.   Go, make you ready.—

[*Exeunt Players.*

Enter POLONIUS, ROSENCRANTZ, *and* GUILDENSTERN.

How now, my lord! will the king hear this
piece of work?   55

Pol. And the queen too, and that presently.

Ham. Bid the players make haste.—

[*Exit Polonius.*

38. *nor man*] Q, *or Norman* F, *nor Turke* Q 1.   40. *men*] Q, F; *them*
Theobald conj., Rann, Furness; *the men*, Farmer conj., Hudson.   44. *sir*]
F, omitted Q.   57. Exit Polonius] F, omitted Q.

38. *nor man*] Farmer needlessly
conjectured "nor Mussulman"; see
Q 1 reading.
44. *indifferently*] see III. i. 123.
46. *clowns*] The "extemporall wit"
of Wilson and of Tarlton is praised
by Stowe.   In Q 1 examples of the
clown's jests are given by Hamlet.

Collier supposed that the passage in
Q 1 might have been levelled at
Kemp, "who about the date quitted
the company of players to which
Shakespeare had always belonged."
See p. 232 *post.*
56. *presently*] immediately, as in
II. ii. 170.

Will you two help to hasten them?

Ros., Guil. We will, my lord.

                [Exeunt Rosencrantz and Guildenstern

Ham. What ho! Horatio!   60

               Enter HORATIO.

Hor. Here, sweet lord, at your service.

Ham. Horatio, thou art e'en as just a man

    As e'er my conversation coped withal.

Hor. O, my dear lord,—

Ham.   Nay, do not think I flatter;

    For what advancement may I hope from thee, 65

    That no revenue hast but thy good spirits,

    To feed and clothe thee? Why should the poor

      be flatter'd?

    No, let the candied tongue lick absurd pomp,

    And crook the pregnant hinges of the knee

    Where thrift may follow fawning. Dost thou

      hear?   70

    Since my dear soul was mistress of her choice,

    And could of men distinguish, her election

    Hath seal'd thee for herself; for thou hast been

---

59. Ros., Guil.] Dyce, Both F, Ros. Q ; *We will*] F, *I*[*=Ay*] Q.   64. *lord,
—*] Rowe, *Lord.* Q, F.   68. *tongue lick*] Q, *tongue, like* F.   70. *fawn-
ing.*] *fauning* ; Q, *faining?* F.   71. *her*] Q, *my* F.   72. *distinguish,
her election*] F, *distinguish her election* Q.   73. *Hath*] F, *S'hath* Q, *She
hath* Malone.

62. *just*] Hamlet, at this moment, needs before all else a man of sound judgment, unswayed by passion. The eulogy that follows has here a dramatic propriety.

63. *coped withal*] as ever my intercourse with men encountered. So *copest* in *Winter's Tale,* IV. iv. 435.

66. *revenue*] accented here on the second syllable. The accent varies in Shakespeare.

68. *candied*] sugared.

69. *pregnant*] Schmidt : "disposed, ready, prompt." Perhaps, quick with meaning. Furness explains, "because untold thrift is born from a cunning use of the knee."

71. *dear*] see I. ii. 182.

Hamlet admired Horatio's fortitude

As one, in suffering all, that suffers nothing;
A man that fortune's buffets and rewards   75
Hath ta'en with equal thanks; and bless'd are those
Whose blood and judgment are so well commingled
That they are not a pipe for fortune's finger
To sound what stop she please.   Give me that man
That is not passion's slave, and I will wear him   80
In my heart's core, ay, in my heart of heart,
As I do thee.   Something too much of this.
There is a play to-night before the king;
One scene of it comes near the circumstance

He has told Horatio everything

Which I have told thee of my father's death: 85
I prithee, when thou seest that act afoot,
Even with the very comment of thy soul
Observe mine uncle; if his occulted guilt
Do not itself unkennel in one speech,
It is a damned ghost that we have seen,   90
And my imaginations are as foul
As Vulcan's stithy.   Give him heedful note;
For I mine eyes will rivet to his face,
And after we will both our judgments join
In censure of his seeming.

Hor.   Well, my lord: 95

---

76. *Hath*] F, *Hast* Q.   77. *commingled*] Dyce, *co-mingled* F, *comedled* Q.
85. *thee of*] Q, *thee, of* F.   87. *thy*] Q, *my* F.   88. *mine*] F, *my* Q.
92. *heedful*] Q, *needfull* F.   95. *In*] Q, *To* F.

77. *blood and judgment*] passion and reason; see I. iii. 6.

80, 81.] Douce: "From this speech Anthony Scoloker, in his *Daiphantus*, 1604 [sig. E], has stolen the following line: 'Oh, I would weare her in my heart's-heart-gore.' "

87. *comment of thy soul*] the emphasis is on *soul*; with the most inward and sagacious criticism. The F *my* would make Hamlet's judgment the text, and Horatio's the comment.

89. *one speech*] Hamlet's dozen or sixteen lines: II. ii. 576.

92. *stithy*] possibly here a forge; often an anvil.

95. *censure*] as in line 32.

If he steal aught the whilst this play is playing,
And 'scape detecting, I will pay the theft.

Ham. They are coming to the play; I must be idle: *mad*
Get you a place.

Danish March. A Flourish. Enter KING, QUEEN,
POLONIUS, OPHELIA, ROSENCRANTZ, GUILDEN-
STERN, *and other Lords attendant, with the Guard,
carrying torches.*

King. How fares our cousin Hamlet?   100

Ham. Excellent, i' faith; of the chameleon's dish: *He is so rude.*
I eat the air, promise-crammed; you cannot
feed capons so.   *hint of ambition, or pretended*

King. I have nothing with this answer, Hamlet;
these words are not mine.   *an answer to*   105

Ham. No, nor mine now.—[*To Polonius.*]   My
lord, you played once i' the university, you
say?

Pol. That did I, my lord, and was accounted a good
actor.   110

Ham. And what did you enact?

97. *detecting*] F, *detected* Q.   Danish March . . . torches] substantially
from F.   Enter Trumpets and Kettle Drummes, King, Queene, Polonius,
Ophelia Q after line 97.   106. *mine now.—My lord,*] Johnson, *mine now
my lord.* Q, *mine. Now my lord,* F.   109. *did I*] Q, *I did* F.   111.
And what] F, *What* Q.

98. *idle*] crazy. In Q 1 Hamlet's
mother, in the interview after the
play, bids him forget these "idle
fits"; he replies:
  "Idle! no mother, my pulse doth
  beate like yours;
  It is not madness that possesseth
  Hamlet."
Perhaps, however, it means here no
more than unoccupied with any
affair.

101. *chameleon's dish*]So Rowlands,
Lett. Humours Blood, 1600: "Can
men feede like camelions on the
ayer?" In Browne's *Vulgar Errors*
the matter is discussed. [See App. III.]
  107. *university*] University plays,
in Latin or in English, form an important group of our elder drama.
The title-page of *Hamlet*, Q 1, states
that it was acted "in the two Universities of Cambridge and Oxford."

8

cross current
of plays.

pun.

Pol. I did enact Julius Cæsar; I was killed i' the
Capitol; Brutus killed me.

Ham. It was a brute part of him to kill so capital
a calf there.——Be the players ready? 115

Ros. Ay, my lord; they stay upon your patience.

Queen. Come hither, my dear Hamlet, sit by me.

Ham. No, good mother, here's metal more at-
tractive.

Pol. [*To the King.*] Oh, ho! do you mark that? 120

Ham. Lady, shall I lie in your lap?

> [*Lying down at Ophelia's feet.*

Oph. No, my lord.

Ham. I mean, my head upon your lap?

Oph. Ay, my lord.

Ham. Do you think I meant country matters? 125

Oph. I think nothing, my lord.

Ham. That's a fair thought to lie between maids' legs.

Oph. What is, my lord?

Ham. Nothing.

Oph. You are merry, my lord. 130

Ham. Who, I?

Oph. Ay, my lord.

---

117. *dear*] Q, *good* F.   120. **To** the **King**] Capell, adding Aside.
121. Lying . . . feet] Rowe.   123, 124. Ham. *I mean . . . lord*]
omitted Q.   125. *country*] Q, F; *contrary* Q I.

---

113. *Capitol*] The error as to the
place of Cæsar's death appears in
Chaucer, *Monkes Tale*, and in Shakespeare's *Julius Cæsar*. So Fletcher,
The Noble Gentleman, v. i.
115. *calf*] dolt, as in v. i. 126.
125. *country matters*] rustic pro-
ceedings. Johnson conjectured
country manners, as in *King John*,
I. i. 156. I suspect that there is

some indelicate suggestion in *country*.
In *Westward Hoe*, v. i., I find:
"Though we lie all night out of the
city, they shall not find country
wenches of us," meaning we will not
wrong our husbands; and in *North-
ward Hoe*, III. i. (spoken of a harlot),
"a good commonwealthes woman
she was borne. For her country, and
has borne her country."

Ham. O God, your only jig-maker. What should
a man do but be merry? for, look you, how
cheerfully my mother looks, and my father 135
died within's two hours.

Oph. Nay, 'tis twice two months, my lord.

Ham. So long? Nay then, let the devil wear black,
for I'll have a suit of sables. O heavens! die
two months ago, and not forgotten yet? 140
Then there's hope a great man's memory may
outlive his life half a year; but, by'r lady, he
must build churches then; or else shall he
suffer not thinking on, with the hobby-horse, *suppressed at*
whose epitaph is "For, O! for, O! the hobby- 145 *Reformation.*
horse is forgot."

Hautboys play.   The dumb-show enters.

136. *within's*] Q, F; *within these* Q 1.

133. *jig-maker*] see II. ii. 531.
136. *within's*] within this.
139. *sables*] Warburton read,
"'fore I'll have a suit of sable."
Johnson observed that the fur of
sables is not black; a suit trimmed
with sables was magnificent, and not
a mourning garment. Hudson adopts
a suggestion of Wightwick, and reads
sabell, flame-colour. But Hamlet's
jest lies in the ambiguity of the word;
sables, the fur and sable, the black of
heraldry. See IV. vii. 81, whence it
appears that sables were the livery of
"settled age." What an age since
my father died! I am quite an old
gentleman! (with an ambiguity of apparent self-contradiction in Hamlet's
manner, on the meaning *black*); I
mean to be rich and comfortable, and
the devil must be the only personage
who always wears black, his accustomed garb.

144. *suffer not thinking on*] undergo oblivion.
144. *hobby-horse*] a figure of May-
games and morris-dances, the figure
of a horse strapped round the actor's
waist, his feet being concealed by a
foot-cloth. "The hobby-horse is
forgot" occurs in *Love's Labour's Lost,*
III. i. 30, and in several Elizabethan
dramas. Probably the Puritans had
for a time succeeded in banishing
him from May sports. See Beaumont
and Fletcher, *Women Pleased,* IV. i.,
for an amusing scene of Puritan *versus*
hobby-horse.
146. dumb-show] The description
of the dumb-show here varies only in
unessential points from that of F.
In Q the differences are not important. But Q 1 deserves to be quoted:
"Enter in a Dumbe Shew, the King
and the Queene, he sits down in an
Arbor, she leaves him: Then enters

Enter a King and a Queen, very lovingly ; the Queen
embracing him, and he her. She kneels, and
makes show of protestation unto him. He takes
her up, and declines his head upon her neck :
lays him down upon a bank of flowers : she,
seeing him asleep, leaves him. Anon comes in
a fellow, takes off his crown, kisses it, and pours
poison in the King's ears, and exit. The Queen
returns ; finds the King dead, and makes
passionate action. The Poisoner, with some two
or three Mutes, comes in again, seeming to
lament with her. The dead body is carried
away. The Poisoner wooes the Queen with
gifts ; she seems loath and unwilling awhile,
but in the end accepts his love. [*Exeunt.*

Lucianus with Poyson in a Viall, and powres it in his eares, and goes away: Then the Queene commeth and finds him dead ; and goes away with the other." In our elder drama dumb-show was employed occasionally to indicate action not developed by subsequent dialogue, or in a kind of allegory to shadow forth what was to follow. Shakespeare's use of it here is singular. Hunter cited an example of Danish soldiers in England, 1688, presenting the action of a sacred drama, given in Danish, in dumb-show before the play, and assumed that this was a common practice of the Danish theatre. Elze conjectured that English actors of Shakespeare's time on the Continent expounded the action of plays in this way. Ophelia suggests that the show may import the argument ; but, according to English practice, such a supposition was not warranted, except in so far that it might symbolically indicate the general tendency of the action.

The King, on the other hand, does not recognise in the dumb-show the argument ; see line 245 : his suspicions would doubtless be aroused, and he would watch the play with keener interest, but he might suppose that the dumb-show presented, in English fashion, action which was not to be developed through dialogue. Hamlet would have thus a double opportunity of catching the conscience of the King. The following passage has perhaps not been quoted in connection with the use of dumb-show : *Ianua Linguarum Quadralinguis; or, A Messe of Tongues,* 1617 [by J. Barbier] ; the writer explains why he puts his " Advertisement" at the end of the volume : " As in a Comedie the Prologue, or in a Tragedie the Chorus, is not for the most acute spectator, able (and more delighted) of himselfe to discerne the pretention of every Act presented, though intimated onely in a dumbe shew." [See Appendix III.]

Oph. What means this, my lord?

Ham. Marry, this is miching mallecho; it means mischief. *skulking mischief*

He might not have known about the dumb-show.

Oph. Belike this show imports the argument of the 150 play?

Enter Prologue.

Ham. We shall know by this fellow; the players cannot keep counsel; they 'll tell all.

Oph. Will he tell us what this show meant?

Ham. Ay, or any show that you 'll show him; be 155 not you ashamed to show, he 'll not shame to tell you what it means.

Oph. You are naught, you are naught: I 'll mark the play.

Pro.   *For us, and for our tragedy,* 160
            Here stooping to your clemency,
            We beg your hearing patiently.   [*Exit.*

Ham. Is this a prologue, or the posy of a ring? *motto*

148. *this is*] F, *this* Q; *miching mallecho*] Malone, *munching Mallico* Q *Miching Malicho* F, *myching Mallico* Q 1; *it*] Q, *that* F.   151. *play?*] F, *play*. Q. Enter Prologue] Theobald; after *fellow*, line 152 Q; after *play*, line 159 F.   152. *this fellow*] Q, *these fellowes* F.   153. *counsel*] F, omitted Q.   154. *he*] Pope, *a* Q, *they* F.   155. *you 'll*] F, *you will* Q. 162. Exit] Globe Sh.; omitted Q, F.

148. *miching mallecho*] skulking mischief. Minsheu gives "To miche, or secretly to hide himself out of the way, as Truants doe from schoole"; Florio has "to miche, to shrug, or sneake in some corner." See "micher," truant, in *1 Henry IV*. ii. iv. 449. "Mallecho," Spanish *malhecho*, mischief. So Shirley, *Gentleman of Venice*: "Be humble, Thou man of mallecho, or thou diest."

158. *naught*] improper, licentious. Bunyan in *Grace Abounding* declares that he never "so much as attempted to be naught with women." So Dekker, *The Honest Whore* (Pearson's *Dekker*, ii. p. 54).

163. *posy*] See *Merchant of Venice*, v. i. 147–150. Posies incised on rings were necessarily brief.

Oph. 'Tis brief, my lord.　　　　　　　　　　　　165

Ham. As woman's love. *He bears all her words.*

Enter two Players, King and Queen.

Rhyming artificial.

P. King. *Full   thirty   times   hath   Phœbus'   cart   gone*
　　　　　　　round
　　　　Neptune's salt wash and Tellus' orbed ground,
　　　　And thirty dozen moons with borrow'd sheen
　　　　About the world have times twelve thirties been, 170
　　　　Since love our hearts and Hymen did our hands
　　　　Unite commutual in most sacred bands. *god of marriage*

P. Queen. *So many journeys may the sun and moon*
　　　　Make us again count o'er ere love be done!
　　　　But, woe is me! you are so sick of late,　　175
　　　　So far from cheer and from your former state,
　　　　That I distrust you.   Yet, though I distrust,
　　　　Discomfort you, my lord, it nothing must;
　　　　For women's fear and love holds quantity,
　　　　In neither aught, or in extremity.　　　180
　　　　Now, what my love is, proof hath made you know,
　　　　And as my love is sized, my fear is so;

166. Enter . . . Queen] Globe, Enter King and Queene Q, Enter King
and his Queene F, Enter the Duke and Dutchesse Q 1.　　168. orbed] F,
orb'd the Q.　　176. your] F, our Q.　　179. For] F, And Q, preceded by
the following unrhymed line: "For women feare too much, even as they
love"; holds] F, hold Q.　　180. In neither aught] F (with spelling ought),
Eyther none, in neither ought Q.　　181. love] F, Lord Q.

167. cart] chariot. Spenser, *Faerie
Queene*, v. viii. 34: "On every side
of his embatteld cart." These lines
resemble lines beginning "Thrice ten
times Phœbus," near the opening of
Act IV. of Greene's *Alphonsus*.

178. must] Perhaps a line, rhyming
with that given in Q, has been lost;
perhaps the Q line had been cancelled
and was printed by mistake.

179. holds quantity] keep proportion to each other. See *Midsummer
Night's Dream*, I. i. 232.

180. In neither aught] Ingleby proposed "In either naught." Hunter
would punctuate "hold quantity Ir.
neither:—aught." Capell explains:
"They either feel none of these
passions, or feel them both in extremity."

Where love is great, the littlest doubts are fear,
Where little fears grow great, great love grows there.

P. King. *'Faith, I must leave thee, love, and shortly too;* 185
My operant powers their functions leave to do;
And thou shalt live in this fair world behind,
Honour'd, beloved; and haply one as kind
For husband shalt thou—

P. Queen.   *Oh, confound the rest!*
Such love must needs be treason in my breast; 190
In second husband let me be accurst!
None wed the second but who kill'd the first.

Ham. [*Aside.*] Wormwood, wormwood!

P. Queen. *The instances that second marriage move*
Are base respects of thrift, but none of love; 195
A second time I kill my husband dead,
When second husband kisses me in bed.

P. King. *I do believe you think what now you speak,*
But what we do determine oft we break.
Purpose is but the slave to memory, 200

183, 184.] Q, omitted F.   186. their functions] Q, my Functions F.
193. Aside] Capell ; omitted Q, F ; *Wormwood, wormwood!*] F, *That's
wormwood.* Q, *O wormwood, wormwood!* Q 1.   198. you think] Q, you.
Think F.

186. leave] cease.

194. instances] motives, induce-
ments, as in *King Henry V.* II. ii. 119.

195. respects] considerations, as in
III. i. 68.

196. kill . . . dead] kill my husband, he being dead (though examples of the tautology "kill dead,"
meaning "kill," occur in Shakespeare). The reading of Q I "lord
that's dead" gives the sense.

200–225.] Furness gives a long
summary of a longer discussion as to
which lines are the dozen or sixteen
written by Hamlet, or whether it is
meant by Shakespeare that any lines

which actually appear should be
identified as his. Lines in the present
speech, it is argued, are singularly
in Hamlet's vein ; they look like an
insertion ; they do not advance the
action ; they are meant to catch the
conscience of Hamlet's mother ; the
plot sufficiently convicts the King.
On the other hand, it is argued, that
the Poisoner's speech (perhaps interrupted before its close) is meant ; that
Hamlet clearly indicates this to
Horatio, and that he warns the player
against mouthing a passionate speech.
Perhaps all this is to inquire too
curiously into a dramatic device of

Of violent birth but poor validity ;
Which now, like fruit unripe, sticks on the tree,
But fall unshaken when they mellow be.
Most necessary 'tis that we forget
To pay ourselves what to ourselves is debt ;　　205
What to ourselves in passion we propose,
The passion ending, doth the purpose lose.
The violence of either grief or joy
Their own enactures with themselves destroy ;
Where joy most revels grief doth most lament ;　210
Grief joys, joy grieves, on slender accident.
This world is not for aye, nor 'tis not strange
That even our loves should with our fortunes change,
For 'tis a question left us yet to prove,
Whether love lead fortune or else fortune love.　215
The great man down, you mark his favourite
　　flies ;
The poor advanced makes friends of enemies ;
And hitherto doth love on fortune tend ;
For who not needs shall never lack a friend ;
And who in want a hollow friend doth try　　220

---

202. like] F, the Q.　　208. either] Q, other F.　　209. enactures] Q,
enactors F.　　211. Grief . . . grieves] F, Greefe ioy, ioy griefes, Q.
216. favourite] Q, fauourites F.

Shakespeare's, designed to lessen the improbability of the "murder of Gonzago" so exactly fitting the occasion ; designed also to show Hamlet as a critic of theatrical art, and indirectly to instruct an Elizabethan audience in theatrical matters. Undoubtedly this speech reflects back on both the Queen and Hamlet himself, but this was Shakespeare's doing, and clearly intentional ; if we were forced to identify Hamlet's lines, we must needs point to the speech of Lucianus. Sir H. Irving, as Hamlet, mutters the Poisoner's words with suppressed passion while they are being delivered by the actor.

204, 205.] Our resolves are debts to ourselves ; why embarrass ourselves by inconvenient payments ?

209. enactures] fulfilments, carrying into act.

> *Directly seasons him his enemy.*
> *But, orderly to end where I begun,*
> *Our wills and fates do so contrary run*
> *That our devices still are overthrown,*
> *Our thoughts are ours, their ends none of our own:* 225
> *So think thou wilt no second husband wed,*
> *But die thy thoughts when thy first lord is dead.*

P. Queen. *Nor earth to me give food nor heaven light!*
> *Sport and repose lock from me day and night!*
> *To desperation turn my trust and hope!*   230
> *An anchor's cheer in prison be my scope!*
> *Each opposite, that blanks the face of joy,*
> *Meet what I would have well and it destroy!*
> *Both here and hence pursue me lasting strife,*
> *If, once a widow, ever I be wife!*   235

Ham. If she should break it now!

P. King. *'Tis deeply sworn.   Sweet, leave me here awhile;*
> *My spirits grow dull, and fain I would beguile*
> *The tedious day with sleep.*   [*Sleeps.*

P. Queen.   *Sleep rock thy brain;*
> *And never come mischance between us twain!*   240
>   [*Exit.*

---

228. to me give] Q, to give me F.   230, 231. To desperation . . . scope] Q, omitted F.   231. An anchor's] Theobald, And anchors Q. 235. once . . . wife] Q 1, F; once I be a widdow, ever I be a wife Q. 236. *now!*] Dyce; *now.* Q, F; *now—* Pope.   239. Sleeps] F (after brain), omitted Q.

221. seasons] Schmidt and Clar. Press: "matures, ripens," see I. iii. 81 ; but perhaps it means qualifies, tempers.

231. anchor's cheer] anchoret's chair. So Bishop Hall, *Satires*, IV. ii. 103 : "Sit seaven yeares pining in an anchores cheyre." *Cheer* is ex-

plained — perhaps rightly — by Clar. Press and others "fare," but "scope" supports the meaning illustrated by Hall.

232. opposite, that blanks] contrary thing that makes pale. So Sylvester's *Du Bartas*, 1605 : "His brow was never blankt with pallid fear."

Ham. Madam, how like you this play?

Queen. The lady doth protest too much, methinks.

Ham. O, but she 'll keep her word.

King. Have you heard the argument? Is there no
　　offence in 't?　　　　　　　　　　　　　　　　245

Ham. No, no; they do but jest, poison in jest; no
　　offence i' the world.

King. What do you call the play?

Ham. The Mouse-trap. Marry, how? Tropically.
　　This play is the image of a murder done in 250
　　Vienna: Gonzago is the duke's name; his
　　wife, Baptista: you shall see anon; 'tis a
　　knavish piece of work; but what o' that?
　　your majesty, and we that have free souls, it
　　touches us not; let the galled jade wince, our 255
　　withers are unwrung.—

242. *doth protest*] Q, *protests* F.　　249. *Tropically*] Q, F; *tropically* Q 1.
253. *o'*] F, *of* Q, *a* Q 1.　　255. *wince*] Q 1; *winch* Q, F.

249. *Tropically*] called The Mouse-trap (catching the conscience of the king) by way of a trope or figure. The "trapically" of Q 1 suggests that a pun is intended.

251. *Gonzago*] In 1538 the Duke of Urbano, married to a Gonzaga, was murdered by Luigi Gonzaga, who dropped poison into his ear. Shakespeare, it is suggested, might have found this writ in choice Italian, might have transferred the name Gonzaga to the murdered man, and formed "Lucianus" from Luigi. "The duke" seems to be an oversight. In Q 1 the murdered man and his wife are Duke and Dutchesse throughout, except in the dumb-show, where they are King and Queen; in the altered form perhaps "duke" was here erroneously retained. It is, how-ever, true, as Walker and Elze point out, that "Duke" and "King" are not always differentiated by Elizabethan writers. As to the name "Baptista," Hunter says he has seen a few instances of the name as borne by women in England. "It had a feminine termination; that was enough. Shakespeare has given it to a man in *The Taming of the Shrew.*" It has been shown by A. von Reumont (*Allgemeine Zeitung,* October 21, 1870) that Baptista was used in Italy as the Christian name of a woman. See *Sh. Jahrbuch,* xxxi. 169, for another Gonzaga murder.

254. *free*] see II. ii. 600.

255. *let the galled jade wince*] a proverbial saying; found in Edwardes, *Damon and Pythias,* and Lyly, *Euphues.*

Enter Player, as LUCIANUS.

This is one Lucianus, nephew to the king.

Oph. You are as good as a chorus, my lord. *[handwritten: Eliz. explanatory chorus]*

Ham. I could interpret between you and your love,

if I could see the puppets dallying. 260

Oph. You are keen, my lord, you are keen.

Ham. It would cost you a groaning to take off my

edge.

Oph. Still better, and worse.

Ham. So you mistake your husbands. — Begin, 265
murderer; pox, leave thy damnable faces, and *[handwritten: Violent language,]*
begin. Come: the croaking raven doth bellow *[handwritten: — probably Hamlet's]*
for revenge. *[handwritten: own insertion.]*

Luc. Thoughts black, hands apt, drugs fit, and time *[handwritten: Luc. has cut it.]*
agreeing ;

Confederate season, else no creature seeing ; 270

---

258. *as good as a*] Q 1, Q ; *a good* F. 262. *my*] F, *mine* Q. 265. *mistake your husbands*] Q, *mistake husbands* F, *must take your husband* Q. 1.
266. *pox*] F, omitted Q, *a poxe* Q 1. 270. Confederate] Q 1, F ; Con-
siderat Q.

258. *chorus*] which explains the
action of a play, as in *Winter's Tale,
Romeo and Juliet, Henry V.*

259, 260. *interpret . . . puppets*]
an interpreter on the stage expounded
the puppet-shows ; see *Two Gentlemen
of Verona*, II. i. 101. Steevens quotes
Greene, *Groatsworth of Wit*: "It was
I that . . . for seven years' space was
absolute interpreter of the puppets."
"Your love," your lover.

264. *better, and worse*] Caldecott :
"more keen and less decorous."

265. *mistake*] Pope read "must
take" with Q 1, and has been followed
by many editors ; but this effaces
Hamlet's insult to womanhood.
Brides, according to the marriage-
service, take their husbands "for
better, for worse." Hamlet means
that women do not take them but
mis-take them (as Capell prints it) in
these words, for the words are not
fulfilled ; you all are faithless wives—
with a thought of his mother.

267. *croaking raven*] Simpson
(*Academy*, December 19, 1874) shows
that Hamlet rolls into one two lines
of *The True Tragedie of Richard the
Third*—ghosts of those whom Richard
has slain in reaching for a crown come
gaping for revenge :
"The screeking raven sits croking for
revenge,
Whole herds of beasts come bellow-
ing for revenge."

Thou mixture rank, of midnight weeds collected,
With Hecate's ban thrice blasted, thrice infected,
Thy natural magic and dire property,
On wholesome life usurp immediately.

　　　　　[Pours the poison into the Sleeper's ears.

Ham. He poisons him i' the garden for 's estate. 275
　　His name 's Gonzago; the story is extant, and
　　writ in choice Italian; you shall see anon how
　　the murderer gets the love of Gonzago's wife.

Oph. The king rises!

Ham. What, frighted with false fire!　　　　　280

Queen. How fares my lord?

Pol. Give o'er the play.

King. Give me some light.—Away!

All. Lights, lights, lights!

　　　　　[Exeunt all but Hamlet and Horatio.

Ham. Why, let the strucken deer go weep,　　285
　　　　The hart ungalled play;
　　For some must watch, while some must sleep;
　　　　So runs the world away.
　　Would not this, sir, and a forest of feathers,—

272. ban] Q, F; bane Q 1.   274. usurp] F; usurps Q 1, Q.   275. *for's*] F; *for his* Q 1, Q.   277. *writ in*] F, *written in very* Q.   280. *What, . . . fire!*] Theobald, *What, . . . fire.* F, omitted Q, *What, . . . fires?* Q 1. 284. All.] F, Pol. Q.   285. *Why, let*] Theobald; *Why let* Q, F; *strucken*] F, *strooken* Q, *stricken* Q 1.   288. *So*] F; *Thus* Q 1, Q.

274. usurp] let them usurp. Compare *Pericles*, III. ii. 82: "Death may usurp on nature many hours."

280. *false fire*] used of fire-works, blank-discharge of firearms, a fire or night-signal made to deceive an enemy. See *A New Eng. Dictionary* under *False* 14 *b*, and under *Fire* 8 *a*.

285-288. *Why . . . away*] Dyce:

"In all probability a quotation from some ballad."

289. *forest of feathers*] So Chapman, *Monsieur D'Olive*, III. i.: "I carry a whole forest of feathers with me." Feathers were much worn on the stage; in Randolph's *The Muses' Looking-Glass*, I. i., Bird, the feather-man, has the custom of the players for all their feathers.

if the rest of my fortunes turn Turk with me—   290
with two Provincial roses on my razed shoes,
get me a fellowship in a cry of players, sir ?

Hor. Half a share.

Ham. A whole one, I.

    For thou dost know, O Damon dear,   295
      This realm dismantled was
    Of Jove himself; and now reigns here
      A very, very—pajock.

Hor. You might have rhymed.

---

291. *two*] F, omitted ; *razed*] *raz'd* Q, *rac'd* F.   292. *sir*] F, omitted Q.   298. *pajock*] Ff 3, 4 ; *paiock* Qq 2–5 ; *Paiocke* F 1, Q 6 ; *Pajocke* F 2.

---

290. *turn Turk*] prove renegade, or turn cruel. See *Much Ado*, III. iv. 57.

291. *Provincial roses*] rosettes of ribbon, like the roses of Provence, or else of Provins (forty miles from Paris), which was celebrated for its roses. "Cotgrave gives both : ' Rose de Provence. The Province rose, the double Damaske Rose,' and ' Rose de Provins, the ordinarie double red Rose.' Gerarde, in his *Herbal*, says that the damask rose is called by some ' Rosa provincialis ' " (Clar. Press).

291. *razed*] slashed, or streaked in patterns. Stubbes, *Anatomie of Abuses*, writes of shoes "razed, carved, cut, and stitched over with silk." Clar. Press quotes Randle Holme, *Academy of Armory*, III. i. p. 14, " Pinked or raised Shooes have the over leathers grain part cut into Roses, or other devices."

292. *cry*] company; transferred from the meaning pack of hounds. Cotgrave, 1611 : " *Meute*, a kennell, or crie, of hounds." Cleveland, *The London Lady*, 35 : "a small Cry of Tenants."

293. *share*] Malone : "The whole receipts of each theatre were divided into shares, of which the proprietors of the theatre, or *house-keepers* . . . had some ; and each actor had one or more shares or part of a share, according to his merit." See Furness for citation of documents from Halliwell.

294. *I*] A whole one, say I. Malone conjectured "A whole one, ay," and several editors adopt the suggestion, "I" and "ay" being both represented in print by "I."

298. *pajock*] Hamlet again probably quotes from some ballad, substituting "pajock" for the rhyming "ass." Q 1676 gave *paicock* ; Q 1695, *pecock* ; Pope and many editors, *peacock*. Dyce says he has heard the lower classes of the north of Scotland call the peacock the *pea-jock* (cf. bubbly-jock, turkey). The peacock had an unenviable reputation in popular belief and current natural history. He was vain, loved not his young, was inordinately lustful, swallowed his own ordure, had " the voice of a feend, the head of a serpent, and the pace of a theefe." Theobald proposed *paddock*, a toad, and *puttock*, a ravenous kite. Spenser, *A View of the Present State of Ireland* (p. 636, Globe ed.), uses *patchocke* for a clown, and perhaps this is Hamlet's word.

Ham. O good Horatio, I'll take the ghost's word   300
for a thousand pound.   Didst perceive?

Hor. Very well, my lord.

Ham. Upon the talk of the poisoning?

Hor. I did very well note him.

Ham. Ah, ha!   Come, some music!   come, the   305
recorders!—

For if the king like not the comedy,
Why then, belike,—he likes it not, perdy.
Come, some music!

Re-enter ROSENCRANTZ *and* GUILDENSTERN.

Guil. Good my lord, vouchsafe me a word with   310
you.

Ham. Sir, a whole history.

Guil. The king, sir,—

Ham. Ay, sir, what of him?

Guil. Is in his retirement marvellous distempered.   315

Ham. With drink, sir?

Guil. No, my lord, rather with choler.

Ham. Your wisdom should show itself more richer
to signify this to his doctor; for, for me to put
him to his purgation would perhaps plunge   320
him into far more choler.

Guil. Good my lord, put your discourse into

303. *poisoning?*] F, *poysning.* Q.   305. *Ah, ha!*] Jennens, *Ah ha,* Q,
Oh, ha? F.   309. Re-enter] Q as here; in F after *note him,* line 304.
317. *rather*] F, omitted Q.   319. *his doctor*] F, *the doctor* Q.   321. *far*]
F, omitted Q.

306. *recorders*] a kind of flageolet.   320. *purgation*] medicinally purg-
315. *distempered*] discomposed in   ing the body, legally clearing from
mind. Hamlet takes it up as if   imputation of guilt, as in *As You
meaning disordered in body; both   Like It,* v. iv. 45. Hamlet plays on
senses occur in Shakespeare.   the two senses.

some frame, and start not so wildly from my
affair.

Ham. I am tame, sir; pronounce.　　　　　　　325

Guil. The queen, your mother, in most great affliction of spirit, hath sent me to you.

Ham. You are welcome.

Guil. Nay, good my lord, this courtesy is not of the
right breed.　If it shall please you to make　330
me a wholesome answer, I will do your mother's
commandment; if not, your pardon and my
return shall be the end of my business.

Ham. Sir, I cannot.

Guil. What, my lord?　　　　　　　　　　335

Ham. Make you a wholesome answer; my wit's
diseased; but, sir, such answer as I can make,
you shall command; or, rather, as you say,
my mother; therefore no more, but to the
matter; my mother, you say,—　　　　　340

Ros. Then thus she says: your behaviour hath
struck her into amazement and admiration.

Ham. O wonderful son, that can so astonish a
mother!　But is there no sequel at the heels
of this mother's admiration?　Impart.　　　345

Ros. She desires to speak with you in her closet ere
you go to bed.

[handwritten margin note:] Courtesy means nothing

[handwritten margin note:] Poor Guildenstern

---

323. *start*] F, *stare* Q.　　333. *of my*] F, *of* Q.　　335. Guil.] F, Ros. Q.
337. *answer*] Q, *answers* F.　　338. *as you*] Q, *you* F.　　343. *astonish*]
F, *stonish* Q.　　345. *mother's*] Q, *Mother* F; *Impart.*] Q, omitted F.

323. *frame*] order, and used specially of an arrangement of words; T.
Spencer, *Logick*, 1628: "This frame
contains a proposition negative universall, &c."
332. *pardon*] see I. ii. 56.

335. Guil.] Evidently this speech
is rightly assigned to Guildenstern by
F.　He then retires and Rosencrantz
tries his hand.
342. *admiration*] wonder, as in I.
ii. 192.

Ham. We shall obey, were she ten times our
    mother.   Have you any further trade with us?

Ros. My lord, you once did love me.   350

Ham. So I do still, by these pickers and stealers.

Ros. Good my lord, what is your cause of dis-
    temper? you do surely bar the door upon
    your own liberty, if you deny your griefs to
    your friend.   355

Ham. Sir, I lack advancement.

Ros. How can that be when you have the voice of
    the king himself for your succession in Den-
    mark?

Ham. Ay, sir, but "While the grass grows,"—the   360
    proverb is something musty.—

Re-enter Players with recorders.

    Oh, the recorders! let me see one. — To
    withdraw with you:—why do you go about

---

351. *So I do*] F, *And do* Q.   353. *surely . . . upon*] Q, *freely . . .
of* F.   360. *sir*] Q, omitted F.   361. Re-enter] Dyce, Enter one with a
Recorder F, Enter the Players with Recorders Q, after line 359.   362. *recorders*] Q, *Recorder* F ; *see one*] Q, *see* F ; a comma after *one* Q, after *see* F.

349. *trade*] business, as in *Twelfth
Night*, III. i. 83.
351. *pickers and stealers*] hands,
which the Church Catechism ad-
monishes us to keep from picking and
stealing.   A mild oath ("by this
hand") found in *Merchant of Venice*,
v. i. 161.   Hamlet wishes to have
done with professions of love, and
swears " by these rogueish hands."
356. *advancement*]   Humouring
their conceit that he is ambitious;
see II. ii. 260.
360, 361. *the proverb*] Malone
quotes the proverb from Whet-
stone, *Promos and Cassandra*, 1578:

" Whylst grass doth growe, oft sterves
the seely steede."
362, 363. *To withdraw with you*]
to have a word in private with you.
Steevens suggests that Guildenstern
has indicated by a gesture his wish
for privacy, and that Hamlet's words
are interrogative.   Mason proposed
"So, withdraw you," or "So, withdraw will you?"   Staunton takes the
words as addressed to the players,
and suggests "So (*taking a recorder*)
withdraw with you."   For the use of
the infinitive compare "to draw" in
III. iv. 216.

to recover the wind of me, as if you would
drive me into a toil? _trap._   365

Guil. O, my lord, if my duty be too bold, my love
is too unmannerly.

Ham. I do not well understand that. Will you
play upon this pipe?

Guil. My lord, I cannot.   370

Ham. I pray you.

Guil. Believe me, I cannot.

Ham. I do beseech you.

Guil. I know no touch of it, my lord.

Ham. 'Tis as easy as lying; govern these ventages 375
with your finger and thumb, give it breath with
your mouth, and it will discourse most eloquent
music. Look you, these are the stops.

Guil. But these cannot I command to any utterance
of harmony; I have not the skill.   380

Ham. Why, look you now, how unworthy a thing
you make of me! You would play upon me;
you would seem to know my stops; you would
pluck out the heart of my mystery; _skill or craft._ you would
sound me from my lowest note to the top of 385
my compass; and there is much music, excellent voice, in this little organ, yet cannot you

Hamlet thinks he has great powers.

375. _'Tis_] F, _It is_ Q.   376. _finger_] F, _fingers_ Q; _and thumb_] F, _& the
vmber_ Q.   377. _eloquent_] Q, _excellent_ F.   385. _the top of_] F, omitted Q.

364. _to recover the wind of me_]
Madden, _The Diary of Master William Silence_, p. 33, note: "In order
to drive a deer into the toils, it was
needful to get to the windward of him,
so that, having you in the wind, he
might break in the opposite direction,"

366, 367. _O . . . unmannerly_] a
duty perhaps too bold may have
forced my love to express itself ill.
Or perhaps—as Clar. Press suggests—
"an unmeaning compliment."

375. _ventages_] vents, holes,

make it speak. 'Sblood, do you think I am
easier to be played on than a pipe?   Call me
what instrument you will, though you can fret *imitate* 390
me, you cannot play upon me.—

Re-enter POLONIUS.

God bless you, sir !

Pol. My lord, the queen would speak with you, and
presently.

Ham. Do you see yonder cloud that's almost in 395
shape of a camel?

Pol. By the mass, and 'tis like a camel, indeed.

Ham. Methinks it is like a weasel.

Pol. It is backed like a weasel.

Ham. Or like a whale?   400

Pol. Very like a whale.

Ham. Then will I come to my mother by and by.—
[*Aside.*] They fool me to the top of my bent.
—I will come by and by.

Pol. I will say so.   [*Exit.* 405

Ham. "By and by" is easily said.—Leave me, friends.

[*Exeunt all but Hamlet.*

388. *speak*] Q, omitted F ; *'Sblood*] Q, *Why* F ; *I*]Q, *that I* F.   390,
391. *can fret me*] Q 1, F ; *fret me not* Q.   391. *you*] Q, F ; *yet you* Q 1,
Globe, Cambridge.   395. *yonder*]Q, *that* F.   396. *of*]Q, *like* F.   397. *'tis
like* Q 4, *'tis, like* Q, *it's like* F.   399. *backed*] Q, F ; *black* Qq 4–6.
402. *will I*] F, *I will* Q.   403–406.] Speeches distributed as in F ; Q omits
the distribution, and the Exit of Polonius ; the Exeunt, line 406, is omitted Q, F.

390. *fret*] Playing on "fret," to
irritate and "fret," the piece of gut,
metal, or wood which regulates the
fingering on certain stringed instru-
ments.

398, 399. *weasel*] Capell transposed
the camel and the weasel, to provide
a hump for the second animal. Pope,
reading with the later Qq *black* for
backed, substituted *ouzle* for *weasel*,
which Theobald approved, noting

that " there is humour in comparing
the same cloud to a beast, a bird,
and a fish."
402. *by and by*] immediately, as
often. [Here=before long, as in
N. C. S., comparing v. ii. 304.
R. H. C.]
403. *bent*] see II. ii. 30.
406. *Leave me, friends*] follows *by
and by* (line 404) in Q.

'Tis now the very witching time of night,

When churchyards yawn, and hell itself breathes
out

Contagion to this world; now could I drink hot
blood,

And do such bitter business as the day   410

Would quake to look on.   Soft! now to my
mother.

O heart, lose not thy nature; let not ever

The soul of Nero enter this firm bosom;

Let me be cruel, not unnatural:

I will speak daggers to her, but use none;   415

My tongue and soul in this be hypocrites;

How in my words soever she be shent, *rebuked* .

To give them seals never, my soul, consent!
                                              deeds
                                                [*Exit.*

Rousing himself to action.

SCENE III.—*A Room in the Castle.*

Enter KING, ROSENCRANTZ, *and* GUILDENSTERN.

King. I like him not, nor stands it safe with us

To let his madness range.   Therefore prepare
you;

I your commission will forthwith dispatch,

And he to England shall along with you;

The terms of our estate may not endure   5

408. *breathes*] F, *breakes* Q.   410. *bitter . . . day*] F, *busines as the bitter day* Q, *better day* Warburton.   411. *Soft! now*] *soft, now* Q, *Soft now,* F.   415. *daggers*] F, *dagger* Q.   417. *soever*] Q 6, *somever* Q, F.

413. *Nero*] The murderer of his mother, Agrippina. See *King John,* v. ii. 152. Perhaps the coincidences are accidental, that Agrippina was the wife of Claudius, was accused of poisoning a husband, and of living in incest with a brother.
417. *shent*] rebuked, as in *Merry Wives,* I. iv. 38.
[418. *seals*] N. C. S. notes the legal diction. R. H. C.]

Hazard so near us as doth hourly grow
Out of his lunacies.

Guil.   We will ourselves provide.
Most holy and religious fear it is
To keep those many many bodies safe
That live and feed upon your majesty.   10

Ros. The single and peculiar life is bound
With all the strength and armour of the mind
To keep itself from noyance; but much more
That spirit upon whose weal depends and rests
The lives of many.   The cease of majesty   15
Dies not alone, but like a gulf doth draw
What's near it with it; it is a massy wheel,
Fix'd on the summit of the highest mount,
To whose huge spokes ten thousand lesser things
Are mortised and adjoin'd; which, when it falls,   20
Each small annexment, petty consequence,
Attends the boisterous ruin.   Never alone
Did the king sigh, but with a general groan.

King. Arm you, I pray you, to this speedy voyage;

6. *near us*] Q 1676, Pope; *neer's* Q; *dangerous* F and many editors.   7.
lunacies] F, *browes* Q, *lunes* Theobald, *braves* Anon.   14. *whose weal*] Q,
whose spirit F.   15. *cease*] F, *cesse* Q.   17. *it is*] F, *or it is* Q.
22. *ruin*] F, *raine* Q.   23. *with*] F, omitted Q.

7. *lunacies*] The Q *brows* may be
right. The word brow is used in the
sense of fronting aspect, countenance,
and also in that of confidence, effron-
tery; see *A New English Dictionary*,
brow, 5 *c* and *d*. The choice of the
word may have been determined by
the fixed gaze of Hamlet upon the
King during the play-scene. It seems
strange that *blows* (in the sense of
injuries, not uncommon in Shakespeare) has not been suggested as an
emendation of *brows*.
    9. *many many*] Ff 2–4 read *many*.

Rolfe compares *King John*, I. i. 183:
"many a many foot of land," and
Clar. Press, *Henry V*. IV. ii. 33:
"A very little little let us do."
    11. *single and peculiar*] individual
and private.
    13. *noyance*] hurt, injury.
    15. *cease*] cessation; cease of ma-
jesty, death of a king. Pope substituted "decease" for "the cease."
    16. *gulf*] whirlpool, as in *King
Richard III*. III. vii. 128.
    24. *Arm you*] prepare yourselves,
as in *Mid. Night's Dream*, I. i. 117.

For we will fetters put upon this fear,   25
Which now goes too free-footed.

Ros., *Guil.*   We will haste us.
    [Exeunt Rosencrantz and Guildenstern.

     Enter POLONIUS.

Pol. My lord, he 's going to his mother's closet;
Behind the arras I 'll convey myself
To hear the process; I 'll warrant she 'll tax him
  home;
And, as you said, and wisely was it said,   30
'Tis meet that some more audience than a mother,
Since nature makes them partial, should o'erhear
The speech, of vantage.   Fare you well, my
  liege;
I 'll call upon you ere you go to bed,
And tell you what I know.

King.   Thanks, dear my lord 35
         [Exit Polonius.
Oh, my offence is rank, it smells to heaven;
It hath the primal eldest curse upon 't,
A brother's murder!   Pray can I not,
Though inclination be as sharp as will:

---

25. *upon*] F, *about* Q.   26. Ros., Guil.] Both F, Ros. Q.   33. *speech, of vantage*] comma inserted by Theobald.   39. *will :*] F, *will*, Q.

33. *of vantage*] from a point or position of vantage. Many editors do not insert the comma before "of vantage." Hudson explains "speech of vantage," a speech having the advantage of such partiality as a mother bears to a son or a son to a mother.
38.] Hanmer needlessly emends the metre by inserting "alas!" after

"Pray." Walker suggests "murderer."
39. *will*] An ingenious gentleman suggested "'twill" to Theobald, which some editors have adopted. Warburton read "th' ill." The King means that his effort to pray was no reluctant resolve; his desire accompanied his act of will.

My stronger guilt defeats my strong intent,   40
And, like a man to double business bound,
I stand in pause where I shall first begin,
And both neglect.   What if this cursed hand,
Were thicker than itself with brother's blood,
Is not there rain enough in the sweet heavens   45
To wash it white as snow?   Whereto serves
        mercy
But to confront the visage of offence?
And what's in prayer but this two-fold force,
To be forestalled ere we come to fall,
Or pardon'd being down?   Then I'll look up;   50
My fault is past.   But, oh, what form of prayer
Can serve my turn?   "Forgive me my foul
        murder?"
That cannot be, since I am still possess'd
Of those effects for which I did the murder,
My crown, mine own ambition, and my queen.   55
May one be pardon'd and retain the offence?
In the corrupted currents of this world
Offence's gilded hand may shove by justice,
And oft 'tis seen the wicked prize itself
Buys out the law; but 'tis not so above;   60
There, is no shuffling; there, the action lies
In his true nature, and we ourselves compell'd
Even to the teeth and forehead of our faults

cf. Macbeth.

50. *pardon'd*] F, *pardon* Q.   52. *murder?*] Caldecott, *murther*, Q,
murther. F.   58. *shove by*] F, *showe by* Q.

57. *currents*] courses.   Dyce and   ii. 368. Occurrents had been sug-
Furness accept Walker's suggestion   gested in 1752.
"'currents" for occurrents; see v.   61. *lies*] Clar. Press: "used in its
        legal sense."

To give in evidence. What then? what rests?
Try what repentance can: what can it not? 65
Yet what can it when one can not repent?
O wretched state! O bosom black as death!
O limèd soul, that struggling to be free
Art more engaged! Help, angels! make assay!
Bow, stubborn knees; and, heart with strings of
    steel, 70
Be soft as sinews of the new-born babe!
All may be well. [*Retires and kneels.*

Enter HAMLET.

ironical. Claudius cannot pray.

Ham. Now might I do it pat, now he is praying;
And now I 'll do 't; and so he goes to heaven;
And so am I revenged. That would be scann'd: 75
A villain kills my father; and for that,
I, his sole son, do this same villain send
To heaven.
Oh, this is hire and salary, not revenge.
He took my father grossly, full of bread, 80
With all his crimes broad blown, as flush as May;
And how his audit stands who knows save heaven?

72. Retires . . .] Malone, omitted Q, F; hee kneeles Q 1. 73. *it pat, now he is praying*] F, *it, but now a is praying* Q. 77. *sole*] Q, *foule* F, *fool*, Capell conject. 79. *Oh*] F, *Why* Q; *hire and salary*] F, *base and silly* Q. 81. *With all*] F, *Withall* Q; *flush*] Q, *fresh* F.

68. *limed*] caught, as with bird-lime.
69. *engaged*] entangled. So Florio, *Montaigne*: "The Barble fishes, if one of them chance to be engaged."
69. *assay*] trial; but *assay* is used by Shakespeare, *King Henry V.* I. ii. 151, for an onset, attack, and perhaps that is the meaning here. It is suggested that "make assay" may

be addressed not to the angels but to the King's own soul.
75. *would be scann'd*] ought to be examined.
80. *bread*] Malone refers to Ezekiel xvi. 49: "pride, fulness of bread."
81. *broad blown*] see the Ghost's words, I. v. 76; *flush*, lusty; full of life; "flush youth," *Ant. and Cleop.* I. iv. 52.

But in our circumstance and course of thought
'Tis heavy with him; and am I then revenged,
To take him in the purging of his soul,   85
When he is fit and season'd for his passage?
No.
Up, sword, and know thou a more horrid hent;
When he is drunk asleep, or in his rage,
Or in the incestuous pleasure of his bed,   90
At gaming, swearing, or about some act
That has no relish of salvation in 't;
Then trip him, that his heels may kick at heaven
And that his soul may be as damn'd and black
As hell, whereto it goes.   My mother stays.—   95
This physic but prolongs thy sickly days.   [*Exit.*
King. [*Rising.*] My words fly up, my thoughts remain below;
Words without thoughts never to heaven go.   [*Exit.*

SCENE IV.—*The Queen's Closet.*

Enter QUEEN *and* POLONIUS.

Pol. He will come straight.   Look you lay home to him;

89. *drunk asleep*] F, *drunke, a sleepe* Q.   91. *gaming, swearing*] F, *game a swearing* Q, *game swearing* Q 1, *game, a-swearing* Cambridge. 97. Rising] omitted Q, F ; Rises Capell.

83. *our . . . thought*] our mortal condition and the course of our thought. Or "circumstance" may be connected with "thought," our thought in its indirect indications and its general tendency.

88. *hent*] seizure, grip. The verb is found in *Measure for Measure*, IV. vi. 14, and *Winter's Tale*, IV. iii. 133, meaning seize, take. F 4 has *bent*, followed by several editors. Warburton conjectured *hest*, command. Why has no "ingenious gentleman" suggested *hunt*, pursuit, and adduced instances of the use of

the hunting-sword in breaking-up the quarry ?

89–96.] Parallels for Hamlet's " infernal sentiment " can be adduced from other dramas. Thus in Beaumont and Fletcher, *Four Plays in One ; The Triumph of Death*, sc. v. (with an evident reminiscence from Hamlet) :

" 'Tis nothing :
No ; take him dead-drunk now, without repentance,
His lechery inseam'd upon him."
[With l. 96 cf. l. 85. *purging* (N. C. S.)   R. H. C.]

Tell him his pranks have been too broad to bear
with,
And that your grace hath screen'd and stood
between
Much heat and him. I 'll silence me e'en here.
Pray you, be round with him.
Ham. [*Within.*]   Mother, mother, mother! 5
Queen. I 'll warrant you ;
Fear me not. Withdraw, I hear him coming.
              [*Polonius hides behind the arras.*

Enter HAMLET.

Ham. Now, mother, what 's the matter?
Queen. Hamlet, thou hast thy father much offended.
Ham. Mother, you have my father much offended. 10
Queen. Come, come, you answer with an idle tongue.
Ham. Go, go, you question with a wicked tongue.
Queen. Why, how now, Hamlet?
Ham.   What 's the matter now?
Queen. Have you forgot me?
Ham.   No, by the rood, not so :
You are the queen, your husband's brother's
wife ;   15

4. *silence me e'en*] F, *silence me even* Q, *'sconce me e'en* Warburton, *sconce me even* Hanmer. 5. Ham. . . . *mother*] F, omitted Q. 6. *warrant*] F, *wait* Q. Polonius hides . . .] omitted Q, F; so with stage directions, line 24, line 25. 12. *a wicked*] Q, *an idle* F.

4. *silence*] Several editors adopt Hanmer's *sconce*. Cf. *Merry Wives*, III. iii. 96: "I will ensconce me behind the arras." Clar. Press reads *sconce* because it is supported by Q 1 : "Ile shrowde my selfe behinde the arras." The "foolish prating knave" Polonius can be "most still" only in death ; his resolve "to silence himself" may have an ironical relation to the occasion of his death, his loud "What, ho !"

5. *round*] see II. ii. 139.

And—would it were not so!—you are my mother.

Queen. Nay then, I 'll set those to you that can speak.

Ham. Come, come, and sit you down; you shall not
      budge;

You go not till I set you up a glass

Where you may see the inmost part of you.   20

Queen. What wilt thou do? thou wilt not murder me?
      Help, help, ho!

Pol. [*Behind.*] What, ho! help, help, help!

Ham. [*Drawing.*] How now! a rat? Dead, for a ducat,
      dead!   [*Makes a pass through the arras.*

Pol. [*Behind.*] Oh, I am slain!   [*Falls and dies.*

Queen.   Oh me, what hast thou done?   25

Ham. Nay, I know not; is it the king?

Queen. Oh, what a rash and bloody deed is this!

Ham. A bloody deed! almost as bad, good mother,

As kill a king, and marry with his brother.

Queen. As kill a king?

Ham.   Ay, lady, 'twas my word.—   30
      [*Lifts up the arras and discovers Polonius.*

Thou wretched, rash, intruding fool, farewell!

I took thee for thy better; take thy fortune;

Thou find'st to be too busy is some danger.—

Leave wringing of your hands. Peace! sit you
      down,

And let me wring your heart; for so I shall   35

If it be made of penetrable stuff;

16. *And . . . you*] Q (no parenthesis, comma after *so*); *But would you were
not so. You* F.   20. *inmost*] F, *most* Q.   22. *Help, help, ho!*] F, *Helpe
how.* Q.   23. *What, ho! . . . help!*] F, *What how helpe* Q.   24. *Makes
. . . arras*] Capell, omitted Q, F.   25. *Behind*] omitted Q, F; *Falls and
dies*] *Killes Polonius* F, omitted Q.   30. *king?*] F, *king.* Q; stage direction
omitted Q, F; *'twas*] F, *it was* Q.   32. *better*] Q, *betters* F.

If damned custom have not braz'd it so

That it is proof and bulwark against sense.

Queen. What have I done that thou darest wag thy tongue

In noise so rude against me?

Ham. Such an act 40

That blurs the grace and blush of modesty,

Calls virtue hypocrite, takes off the rose

From the fair forehead of an innocent love,

And sets a blister there; makes marriage vows

As false as dicers' oaths; oh, such a deed 45

As from the body of contraction plucks

The very soul, and sweet religion makes

A rhapsody of words; heaven's face doth glow,

Yea, this solidity and compound mass,

With tristful visage, as against the doom, 50

Is thought-sick at the act.

Queen. Ay me, what act,

That roars so loud and thunders in the index?

37. *braz'd*] F, *brasd* Q, *brass'd* Globe.   38 *is*] F, *be* Q.   44. *sets*] Q,
makes F.   48. *doth*] F, *dooes* Q.   48, 49. *glow, Yea*] F, *glowe Ore* Q.
50. *tristful*] F, *heated* Q.   51, 52. *Ay . . . index*] given to the Queen F;
Ay . . . act? given to Queen; *That roars*, &c., to Hamlet Q.

37. *braz'd*] hardened like brass. So
Armin, *Nest of Ninnies*, 1608: "I am
brazed by your favours, made bold in
your ostended curtesies."

38. *proof and bulwark*] armour of
proof and rampart against sense, that
is, feeling. For *proof* compare *Macbeth*, I. ii. 54: "Bellona's bridegroom
lapp'd in proof." Clar. Press takes
"proof" and "bulwark" as adjectives.

44. *sets a blister*] Clar. Press:
"brands as a harlot." Compare IV.
v. 117, and *Comedy of Errors*, II. ii.
138.

46. *contraction*] act of contracting,
specially of the marriage-contract.

Hakluyt, *Voyages*, 1598: "The
mutual contraction of a perpetuall
league." Cotton Mather, *Magnalia
Christi*, 1702: "After his 'contraction'... unto the daughter of
Mr. Wilson."

49. *this solidity*] the earth.

50. *tristful*] sorrowful, as in *1
Henry IV.* II. iv. 433: *doom*, doomsday.

51. *thought-sick*] see III. i. 85.

52 *index*] prelude; the index or
"table" was usually placed at the
beginning of books. So *Othello*, II. i.
263: "an index and obscure prologue."

Ham. Look here, upon this picture, and on this;
 The counterfeit presentment of two brothers.
 See what a grace was seated on this brow;   55
 Hyperion's curls, the front of Jove himself,
 An eye like Mars, to threaten and command;
 A station like the herald Mercury
 New-lighted on a heaven-kissing hill;
 A combination and a form indeed,   60
 Where every god did seem to set his seal
 To give the world assurance of a man:
 This was your husband. Look you now, what
   follows:
 Here is your husband; like a mildew'd ear,
 Blasting his wholesome brother. Have you eyes? 65
 Could you on this fair mountain leave to feed,
 And batten on this moor? Ha! have you eyes?
 You cannot call it love, for at your age
 The hey-day in the blood is tame, it's humble,
 And waits upon the judgment; and what judg-
   ment   70

55. *this*] Q, *his* F.   57. *and*] Q, *or* F.   65. *brother*] Q, *breath* F.

53. *Look here,*] Restoration actors made Hamlet produce two miniatures; but miniatures could hardly represent Hamlet's father at full-length, as he is described. A print, prefixed to Rowe's ed. of *Hamlet*, 1709, exhibits half-lengths hanging on the wall. The actor Holman had a picture of Claudius on the wall, and a miniature of the dead king produced from Hamlet's bosom. Fechter had two miniatures, one worn round Gertrude's neck, the other by Hamlet; he tore the miniature from Gertrude and flung it away; so Rossi, who stamped upon it. Edwin Booth used two miniatures. Sir H. Irving and Salvini have represented the portraits as seen only by the mind's eye.

54. *counterfeit presentment*] portrayed representation. Compare "Fair Portia's counterfeit," *Merchant of Venice*, III. ii. 116.

58. *station*] attitude in standing, as in *Ant. and Cleop.* III. iii. 22.

59.] Malone conjectured that this image was caught from Phaer's *Æneid*, IV. 246, Mercury arriving on Atlas.

67. *batten*] feed gluttonously. *Coriolanus*, IV. v. 35: "batten on cold bits."

Would step from this to this? Sense sure you
 have,
Else could you not have motion; but sure, that
 sense
Is apoplex'd; for madness would not err,
Nor sense to ecstasy was ne'er so thrall'd
But it reserved some quantity of choice,   75
To serve in such a difference. What devil was 't
That thus hath cozen'd you at hoodman-blind?
Eyes without feeling, feeling without sight,
Ears without hands or eyes, smelling sans all,
Or but a sickly part of one true sense   80
Could not so mope.
O shame! where is thy blush? Rebellious hell,
If thou canst mutine in a matron's bones,
To flaming youth let virtue be as wax
And melt in her own fire; proclaim no shame   85
When the compulsive ardour gives the charge,
Since frost itself as actively doth burn,
And reason panders will.

Queen.   O Hamlet, speak no more;
Thou turn'st mine eyes into my very soul,

71. *step*] Q, F; *stoop* Collier MS., and MS. in Ingleby's copy of Q 1637.
71–76. *Sense . . . difference*] Q, omitted F.   78–81. *Eyes . . . mope*] Q,
omitted F.   88. *And*] Q, *As* F; *panders*] F, *pardons* Q.   89. *eyes
. . . very*] F, *very eyes into my* Q.

71, 72. *Sense . . . motion*] sense,
feeling; motion, impulse, desire, as
frequently in Shakespeare.
74. *ecstasy*] madness, as in II. i.
102.
75. *quantity*] portion; used sometimes by Shakespeare contemptuously
for a small portion or anything dim-
inutive, as in *King John*, v. iv. 23.

77. *hoodman - blind*] blind - man's
buff. Singer quotes Baret's *Alvearie*:
"The Hoodwinke play, or hoodman-
blind, in some places called the blind-
manbuff."
81. *mope*] be stupid, as in *Tempest*,
v. i. 239.
83. *mutine*] mutiny. Cotgrave;
"Mutiner, to mutine."

And there I see such black and grained spots   90
As will not leave their tinct.

Ham.   Nay, but to live
In the rank sweat of an enseamed bed,
Stew'd in corruption, honeying and making love
Over the nasty sty,—

Queen.   O, speak to me no more;
These words like daggers enter in mine ears;   95
No more, sweet Hamlet!

Ham.   A murderer and a villain;
A slave that is not twentieth part the tithe
Of your precedent lord; a vice of kings;
A cut-purse of the empire and the rule,
That from a shelf the precious diadem stole,   100
And put it in his pocket!

Queen.   No more!

Ham. A king of shreds and patches—

Enter GHOST.

Save me, and hover o'er me with your wings,
You heavenly guards!—What would your gracious
    figure?

Queen. Alas, he's mad!   105

90. *grained*] F, *greeued* Q.   91. *not leave*] F, *leave there* Q.   94 *sty,—*]
sty. Q, F.   95. *mine*] F, *my* Q.   102. *patches—*] Rowe, *patches,* Q,
patches. F.   103. Enter Ghost.] before line 102 Q, F ; Enter the Ghost in
his night gowne Q 1.   104. *your*] Q, *you* F.

90. *grained*] dyed in grain.
92. *enseamed*] loaded with grease.
French, *enseimer* (now *ensimer*). *New
English Dictionary*: "The French
word is now used only in sense 'to
grease cloth,' whence perhaps the
fig. use in Shaks." See note on III.
iii. 89-95.

98. *vice*] the vice of the old
moralities was commonly a mis-
chievous buffoon ; he wore sometimes
the parti-coloured dress of a fool,
whence, Dyce supposes, "a king of
shreds and patches,"

Ham. Do you not come your tardy son to chide,
    That, lapsed in time and passion, lets go by
    The important acting of your dread command?
    Oh, say!

Ghost. Do not forget: this visitation   110
    Is but to whet thy almost blunted purpose.
    But look, amazement on thy mother sits;
    Oh, step between her and her fighting soul;
    Conceit in weakest bodies strongest works:
    Speak to her, Hamlet.

Ham.   How is it with you, lady? 115
Queen. Alas, how is 't with you,
    That you do bend your eye on vacancy
    And with the incorporal air do hold discourse?
    Forth at your eyes your spirits wildly peep;
    And, as the sleeping soldiers in the alarm,   120
    Your bedded hair, like life in excrements,
    Starts up and stands an end.   O gentle son,
    Upon the heat and flame of thy distemper
    Sprinkle cool patience.   Whereon do you look?

Ham. On him, on him!   Look you, how pale he
    glares!   125

117. *you do*] Q, *you* F.   118. *the incorporal*] Q, *their corporall* F.
122. *Starts . . . stands*] Q 4, *Start . . . stand* Q, F.

107. *lapsed . . . passion*] Johnson:
"having suffered time to slip and passion to cool." Rolfe: "having let time
slip by while indulging in mere passion." Schmidt (guided by the use of
lapsed in *Twelfth Night*, III. iii. 36):
"surprised by you in a time and passion
fit for the execution of your command."
Collier MS. has "fume" for "time."
    108. *important*] urgent, as in *All's
Well*, III. vii. 21.

112. *amazement*] bewilderment, as
in *Measure for Measure*, IV. ii. 220.
    114. *Conceit*] imagination, as in II.
ii. 593.
    121. *excrements*] outgrowths; used
especially of hair, nails, feathers; used
of the beard in *Merchant of Venice*,
III. ii. 87.   Rowe read *hairs*, and is
followed by several editors.
    122. *an end*] see I. v. 19.

His form and cause conjoin'd, preaching to stones,
Would make them capable.—Do not look upon
　me,
Lest with this piteous action you convert
My stern effects; then what I have to do
Will want true colour; tears perchance for
　blood.　　　　　　　　　　　　　　130

Queen. To whom do you speak this?
Ham.　　　　　　　　Do you see nothing there?
Queen. Nothing at all; yet all that is I see.
Ham. Nor did you nothing hear?
Queen.　　　　　　　No, nothing but ourselves.
Ham. Why, look you there! look, how it steals away!
My father, in his habit as he lived!　　　135
Look, where he goes, even now, out at the portal!
　　　　　　　　　　　　　　[*Exit Ghost.*
Queen. This is the very coinage of your brain;
This bodiless creation ecstasy
Is very cunning in.
Ham.　　　　　　　Ecstasy?
My pulse, as yours, doth temperately keep time,　140
And makes as healthful music; it is not madness
That I have utter'd; bring me to the test,
And I the matter will re-word, which madness
Would gambol from.　Mother, for love of grace,

129. *effects*] Q, F; *affects*, Singer. 131. *whom*] Q, *who* F.　139. *Ecstasy?*] F, omitted Q.

127. *capable*] susceptible, as in III. ii. 14.
129. *effects*] action, as in *Venus and Adonis*, 605, and *Lear*, II. iv. 182. Singer's proposal *affects*, affections of the mind, is perhaps right.
135. *his habit*] Q 1 directs that the Ghost shall appear in his night-gown, that is, dressing-gown.
138. *ecstasy*] see II. i. 102.

[In the German play (see p. xiv. *ante*) Hamlet accounts for the Ghost's invisibility to his mother by her "unworthiness to look upon his form." N. C. S. refers to Heywood's *Iron Age*, pt. ii. v. i., to show that such a consequence of guilt was probably a common belief in Shakespeare's time. R. H. C.]

Lay not that flattering unction to your soul,　145
That not your trespass but my madness speaks;
It will but skin and film the ulcerous place, *cover it over – appearance*
Whilst rank corruption, mining all within,　*of healing.*
Infects unseen.　Confess yourself to heaven;
Repent what's past, avoid what is to come;　150
And do not spread the compost on the weeds,
To make them ranker.　Forgive me this my virtue,
For in the fatness of these pursy times
Virtue itself of vice must pardon beg,
Yea, curb and woo for leave to do him good.　155
Queen. O Hamlet, thou hast cleft my heart in twain.
Ham. O, throw away the worser part of it,
And live the purer with the other half.
Good night: but go not to mine uncle's bed;
Assume a virtue, if you have it not.　160
That monster, custom, who all sense doth eat, *consciousness as in*
Of habits devil, is angel yet in this,
That to the use of actions fair and good
He likewise gives a frock or livery,
That aptly is put on.　Refrain to-night,　165

readily

145. *that*] Q, *a* F.　148. *Whilst*] F, *Whiles* Q.　151. *on*] Q, *or* F, *o'er* Caldecott.　152. *ranker*] Q, *ranke* F.　153. *these*] Q, *this* F. 155. *curb*] Q, *courb* F.　158. *live*] F, *leaue* Q.　159. *mine*] F, *my* Q. 161–165. *That . . . put on*] Q, omitted F.　161, 162. *eat, Of habits devil,*] Q 6, *eate Of habits deuill* Q.　165. *on. Refrain to-night*] Q 6 (with semi-colon after *on*), *on to refraine night* Q.

152. *Forgive*] Staunton regards these words to the close of the speech as addressed to "my virtue," and marks them "aside"; but how does this agree with virtue begging pardon of vice?　Evidently the words are spoken to his mother.
155. *curb*] The modern spelling of F *courb*, French *courber*, to bow or

bend. Drummond of Hawthornden, *Cypress Grove*: "bodies languishing and curbing."
161–165.] With the pointing above, no emendation is required: Custom, who destroys all sensibility, the evil spirit of our habits, is yet an angel in this, etc.　The emendation suggested by Thirlby to Theobald "of habits

10

And that shall lend a kind of easiness

To the next abstinence; the next more easy;

For use almost can change the stamp of nature,

And either master the devil, or throw him out

With wondrous potency.   Once more, good night;

And when you are desirous to be bless'd,   171

I 'll blessing beg of you.——For this same lord,

> [*Pointing to Polonius.*

I do repent; but heaven hath pleased it so,

To punish me with this, and this with me,

That I must be their scourge and minister.   175

I will bestow him, and will answer well

The death I gave him.——So, again, good night.

I must be cruel, only to be kind;

Thus bad begins, and worse remains behind.

One word more, good lady.

Queen.   What shall I do? 180

Ham. Not this, by no means, that I bid you do:

Let the bloat king tempt you again to bed;

Pinch wanton on your cheek; call you his mouse;

167-170. *the next more . . . potency*] Q, omitted F.   169. *And . . . the*] Jennens, Steevens (1785), Dyce (ed. 2), Furness; *And either the* Qq 2, 3; *And Maister the* Q 4.   179. *Thus*] F, *This* Q.   180. *One . . . lady*] Q, omitted F.   182. *bloat*] Warburton, *blowt* Q, *blunt* F.

evil" is plausible; but it effaces the opposition of "angel" to "devil." Staunton reads "eat, Oft habits' devil"; Grant White, "eat of habit's evil"; Johnson, "eat Of habits, devil." Clar. Press notes: "The double meaning of the word 'habits' suggested the frock or livery."

169. *And either master*] Q omits the verb; Q 4 omits *either* and inserts *master*. Several editors follow Q 4. Pope and Capell, "And master even" (or ev'n); Malone, "And either

curb." Quell, lay, shame, and other verbs have been proposed. "Master" may be derived from the early stage, and has somewhat more authority than any other word.

178, 179.] Delius supposes that the lines are spoken aside.

183. *mouse*] a pet name, as in *Love's Labour's Lost*, v. ii. 19; Burton, *Anatomy of Melancholy*: "pleasant names may be invented, bird, mouse, lamb, pus, pigeon, &c."

And let him, for a pair of reechy kisses,

Or paddling in your neck with his damn'd
    fingers,   185

Make you to ravel all this matter out,

That I essentially am not in madness,

But mad in craft.   'Twere good you let him
    know;

For who that's but a queen, fair, sober, wise,

Would from a paddock, from a bat, a gib,   190

Such dear concernings hide? who would do so?

No, in despite of sense and secrecy,

Unpeg the basket on the house's top,

Let the birds fly, and, like the famous ape,

To try conclusions, in the basket creep,   195

And break your own neck down.

Queen. Be thou assured, if words be made of breath,

And breath of life, I have no life to breathe

What thou hast said to me.

Ham. I must to England; you know that?

Queen.   Alack, 200

I had forgot; 'tis so concluded on.

---

188. *craft. 'Twere*] F, *craft, 'twere* Q.   195. *conclusions, in the basket*] F
3, no pointing in Q, comma only after *basket* F.   200. *that ?*] F, *that.* Q.

184. *reechy*] another form of *reeky*, smoky; hence foul; but reek is also used to mean emit vapour, commonly malodorous, and perhaps the word may mean stinking. We have "reeky shanks and yellow chapless skulls" in *Romeo and Juliet*, IV. i. 83.

190. *paddock*] toad, as in *Macbeth*, I. i. 9.

190. *gib*] tom-cat; so "gib-cat," *1 Henry IV.* I. ii. 83. Clar. Press notes: "The toad, bat, and cat were supposed to be familiars of witches and acquainted with their mistresses'

secrets." Perhaps the ideas of venom, blindness, and lust are suggested.

193-196] The famous ape is now unknown. Warner suggests that Suckling alludes to the forgotten story in a letter, where he speaks of the jackanapes and the partridges; but Suckling's jackanapes, though he lets out the partridges, does not break his neck.

195. *try conclusions*] try experiments, as in *Lucrece*, 1160.

200. *England*] How Hamlet had learnt this is left untold.

Ham. There's letters seal'd; and my two school-
    fellows,
Whom I will trust as I will adders fang'd,
They bear the mandate; they must sweep my
    way,
And marshal me to knavery. Let it work;   205
For 'tis the sport to have the enginer
Hoist with his own petar; and 't shall go hard
But I will delve one yard below their mines,
And blow them at the moon; oh, 'tis most
    sweet
When in one line two crafts directly meet.   210
This man shall set me packing;
I 'll lug the guts into the neighbour room.
Mother, good night. Indeed this counsellor
Is now most still, most secret, and most grave,
Who was in life a foolish prating knave.—   215
Come, sir, to draw toward an end with you.—
Good night, mother.
    [Exeunt severally; Hamlet dragging in Polonius.

202–210. *There's . . . meet*] Q, omitted F.   207. *and 't*] Theobald,
an 't Q.   213. *good night. Indeed*] F, *good night indeed*, Q.   215. *foolish*]
Q 1, F; *most foolish* Q.   217. Exeunt . . .] Steevens; Exit Q; Exit
Hamlet tugging in Polonius F; Exit Hamlet with the dead body Q 1.

206. *enginer*] constructor of military works; accent on *en*, as in *Othello*, II. i. 65. Compare *pioner*, I. v. 163.

207. *Hoist*] Shakespeare has both the forms *hoise* and *hoist*, to either of which forms of the verb this may belong.

207. *petar*] Clar. Press quotes Cotgrave: "Petart: a Petard or Petarre; an Engine . . . wherewith strong gates are burst open."

211. *packing*] Schmidt: departing in a hurry. Clar. Press: contriving, plotting, with a play on the other sense. "Pack" occurs in both senses in Shakespeare.

ACT IV

SCENE I.—*A Room in the Castle.*

Enter KING, QUEEN, ROSENCRANTZ, *and*
GUILDENSTERN.

King. There's matter in these sighs; these profound
 heaves
 You must translate; 'tis fit we understand them.
 Where is your son?
Queen. Bestow this place on us a little while.
     [*Exeunt Rosencrantz and Guildenstern.*
 Ah, my good lord, what have I seen to-night! 5
King. What, Gertrude? How does Hamlet?
Queen. Mad as the sea and wind, when both contend
 Which is the mightier: in his lawless fit,
 Behind the arras hearing something stir,
 Whips out his rapier, cries, " A rat, a rat!" 10
 And in this brainish apprehension kills
 The unseen good old man.
King.   O heavy deed!
 It had been so with us had we been there;
 His liberty is full of threats to all,
 To you yourself, to us, to every one. 15

Enter . . . Guldenstern] substantially Q, Enter King F. 1. *matter*] Q,
matters F. 1, 2. *There's . . . translate*] F has full stop after *sighs*,
Q has comma after *sighs*, *heaves*, and *translate*. 4. *Bestow . . . while*]
Q, omitted F. Exeunt . . .] omitted Q, F. 5. *my good*] F, *mine own* Q;
to-night !] Hanmer; *to-night ?* Q, F. 7. *sea*] Q, *seas* F. 10. *Whips* . . .
cries] Q, *He whips his Rapier out, and cries* F. 11. *this*] Q, *his* F.

11. *brainish*] headstrong, passion- " Braynisshe, **hedy,** selfe
ate. Palsgrave, *Lesclarcissement*, 1530: wylled."

Alas, how shall this bloody deed be answer'd?
It will be laid to us, whose providence
Should have kept short, restrain'd and out of haunt,
This mad young man; but so much was our love,
We would not understand what was most fit,　　20
But, like the owner of a foul disease,
To keep it from divulging, let it feed
Even on the pith of life.　Where is he gone?

Queen. To draw apart the body he hath kill'd;
O'er whom his very madness, like some ore　　25
Among a mineral of metals base,
Shows itself pure; he weeps for what is done.

King. O Gertrude, come away!
The sun no sooner shall the mountains touch
But we will ship him hence; and this vile deed　　30
We must, with all our majesty and skill,
Both countenance and excuse.—Ho! Guildenstern!

Re-enter ROSENCRANTZ *and* GUILDENSTERN.

Friends both, go join you with some further aid;
Hamlet in madness hath Polonius slain,
And from his mother's closet hath he dragg'd
　him:　　　　　　　　　　　　　　　　35

---

22. *let*] Q, *let's* F.　　31. *must*] F, *most* Q.

18. *kept short*] So in Florio's *Mon-taigne*: "When his soldiers were nearest unto their enemies he re-strained and kept them very short" (II. 34).

18. *haunt*] resort, as in *As You Like It*, II. i. 15.

25. *ore*] Schmidt gives no meaning for *ore* in Shakespeare except "a vein of gold." Clar. Press: "in the English-French Dictionary appended to Cotgrave *ore* is confined to gold." Walker proposed and Furness reads "like fine ore."

26. *mineral*] Malone: "Minsheu defines 'mineral' to be 'anything that grows in mines and contains metals.'" It is used in Hall's *Satires*, b. vi. for mine.

Go seek him out; speak fair, and bring the body
Into the chapel.   I pray you, haste in this.—
    [Exeunt Rosencrantz and Guildenstern.
Come, Gertrude, we'll call up our wisest friends
And let them know both what we mean to do,
And what's untimely done : [so, haply, slander,] 40
Whose whisper o'er the world's diameter,
As level as the cannon to his blank
Transports his poison'd shot, may miss our name
And hit the woundless air.   O, come away!
My soul is full of discord and dismay. 45
        [Exeunt.

SCENE II.—*Another Room in the Castle.*

Enter HAMLET.

Ham. Safely stowed.

Ros., Guil. [*Within.*] Hamlet! Lord Hamlet!

Ham. But soft, what noise? who calls on Hamlet?
  O, here they come.

Enter ROSENCRANTZ *and* GUILDENSTERN.

Ros. What have you done, my lord, with the dead 5
  body?

39. *And let*] Q, *To let* F. 40–44.] see note below.

Scene II.

Enter Hamlet] F ; Enter Hamlet, Rosencraus, and others Q. **2.** Ros.
Guil. [Within.] *Hamlet! Lord Hamlet!*] substantially F, omitted Q. **3.** *But
soft,*] Q, omitted F. 4. Enter . . .] F, omitted Q.

40. *so haply slander*] F omits all between *done* and *O*, line 44 ; Q reads :
 "And whats vntimely doone,
 Whose whisper."
Theobald suggested "Happily, slander," or *rumour*, and read "For,
haply, slander."   Capell read as
above, and is followed by many
editors.   Malone 1790: "So viper-
ous slander."   Staunton suggested
"thus calumny."
 42. *blank*] the white spot in the
centre of a target ; mark.   Compare
Othello, III. iv. 128.

Ham. Compounded it with dust, whereto 'tis kin.

Ros. Tell us where 'tis, that we may take it thence
and bear it to the chapel.

Ham. Do not believe it.   10

Ros. Believe what?

Ham. That I can keep your counsel and not mine
own. Besides, to be demanded of a sponge,
what replication should be made by the son
of a king?   15

Ros. Take you me for a sponge, my lord?

Ham. Ay, sir; that soaks up the king's countenance,
his rewards, his authorities. But such officers
do the king best service in the end; he keeps
them, like an ape, in the corner of his jaw;   20
first mouthed, to be last swallowed; when he
needs what you have gleaned, it is but squeez-
ing you, and, sponge, you shall be dry
again.

Ros. I understand you not, my lord.   25

Ham. I am glad of it; a knavish speech sleeps in
a foolish ear.

---

7. *Compounded*] F, *Compound* Q.   13. *sponge*,] Q, F; *spunge!*—
Steevens; *spunge!* Caldecott.   20. *like an ape*] F, *like an apple* Q, as
an Ape doth nuttes Q 1, *like an ape, an apple* Farmer conject.

7. *Compounded*] The Q *Compound*
may be right, as an imperative. So
2 Henry IV. IV. v. 116.

12. *keep your counsel*] Hamlet
knows of the commission to England.
Or perhaps the reference is to his
not betraying their confession that
they had been sent for by the King.
See II. ii. 305. Possibly there is a
play on the word *counsel* meaning
councillor, as elsewhere in Shakespeare. See stage direction in Q 1,

I. ii. (opening) " Counsaile ; as Polonius."

13. *sponge*] The same image was
used, in nearly the same way, by
Vespasian, as recorded by Suetonius.
Caldecott quotes from R. C.'s Henr.
Steph. *Apology for Herodotus*, 1608,
and Barnabe Riche, *Faultes, faults*,
1606, in illustration of the image.
Steevens quotes Marston, *Satires*, vii.

17. *countenance*] patronage, favour,
as in *2 Henry IV.* IV. ii. 13.

Ros. My lord, you must tell us where the body is,
  and go with us to the king.

Ham. The body is with the king, but the king is 30
  not with the body. The king is a thing—

Guil. "A thing," my lord?

Ham. Of nothing: bring me to him. Hide fox, *— he rushes out*
  and all after. *[Exeunt. and they run after him*

SCENE III.—*Another Room in the Castle.*

Enter KING, *attended.*

King. I have sent to seek him, and to find the body.
  How dangerous is it that this man goes loose!
  Yet must not we put the strong law on him:
  He's loved of the distracted multitude,
  Who like not in their judgment, but their eyes; 5
  And where 'tis so, the offender's scourge is weigh'd,
  But never the offence. To bear all smooth and even,
  This sudden sending him away must seem

---

31. *a thing*—] F, *a thing.* Q.   33, 34. *Hide . . . after*] F, omitted Q.

Scene III.

7. *never*] Q, *neerer* F.

30, 31. *The body . . . thing*—] Clar. Press: "Hamlet is talking nonsense designedly." He wishes to baffle the courtiers, and have a private meaning, as often before. He has just called himself "the son of a king"; he has seen his father in his own castle. To the courtiers his words are nonsense; for himself they mean "the body lies in death with the King my father, but my father walks disembodied." He might have added something, but he is interrupted, and adopting Rosencrantz's meaning of "King," completes his sentence otherwise than intended, yet so as to express a part of his mind; "the King—as you mean King—is for me a negligible quantity, a thing of nothing." In v. ii. 64. Hamlet speaks of his father as my "king."

33, 34. *Hide fox, and all after*] Hanmer says that there is a play among children so named. Dekker, *Satiromastix* has: "does play at bo-peep with your grace, and cries—All hid, as boys do." Whether the reference is to a children's game or to a fox-hunt, the meaning seems to be: "The old fox, Polonius, is hidden; come, let us all follow the sport and hunt him out." See App. III.

Deliberate pause; diseases desperate grown
By desperate appliance are relieved,   10
Or not at all.—

Enter ROSENCRANTZ.

                  How now! what hath befall'n?

Ros. Where the dead body is bestow'd, my lord,
We cannot get from him.

King.   But where is he?

Ros. Without, my lord; guarded, to know your
pleasure.

King. Bring him before us.   15

Ros. Ho, Guildenstern! bring in my lord.

Enter HAMLET *and* GUILDENSTERN.

King. Now, Hamlet, where's Polonius?

Ham. At supper.

King. At supper? where?

Ham. Not where he eats, but where he is eaten; a 20
certain convocation of politic worms are e'en
at him. Your worm is your only emperor for
diet; we fat all creatures else to fat us, and
we fat ourselves for maggots: your fat king
and your lean beggar is but variable service, 25
two dishes, but to one table; that's the
end.

---

11. Enter Rosencrantz] F, Enter Rosencraus and all the rest Q.   16. *Ho,*
Guildenstern] F, *How,* Q; *my lord*] F, *the lord* Q.   21. *politic*] Q,
omitted F.   24. *ourselves*] Q, *our selfe,* F.

21. *politic worms*] such worms as | Diet of Worms. W. Hall Griffin
might breed in a politician's corpse. | adds, "the mention of 'emperor'
Singer suggests an allusion to the | makes it very probable."

King. Alas, alas!

Ham. A man may fish with the worm that hath
    eat of a king, and eat of the fish that hath   30
    fed of that worm.

King. What dost thou mean by this?

Ham. Nothing but to show you how a king may
    go a progress through the guts of a beggar.

King. Where is Polonius?   35

Ham. In heaven; send thither to see; if your
    messenger find him not there, seek him i' the
    other place yourself. But indeed, if you find
    him not within this month, you shall nose
    him as you go up the stairs into the lobby.   40

King. [*To some Attendants.*] Go seek him there.

Ham. He will stay till you come.

                           [*Exeunt Attendants.*

King. Hamlet, this deed, for thine especial safety,
    Which we do tender, as we dearly grieve
    For that which thou hast done, must send thee hence 45
    With fiery quickness; therefore prepare thyself;
    The bark is ready, and the wind at help,
    The associates tend, and every thing is bent
    For England.

Ham.   For England?

King.   Ay, Hamlet.

Ham.   Good.

28–31. King. *Alas . . . worm*] Q, omitted F.   38. *indeed, if*] F, *if
indeed* Q.   39. *within*] Q, omitted F.   41, 42. stage directions inserted
by Capell.   42. *you*] Q, *ye* F.   43. *deed, for thine*] Q, *deed of thine, for
thine* F.   46. *With fiery quickness*] F, omitted Q.   48. *is bent*] Q,
at bent F.   49. *England ?*] F, *England.* Q.

34. *progress*] a royal journey of state, as in *2 Henry VI.* I. iv. 76.

King. So is it, if thou knew'st our purposes.　　　　50

Ham. I see a cherub that sees them.—But, come;
　　for England!—Farewell, dear mother.

King. Thy loving father, Hamlet.

Ham. My mother: father and mother is man and
　　wife; man and wife is one flesh, and so, my　55
　　mother.—Come, for England!　　　　　[*Exit.*

King. Follow him at foot; tempt him with speed aboard;
　　Delay it not, I'll have him hence to-night;
　　Away! for every thing is seal'd and done
　　That else leans on the affair: pray you, make
　　haste.—　　　　　　　　　　　　　　60
　　　　　　　[*Exeunt Rosencrantz and Guildenstern.*
　　And, England, if my love thou hold'st at aught,—
　　As my great power thereof may give thee sense,
　　Since yet thy cicatrice looks raw and red
　　After the Danish sword, and thy free awe
　　Pays homage to us,—thou may'st not coldly set　65
　　Our sovereign process; which imports at full,
　　By letters conjuring to that effect,
　　The present death of Hamlet. Do it, England:
　　For like the hectic in my blood he rages,

[In left margin, handwritten:] Apostrophizing To England

[Handwritten above "cicatrice":] scar

---

51. *them*] Q, *him* F.　　55. *and so*] F, Q 1 ; *so* Q.　　60. Exeunt . . .]
Theobald ; omitted Q, F.　　67. *conjuring*] F, *congruing* Q.

51. *a cherub*] The cherubim are
angels of knowledge, and so they see
the King's purposes.
57. *at foot*] close, at heel.
65. *set*] Pope (ed. 2) read *let, i.e.*
hinder ; Hanmer *set by*. "Coldly
set" is explained by Schmidt "regard
with indifference." "Set me light,"
esteem me lightly, occurs in *Sonnets*,
lxxxviii., and "sets it light" in *King
Richard II.* I. iii. 293.

66. *process*] procedure.
67. *conjuring*] This word, rather
than Q *congruing*, corresponds with the
"earnest conjuration" of the document, described by Hamlet in v.
ii. 38. The accent on the first
syllable is found in *Measure for
Measure*, v. i. 48.
69. *hectic*] Cotgrave has "Ectique
. . . a fever called Hecticke," and
"sick of an Heckticke fever."

And thou must cure me.   Till I know 'tis done, 70
Howe'er my haps, my joys were ne'er begun. [*Exit.*

SCENE IV.—*A Plain in Denmark.*

Enter FORTINBRAS, *a Captain and Soldiers, marching.*

For. Go, captain, from me greet the Danish king;
Tell him that, by his license, Fortinbras
Claims the conveyance of a promised march
Over his kingdom.   You know the rendezvous.
If that his majesty would aught with us,   5
We shall express our duty in his eye; *in his presence*
And let him know so.

Cap.   I will do 't, my lord.

For. Go softly on.

[*Exeunt Fortinbras and Soldiers.*

Enter HAMLET, ROSENCRANTZ, GUILDENSTERN, *and
others.*

Ham. Good sir, whose powers are these?

Cap. They are of Norway, sir.   10

71. *joys . . . begun*] F, *joys will nere begin* Q.

Scene IV.

A Plain . . .] Capell; A Camp Rowe.   Enter . . .] Globe ed.   Enter
Fortinbrasse with his Army over the stage Q.   Enter Fortinbras with an
Armie F.   3. *Claims*] F, *Craves* Q.   6. *eye;*] Collier; *eye*, Q, F.   8.
softly] Q, *safely* F.   Exeunt . . .] omitted Q, Exit F.   Enter . . .] Dyce;
Enter Hamlet, Rosencraus, etc. Q, omitted F.   9–66. *Good sir, . . . worth*]
Q, omitted F.

71. *haps*] Johnson suggested and
Collier's MS. has "hopes."

Scene IV.

6. *in his eye*] in his presence;
Steevens compares *Antony and Cleo-*
patra, II. ii. 212.   Collier's semicolon
after *eye* is meant to make it clear
that the words which follow are a
direction to the Captain.

8. *softly*] leisurely, slowly, as in
Julius Cæsar, v. i. 16.

Ham. How purposed, sir, I pray you?

Cap. Against some part of Poland.

Ham. Who commands them, sir?

Cap. The nephew to old Norway, Fortinbras.

Ham. Goes it against the main of Poland, sir,   15
      Or for some frontier?

Cap. Truly to speak, and with no addition,
      We go to gain a little patch of ground
      That hath in it no profit but the name.
      To pay five ducats, five, I would not farm it;   20
      Nor will it yield to Norway or the Pole
      A ranker rate, should it be sold in fee.

more abundant

Ham. Why, then the Polack never will defend it.

Cap. Yes, 'tis already garrison'd.

Ham. Two thousand souls and twenty thousand ducats   25
      Will not debate the question of this straw;
      This is the imposthume of much wealth and peace,
      That inward breaks, and shows no cause without
      Why the man dies.—I humbly thank you, sir.

Cap. God be wi' you, sir.   [*Exit.*

Ros.   Will 't please you go, my lord?   30

Ham. I 'll be with you straight.   Go a little before.
                       [*Exeunt all except Hamlet.*
      How all occasions do inform against me,

17. *speak*] Q, *speak it* Pope, *speak, sir* Capell.   24. *'tis*] Pope, *it is* Q.
30. Exit] omitted Q.   31. Exeunt . . .] omitted Q.

15. *main*] Clar. Press: "the chief power"; Schmidt: "the whole."
20. *five . . . it*] Theobald suggested "five ducats fine," but did not adopt it in his edition; *farm it,* "rent it," contrasted with *sold in fee,* line 22, *i.e.* in absolute possession.
22. *ranker*] more abundant.

25, 26.] It has been suggested (*Gent. Magazine,* lx. 403) that these lines belong to the Captain.
27. *imposthume*] Minsheu defines the word "a course of evill humours gathered to some part of the bodie"; Cotgrave: "an inward swelling full of corrupt matter."

And spur my dull revenge! What is a man,
If his chief good and market of his time
Be but to sleep and feed? a beast, no more.   35
Sure he that made us with such large discourse, *power of thought*
Looking before and after, gave us not
That capability and god-like reason
To fust in us unused. Now, whether it be
Bestial oblivion, or some craven scruple   40 *Applies it to himself*
Of thinking too precisely on the event,—
A thought which, quarter'd, hath but one part wisdom
And ever three parts coward,—I do not know
Why yet I live to say "This thing's to do,"
since Sith I have cause, and will, and strength, and
   means,   45
To do 't. Examples, gross as earth, exhort me;
Witness this army, of such mass and charge,
Led by a delicate and tender prince,   *Fortinbras, doing bravely*
Whose spirit with divine ambition puff'd   *for a very small cause*
Makes mouths at the invisible event;   50
Exposing what is mortal and unsure
To all that fortune, death and danger dare,   *concrete words*
Even for an egg-shell. Rightly to be great
Is not to stir without great argument,

39. *fust*] Q, *rust* Rowe.

34. *market*] that which he pur-
chases with his time.
36. *discourse*] power of thought
and reasoning; see I. ii. 150.
39. *fust*] grow mouldy; Cotgrave
explains *fuste*, "fustie, tasting of the
cask." Fr. *fuste*, a cask.
41. *event*] issue, consequences, as
in line 50.
47. *charge*] cost.
50. *mouths*] a common corruption

of "mows," grimaces, found in *Midsummer Night's Dream*, III. ii. 238;
see II. ii. 386, *ante*.
53–56.] To stir without great
argument (matter in dispute) is not
rightly to be great, but to find quarrel
in a straw when honour's at the stake
is an attribute of true greatness. The
"not," as Furness argues, belongs to
the copula, not to the predicate.

But greatly to find quarrel in a straw   55
When honour's at the stake.   How stand I then,
That have a father kill'd, a mother stain'd,
Excitements of my reason and my blood,
And let all sleep, while, to my shame, I see
The imminent death of twenty thousand men,   60
That, for a fantasy and trick of fame,
Go to their graves like beds, fight for a plot
Whereon the numbers cannot try the cause,
Which is not tomb enough and continent
To hide the slain?   Oh, from this time forth,   65
My thoughts be bloody, or be nothing worth!

[*Exit.*

SCENE V.—*Elsinore.   A Room in the Castle.*

Enter QUEEN, HORATIO, *and a Gentleman.*

Queen. I will not speak with her.
Gent. She is importunate, indeed distract;
  Her mood will needs be pitied.
Queen.   What would she have?
Gent. She speaks much of her father; says she hears
  There's tricks i' the world; and hems, and beats
    her heart;   5

Scene V.
Enter . . .] Pope; Enter Horatio, Gertrard, and a Gentleman Q; Enter
Queene and Horatio F.   2, 4. Gent.] Q, Hor. F.

61. *trick of fame*] toy or trifle of
fame; *Taming of the Shrew*, IV. iii.
67: "a knack, a toy, a trick, a
baby's cap." Perhaps "fantasy"
also should be connected with "of
fame."
  64. *continent*] receptacle, that which
contains, as in *Midsummer Night's
Dream*, II. i. 92.

Scene V.
1–16. The only variation here from
the distribution of speeches in Q is
the assignment of the words "Let
her come in" (line 16) to the Queen
instead of to Horatio. Collier suggests
that the omission in F of the Gentleman was to avoid the employment of
another actor.

Spurns enviously at straws; speaks things in doubt,
That carry but half sense: her speech is nothing,
Yet the unshaped use of it doth move
The hearers to collection; they aim at it,
And   botch   the   words   up   fit   to   their   own
   thoughts;   10
Which, as her winks and nods and gestures yield
   them,
Indeed   would   make   one   think   there   might   be
   thought,
Though nothing sure, yet much unhappily.
Hor. 'Twere good she were spoken with, for she may strew
   Dangerous conjectures in ill-breeding minds.   15
Queen. Let her come in.   *[Exit Gentleman.*
[Aside.] To my sick soul, as sin's true nature is,
   Each toy seems prologue to some great amiss;
   So full of artless jealousy is guilt,
   It spills itself in fearing to be spilt.   20

Re-enter Gentleman, with OPHELIA.

Oph. Where is the beauteous majesty of Denmark?

9. *aim*] F (*ayme*), *yawne* Q.   12. *might*] Q, *would* F.   14–16.] given
to Horatio Q, given to Queen F. Arranged here as conjectured by Blackstone; lines 14, 15 are continued to Gentleman by Hanmer and several
editors.   16. Exit Gentleman] Hanmer and several editors; Exit Hor.
Johnson and others; omitted Q, F.   17. Aside] Capell; omitted Q, F.
21. Re-enter . . .] Cambridge; Enter Ophelia Q (after line 16); Enter Ophelia,
distracted F.

6. *Spurns enviously*] kicks spite-
fully. Compare *Antony and Cleopatra*, III. v. 17, where Antony
" spurns the rush that lies before him."
   9. *collection*] inference, but here
with the idea of a preliminary gathering together of Ophelia's distracted
thoughts. Compare *Cymbeline*, v. v.
432.

19. *jealousy*] suspicion, as in II. i.
113.
   21. Oph.] The stage direction of
Q 1 is: " Enter Ofelia playing on a
Lute, and her haire downe singing."
For the traditional music of Ophelia's
songs, see Furness, *Hamlet*, or E.
W. Naylor, *Shakespeare and Music*,
1896.

11

Queen. How now, Ophelia?

Oph. [Sings.] *How should I your true love know*
　　　　　　From another one?
　　　　　　By his cockle hat and staff　　　25
　　　　　　And his sandal shoon.

Queen. Alas, sweet lady, what imports this song?

Oph. Say you? nay, pray you, mark.

　　[Sings.] *He is dead and gone, lady,*
　　　　　　He is dead and gone;　　　30
　　　　　　At his head a grass-green turf,
　　　　　　At his heels a stone.

　　　O, ho!

Queen.　　　Nay, but, Ophelia,—

Oph.　　　　　　　　Pray you, mark.

　　[Sings.] *White his shroud as the mountain snow,—*

Enter KING.

Queen. Alas, look here, my lord.　　　35

Oph. [Sings.]　*Larded with sweet flowers;*
　　　　　　Which bewept to the grave did not go
　　　　　　With true-love showers.

King. How do you, pretty lady?

23. *Sings*] *shee sings* Q, omitted F.　　28. *Say you?*] F, *Say you,* Q.
29. *Sings*] *Song* Q, omitted F.　　33. *O, ho!*] Q, omitted F, *Oh, oh!* Cambridge.　　34. *Sings*] omitted Q, F.　Enter King] Q; after *stone,* line 32, F.
36. *Sings*] *Song* Q, opposite line 37; Larded] Q 1, F; Larded all Q.
37. grave] Q 1, F; ground Q; did not] Q, F, Q 1; did Pope and many
editors.　　39. *you*] Q, *ye* F.

25. cockle hat] a hat with a scallop-shell stuck in it, the sign of a pilgrim having been at the shrine of St. James of Compostella. For the disguise of a lover as pilgrim compare *Romeo and Juliet*, I. v.
36. Larded] garnished, as in **v**, ii. 20.

37. did not go] It seems rash—Q 1, Q, and F agreeing—to adopt Pope's emendation "did go," lest Shakespeare may have meant a distracted allusion to the "obscure burial" (line 212) of Polonius.

Oph. Well, God 'ild you! They say the owl was a   40
baker's daughter. Lord, we know what we
are, but know not what we may be. God be
at your table!

King. Conceit upon her father.

Oph. Pray you, let's have no words of this; but when   45
they ask you what it means, say you this:

[*Sings.*] *To-morrow is Saint Valentine's day,*
          All in the morning betime,
          And I a maid at your window,
             To be your Valentine.   50
          Then up he rose, and donn'd his clothes,
             And dupp'd the chamber door;
          Let in the maid, that out a maid
             Never departed more.

King. Pretty Ophelia!   55

Oph. Indeed, la, without an oath, I'll make an end on't:

40. *God 'ild*] Capell, *good dild* Q, *God dil'd* F.   44] marked Aside
Furness.   45. *Pray you*] F, *Pray* Q.   47. *Sings*] *Song* Q, omitted F.
56. *Indeed, la,*] Johnson, *Indeede* Q, *Indeed la?* F.

40. *'ild*] yield, reward, as in *As
You Like It*, III. iii. 76.

40. *owl*] Douce records a story
"among the vulgar in Gloucester-
shire": Jesus asked for bread at a
baker's shop; the mistress put dough
in the oven, was reprimanded by
her daughter, who reduced its size;
the dough miraculously grew huge;
the daughter cried out "Heugh,
heugh, heugh," like an owl, where-
upon Jesus transformed her to an
owl. In Fletcher, *The Nice Valour*,
III. iii. we find:
  "Give me a nest of owls,
 and take 'em:
Happy is he, say I, whose window
 opens

To a brown baker's chimney! he
 shall be sure there
To hear the bird sometimes after
 twilight."
The idea of Ophelia's own transformation, suggested by that of the
baker's daughter, is touched on in the
words "Lord, etc."

44. *Conceit*] imagination, as frequently.

50. Valentine] Halliwell: "This
song alludes to the custom of the first
girl seen by a man on the morning of
this day being considered his Valentine, or true-love."

52. dupp'd] dup, do up, open.
Edwardes, *Damon and Pitheas*, 1564:
"Will they not dup the gate to-
day?"

[Sings.] *By Gis and by Saint Charity,*
    Alack, and fie for shame!
    Young men will do't, if they come to't;
      By Cock, they are to blame.   60
    Quoth she, before you tumbled me,
      You promised me to wed:
He answers:
    So would I ha' done, by yonder sun,
      An thou hadst not come to my bed.   65

King. How long hath she been thus?

Oph. I hope all will be well. We must be patient;
but I cannot choose but weep, to think they
should lay him i' the cold ground. My
brother shall know of it: and so I thank you   70
for your good counsel.—Come, my coach!—
Good night, ladies; good night, sweet ladies;
good night, good night.   [*Exit.*

King. Follow her close; give her good watch, I pray
    you.—   [*Exit Horatio.*
Oh, this is the poison of deep grief; it springs   75
All from her father's death. O Gertrude, Gertrude,
When sorrows come, they come not single spies,
But in battalions! First, her father slain;

57. *Sings*] omitted Q, F.   63. *He answers*] (*He answers*) Q, omitted F.
65. *An*] Hanmer; And Q, F.   66. *thus*] Q, *this* F.   69. *should*] F,
would Q.   72, 73. *Good . . . night*] F substantially; *God night, Ladies, god
night. Sweet Ladyes god night, god night.* Q.   74. Exit Hor.] Theobald;
omitted Q, F.   76. *death.* O] F, *death, and now behold, ô* Q.   77. *sorrows
come*] Q, *sorrowes comes* F.   78. *battalions*] Q, *Battaliaes* F.

57. Gis] an abbreviation or pious
disguise of "Jesus"; spelt also *jis*
and *jysse*; for examples see Nares'
Glossary.
57. Saint Charity] the grace per-
sonified. E. K. glosses "Saint

Charitie," in Spenser, *Shepherd's Calendar, May*: "the Catholiques comen
othe."
60. Cock] a perversion of "God."
In the *Canterbury Tales*, Manciple's
Prologue, we have "Cockes bones."

Next, your son gone; and he most violent author
Of his own just remove: the people muddied, 80
Thick and unwholesome in their thoughts and
  whispers,
For good Polonius' death; and we have done but
  greenly,
In hugger-mugger to inter him; poor Ophelia
Divided from herself and her fair judgment,
Without the which we are pictures, or mere beasts;
Last, and as much containing as all these, 86
Her brother is in secret come from France,
Feeds on his wonder, keeps himself in clouds,
And wants not buzzers to infect his ear
With pestilent speeches of his father's death; 90
Wherein necessity, of matter beggar'd,
Will nothing stick our person to arraign
In ear and ear. O my dear Gertrude, this,
Like to a murdering-piece, in many places
Gives me superfluous death. [*A noise within.*

Queen. Alack, what noise is this? 95
King. Where are my Switzers? Let them guard the
  door.—

81. *their*] F, omitted Q. 88. *Feeds on his wonder*] Johnson, *Feeds on this wonder* Q, *Keepes on his wonder* F. 92. *person*] Q, *persons* F. 95. *Alack . . . this*] F, omitted Q. 96. *Where are*] F, *Attend, where is* Q.

83. *In hugger-mugger*] secretly. Steevens quotes North's *Plutarch* (Brutus): "Antonius thinking good . . . that his bodie should be honourably buried, and not in hugger-mugger."
94. *murdering-piece*] a cannon loaded with case-shot (small projectiles put up in cases). Steevens quotes Beaumont and Fletcher, *The Double Marriage*, IV. ii.: "A father's curses . . . like a murdering-piece aim not at one, But all that stand within the dangerous level."
96. *Switzers*] Malone quotes Nash, *Christ's Tears over Jerusalem*, 1594: "Law, logicke, and the Switzers may be hired to fight for any body."

Enter another Gentleman.

What is the matter?

Gent.　　　　　　　Save yourself, my lord;
The ocean, overpeering of his list,
Eats not the flats with more impetuous haste
Than young Laertes, in a riotous head,　　　　100
O'erbears your officers.　The rabble call him lord;
And, as the world were now but to begin,
Antiquity forgot, custom not known,
The ratifiers and props of every word,
They cry "Choose we; Laertes shall be king!"　105
Caps, hands, and tongues applaud it to the clouds,
"Laertes shall be king, Laertes king!"

Queen. How cheerfully on the false trail they cry!
Oh, this is counter, you false Danish dogs!

King. The doors are broke.　　　　[*Noise within.* 110

Enter LAERTES, *armed; Danes following.*

Laer. Where is this king?—Sirs, stand you all without.

Enter . . .] Staunton, Enter a Messenger Q, F after *death*, line 95.
99. *impetuous*] *impitious* Q, *impittious* F.　　105. *They*] F, *The* Q.
110. Noise within] F (after line 109), A noise within Q (opposite line 108).
Enter Laertes . . .] Enter Laertes with others Q (after line 109), Enter
Laertes F (after line 109).　　111. *this king? Sirs*] Q, *the King, sirs?* F.

98. *list*] boundary, as in *Othello*, IV.
i. 76.

100. *head*] a force raised, or body of
people gathered, especially in insur-
rection; as in *1 Henry IV.* III. ii.
167. Pepys, *Diary*, 8 Jan. 1661:
"Some talk to-day of a head of
Fanatiques, that do appear about
Barnett."

104. *word*] Ward, weal, and work
have been proposed instead of "word";
no emendation is required; antiquity
and custom are the true ratifiers and
props of every word (perhaps in the
sense of title); or—less probably—the
rabble, ready to make good and to
support every word they utter, cry, etc.

109. *counter*] Clar. Press quotes the
definition of "counter" in Holme's
Academy of Armory, II. ix.: "When
a hound hunteth backwards, the
same way that the chase is come."
"The huntsmen," writes Turbervile
(*Venerie*), ". . . must take heede that
their houndes take not the counter by
cause the harte is fledde backwards."

Danes. No, let's come in.

Laer.   I pray you, give me leave.

Danes. We will, we will.

                   [*They retire without the door.*

Laer. I thank you: keep the door.—O thou vile king,
  Give me my father!

Queen.   Calmly, good Laertes.   115

Laer. That drop of blood that's calm proclaims me
      bastard,
  Cries cuckold to my father, brands the harlot
  Even here, between the chaste unsmirched brows
  Of my true mother.

King.   What is the cause, Laertes,
  That thy rebellion looks so giant-like?—   120
  Let him go, Gertrude; do not fear our person;
  There's such divinity doth hedge a king,
  That treason can but peep to what it would,
  Acts little of his will.—Tell me, Laertes,
  Why thou art thus incensed.—Let him go,
      Gertrude.—   125
  Speak, man.

Laer. Where's my father?

King.   Dead.

Queen.   But not by him.

King. Let him demand his fill.

Laer. How came he dead?   I'll not be juggled with.

---

113. They retire . . .] Capell; omitted Q, F.   116. *that's calm*] Q, *that calmes* F.   118. *brows*] Grant White; *brow* Q, F.   127. *Where's*] F, *Where is* Q.

118. *brows*] Grant White (followed   121. *fear*] fear for.
by Cambridge and Furness), as re-
quired by *between*.

To hell, allegiance! vows, to the blackest devil! 130
Conscience and grace, to the profoundest pit!
I dare damnation.　To this point I stand,
That both the worlds I give to negligence,
Let come what comes; only I'll be revenged
Most throughly for my father.

King.　　　　　　　　　Who shall stay you? 135
Laer. My will, not all the world; ('s Dover Wilson)
And for my means, I'll husband them so well,
They shall go far with little.

King.　　　　　　　　　Good Laertes.
If you desire to know the certainty
Of your dear father's death, is't writ in your
　　revenge,　　　　　　　　　　　　140
That, swoopstake, you will draw both friend and foe,
Winner and loser?

Laer. None but his enemies.

King.　　　　　　　　　Will you know them then?
Laer. To his good friends thus wide I'll ope my arms;
And, like the kind life-rendering pelican, 145
Repast them with my blood.

King.　　　　　　　　　Why, now you speak
Like a good child and a true gentleman.

131. *pit!*] *pit* Q, *pit.* F.　　　136. *world*] F, *worlds* Q, *world's* Pope.
140. *father's death*] F, *father* Q; *is't*] Q, *if* F.　　142. *loser ?*] Q 6; *looser.*
Q, F.　　145. *pelican*] Q, *politician* F.

141. *swoopstake*] Q, F print *soop-stake*; Q 1 has—
"Therefore will you like a most
　　desperate gamster,
Swoop-stake-like, draw at friend,
　　and foe, and all?"
Sweepstakes is a game of cards in
which a player may win all the stakes
or take all the tricks.

145. *pelican*] Sir Thomas Browne
in *Vulgar Errors*, v. chap. i. dis-
cusses "the picture of the Pelican
opening her breast with her bill, and
feeding her young ones with the blood
distilled from her." Allusions occur
in *Richard II.* II. i. 126, and *Lear*,
III. iv. 77.

That I am guiltless of your father's death,
And am most sensibly in grief for it,
It shall as level to your judgment pierce   150
As day does to your eye.

Danes. [*Within.*]   Let her come in.

Laer. How now! what noise is that?—

> *Re-enter* OPHELIA.

O heat, dry up my brains! tears seven times
    salt,
Burn out the sense and virtue of mine eye!—
By heaven, thy madness shall be paid by weight, 155
Till our scale turn the beam.   O rose of May!
Dear maid, kind sister, sweet Ophelia!—
O heavens! is 't possible a young maid's wits
Should be as mortal as an old man's life?
Nature is fine in love, and where 'tis fine   160
It sends some precious instance of itself
After the thing it loves.

Oph. [Sings.] *They bore him barefaced on the bier;*

> *Hey non nonny, nonny, hey nonny;*

> *And in his grave rain'd many a tear;—* 165

Fare you well, my dove!

---

149. *sensibly*] Q, *sensible* F.   150. *pierce*] F, *peare* Q, *'pear* Johnson.
151. *Danes . . . in*] Capell; Q has stage direction A noyse within, opposite
eye, and gives *Let her come in* to Laertes; F has "A noise within. Let her
come in," as if a stage-direction, after *eye*.   155. *by*] F, *with* Q.
156. *Till*] F, *Tell* Q; *turn*] Q, *turnes* F.   159. *an old*] F, *a poore* Q.
160–162. *Nature . . . loves*] F, omitted Q.   163. *Sings*] *Song* Q, omitted F.
164] F, omitted Q.   165. *in*] Q, *on* F; *rain'd*] Q, *raines* F.   166. *Fare
. . . dove*] Capell; in italics (as if last line of song) F; using Roman for
the whole speech, Q leaves it doubtful.

160–162] Nature is delicate (or Ophelia's sanity after Polonius as a
accomplished) in love, and sends precious token (or sample) of itself.

Laer. Hadst thou thy wits, and didst persuade revenge,
It could not move thus.

Oph. You must sing, *Down a-down, and you call
him a-down-a.* Oh, how the wheel becomes it! 170
It is the false steward that stole his master's
daughter.

Laer. This nothing's more than matter.

Oph. There's rosemary, that's for remembrance;
pray you, love, remember; and there is pansies, 175
that's for thoughts.

Laer. A document in madness: thoughts and remembrance fitted.

[margin note left: used at weddings & funerals, to Laertes]

[margin note right: keeps for herse]

169, 170.] see note below ; Q for Down a-down has a downe a downe.
175. *pray you*] Q, *Pray* F.

169, 170. *You* . . . a-down-a] Q, F print the whole speech in Roman type. Johnson used italics for *You* . . . *a-down-a* ; (Capell had printed *Down* with a capital). Staunton, Globe, Cambridge print the same words as verse. The above follows Steevens. It has been suggested that *You* and *and you* should be in Roman, as instructions to two supposed singers.

170. *wheel*] Guest, *English Rhythms*, bk. IV. chap. iv., uses *wheel* for a kind of refrain, the return of some peculiar rhythm at the end of each stanza. Steevens quoted from memory an example of this use of the word from a book of which he had forgotten the title and date. No early example appears to have been found. Cotgrave explains French *refrain* as "the Refret, burthen, or downe of a ballade." F 2 has "wheeles become." Perhaps Malone was right in thinking that the reference is to a song sung at the spinning-wheel ; he refers aptly to *Twelfth Night*, II. iv. 45, and quotes a men-

tion of ballads "sung to the wheel," from Hall, *Virgidemiarum*, IV. vi.

174. *rosemary*] Used as a symbol of remembrance, both at weddings and funerals. Compare *Romeo and Juliet*, IV. v. 79, and *Winter's Tale*, IV. iv. 74-76. See Ellacombe's *Plant Lore of Shakespeare* for this and the other flowers. Perhaps the rosemary is given to Laertes, mistaken by Ophelia for her lover. Delius supposes the flowers to exist only in Ophelia's distracted imagination. In Q 1 her first words, after re-entrance, are "Wel God a mercy, I a bin gathering of floures."

175. *pansies*] for thoughts, Fr. *pensées*. Ellacombe states that still in Warwickshire the pansy is named love-in-idleness, signifying love in vain. Chapman in *All Fools*, II. i., refers to the pansy as "for lover's thoughts."

177. *document*] a piece of instruction, lesson. So Spenser, *Faerie Queene*, I. x. 19: "And heavenly documents thereout did preach."

Oph. There's fennel for you, and columbines;
  there's rue for you; and here's some for me; 180
  we may call it herb of grace o' Sundays; oh,
  you must wear your rue with a difference.
  There's a daisy; I would give you some
  violets, but they withered all when my father
  died; they say he made a good end,— 185
  [Sings.] *For bonny sweet Robin is all my joy.*

Laer. Thought and affliction, passion, hell itself,
  She turns to favour and to prettiness.

Oph. [Sings.] *And will he not come again?*
  And will he not come again? 190

181. *herb of grace*] Q, *Herbe-Grace* F, *hearb a' grace* Q 1. 181, 182. *oh, you must*] F, *you may* Q, *you must* Q 1. 186. *Sings*] Capell; omitted Q, F. 187. *Thought*] Q, F; *Thoughts* Q 1; *affliction*] F; *afflictions* Q 1, Q. 189. *Sings*] *Song* Q, omitted F.

179. *fennel*] Malone quotes *A Handfull of Pleasant Delites*, 1584: "Fennel is for flatterers"; Florio has "Dare finocchio, to flatter, or give Fennell." Given probably to the King.

179. *columbines*] Steevens says: "It should seem as if this flower was the emblem of cuckoldom." Quotations from Chapman's *All Fools*, II. i. (misunderstood through abbreviation), and *Caltha Poetarum*, 1599, verify the statement. Given probably to the King.

180. *rue*] the emblem of sorrow and repentance. See *Richard II.* III. iv. 105. The name herb-grace or herb of grace is found in the herbals and dictionaries. Given to the Queen. Ophelia wears her rue as the emblem of sorrow and of grace. "With a difference" had a heraldic meaning (slight distinctions in coats of arms borne by members of the same family), but that meaning is not required here. Skeat suggests that the difference is

that of "rue" and "ruth" (referring to the passage in *Richard II.*).

183. *daisy*] Henley quotes Greene, *Quip for an Upstart Courtier*: "Next them grew the dissembling daisie, to warne such light-of-love wenches not to trust every faire promise that such amorous batchelors make them." But perhaps Chaucer's flower of the loyal Alcestis has here no such significance; perhaps it is not given away.

184. *violets*] Malone quotes *A Handfull of Pleasant Delites*: "Violet is for faithfulness." Perhaps, as Clar. Press suggests, these words are spoken to Horatio.

186. Robin] *Two Noble Kinsmen*, IV. i: "I can sing the Broom, And Bonny Robin." Chappell (*Popular Music of the Olden Times*) identifies the song with one given in Holborne's *Cittharn Schoole*, 1597, and elsewhere.

187. *Thought*] careful or melancholy thought, as in III. i. 85.

> *No, no, he is dead,*
> *Go to thy death-bed,*
> *He never will come again.*
>
> *His beard was as white as snow,*
> *All flaxen was his poll;*   195
> *He is gone, he is gone,*
> *And we cast away moan:*
> *God ha' mercy on his soul!*

And of all Christian souls, I pray God. God be
wi' you!   [*Exit.*

Laer. Do you see this, O God!   200

King. Laertes, I must commune with your grief,
Or you deny me right. Go but apart,
Make choice of whom your wisest friends you will,
And they shall hear and judge 'twixt you and me.
If by direct or by collateral hand   205
They find us touch'd, we will our kingdom give,
Our crown, our life, and all that we call ours,
To you in satisfaction; but if not,
Be you content to lend your patience to us,
And we shall jointly labour with your soul   210
To give it due content.

Laer.   Let this be so:

194 was as] Q, as F, was Johnson.   195. All] F, omitted Q.   198. God ha' mercy] Collier, God a mercy Q, Gramercy F.   199. *Christian*] F, *Christians* Q; *I pray God*] F, omitted Q; *you*] Q, *ye* F. Exit] Exeunt Ophelia F, omitted Q.   200. *Do . . . God!*] Capell, *Doe you this ô God.* Q, *Do you see this, you gods?* F.

198, 199. God . . . *souls*] A common conclusion, says Steevens, to monumental inscriptions. Sir Thomas More's *Workes*, 1557, p. 337: "We see there [in purgatory] our chyldren too, whom we loved so well, pipe, sing, and daunce, and no more thinke on their fathers soules than on their old shone, saving that sometime cometh out *God have mercy on all christen soules.*"

His means of death, his obscure burial,
No trophy, sword, nor hatchment o'er his bones,
No noble rite, nor formal ostentation,
Cry to be heard, as 'twere from heaven to earth, 215
That I must call 't in question.

King.   So you shall;
And where the offence is let the great axe fall.
I pray you, go with me.   [*Exeunt.*

SCENE VI.—*Another Room in the Castle.*

Enter HORATIO *and a Servant.*

Hor. What are they that would speak with me?
Serv. Sailors, sir; they say they have letters for you.
Hor. Let them come in.—   [*Exit Servant.*
I do not know from what part of the world
I should be greeted, if not from Lord Hamlet.   5

Enter Sailors.

First Sail. God bless you, sir.
Hor. Let him bless thee too.
First Sail. He shall, sir, an't please him.   There's
      a letter for you, sir,—it comes from the

212. *burial*] F, *funerall* Q.   213. *trophy, sword,*] F, *trophe sword,* Q,
trophy sword, Pope.   214. *rite*] F, *right* Q.   216. *call 't*] Q, *call* F.

Scene VI.

Enter . . .] Capell; Enter *Horatio* and others Q; Enter *Horatio,*
with an Attendant F.   2. Serv.] F, Gent. Q; *Sailors*] F, *Seafaring
men* Q.   5. Enter Sailors] Q; Enter Sailor F.   6, 8. First Sail.]
1. S. Capell; Say. Q, F.   8. *an't*] Q 6, *and* Q, *and't* F.   9. *comes*] F,
came Q.

212. *obscure*] accented in different   216. *That*] so that, as in IV. vii.
places by Shakespeare on the first or   148.
on the second syllable.

ambassador that was bound for England,—if   10
your name be Horatio, as I am let to know
it is.

Hor. [Reads.] *Horatio, when thou shalt have overlooked*
this, give these fellows some means to the king;
they have letters for him. Ere we were two days   15
old at sea, a pirate of very warlike appointment
gave us chase. Finding ourselves too slow of
sail, we put on a compelled valour, and in the
grapple I boarded them; on the instant they
got clear of our ship, so I alone became their   20
prisoner. They have dealt with me like thieves
of mercy; but they knew what they did; I am
to do a good turn for them. Let the king have
the letters I have sent; and repair thou to me
with as much haste as thou would'st fly death.   25
I have words to speak in thine ear will make
thee dumb; yet are they much too light for the
bore of the matter. These good fellows will
bring thee where I am. Rosencrantz and
Guildenstern hold their course for England; of   30
them I have much to tell thee. Farewell.

         He that thou knowest thine,   HAMLET.

Come, I will give you way for these your letters;

---

10. *ambassador*] Q, *Ambassadours* F.   18. and in] Q, in F.   23. good]
F, omitted Q.   25. haste] F, speede Q.   26. thine] Q, your F.   28.
bore] F, bord Q.   32. He] F, So Q (with no point before *Hamlet*).
33. *give*] F, omitted Q, *make* Q 4 and several editors.

22. knew what they did] Miles,   ing the enginer with his own petar,
Southern Review, April and July   this was in his mind.
1870, suggests that the pursuit was   28. bore] calibre, figurative from
prearranged by Hamlet, and that   bore of gun.
when he spoke to his mother of hoist-

And do't the speedier, that you may direct me
To him from whom you brought them.   [*Exeunt.*

SCENE VII.—*Another Room in the Castle.*

Enter KING *and* LAERTES.

King. Now must your conscience my acquittance seal,
    And you must put me in your heart for friend,
    Sith you have heard, and with a knowing ear,
    That he which hath your noble father slain
    Pursued my life.

Laer.   It well appears; but tell me   5
    Why you proceeded not against these feats,
    So crimeful and so capital in nature,
    As by your safety, wisdom, all things else,
    You mainly were stirr'd up.

King.   Oh, for two special reasons,
    Which may to you perhaps seem much unsinew'd, 10
    And yet to me they are strong. The queen his mother
    Lives almost by his looks; and for myself,—
    My virtue or my plague, be it either which,—
    She's so conjunctive to my life and soul,
    That, as the star moves not but in his sphere,   15
    I could not but by her. The other motive,
    Why to a public count I might not go,
    Is the great love the general gender bear him;
    Who, dipping all his faults in their affection,

6. *proceeded*] F, *proceede* Q.   7. *crimeful*] F, *criminall* Q.   8. *safety*]
F, *safetie, greatnes* Q.   11. *And*] F, *But* Q; *they are*] F, *tha'r* Q.
14. *She's so conjunctive*] F, *She is so conclive* Q.

14. *conjunctive*] The idea of plane-   17. *count*] account, reckoning.
tary conjunction seems to have sug-   18. *general gender*] common species,
gested the line that follows.   community of men.

Would, like the spring that turneth wood to stone, 20
Convert his gyves to graces; so that my arrows,
Too slightly timber'd for so loud a wind,
Would have reverted to my bow again,
And not where I had aim'd them.

Laer. And so have I a noble father lost;   25
A sister driven into desperate terms,
Whose worth, if praises may go back again,
Stood challenger on mount of all the age
For her perfections. But my revenge will come.

King. Break not your sleeps for that; you must not
think   30
That we are made of stuff so flat and dull
That we can let our beard be shook with danger
And think it pastime. You shortly shall hear more;
I loved your father, and we love ourself;
And that, I hope, will teach you to imagine,— 35

Enter a Messenger.

How now! what news?

Mess.   Letters, my lord, from Hamlet;
This to your majesty; this to the queen.

20. *Would*] F, *Worke* Q.   22. *loud a wind*] F, *loved Arm'd* Q.   24. *And*] F, *But* Q ; *had*] F, *have* Q ; *aim'd*] Q, *arm'd* F.   27. *Whose worth*] Q, *Who was* F.   36. *How . . . Hamlet*] F, omitted Q.   37. *This*] F, *These* Q.

20. *spring*] In Harrison's *Description of England* (ed. Furnivall, p. 349) it is stated that the baths of King's Newnham, in Shakespeare's county, Warwickshire, have the property of turning wood to stone. The reference was supposed by Reed to be to the dropping well at Knaresborough.

21. *gyves*] Daniel would read *gyres*, wild and whirling actions. Elze

would read *greaves* (? he prints it *graves*).

22. *loud a wind*] Jennens would maintain the Q misprint "loved arm'd," explaining it "one so loved and armed with the affections . . . of the people." Elze suggests "solid arms," which he connects with his reading *greaves* in line 21.

27. *praises*] if I may return in praise to Ophelia's better days.

King. From Hamlet? who brought them?

Mess. Sailors, my lord, they say; I saw them not;
　　They were given me by Claudio; he received
　　　them　　　　　　　　　　　　　　　40
　　Of him that brought them.

King.　　　　　　　　　Laertes, you shall hear them.—
　　Leave us.　　　　　　　　　　　[*Exit Messenger.*

[Reads.] *High and mighty, you shall know I am
　　set naked on your kingdom.　To-morrow shall I
　　beg leave to see your kingly eyes; when I shall,　45
　　first asking your pardon thereunto, recount the
　　occasion of my sudden and more strange return.*

　　　　　　　　　　　　　　　　　Hamlet.

　　What should this mean?　Are all the rest come back?
　　Or is it some abuse, and no such thing?　　50

Laer. Know you the hand?

King. 'Tis Hamlet's character.　"Naked!"
　　And in a postscript here, he says " alone."
　　Can you advise me?

Laer. I'm lost in it, my lord.　But let him come:　55
　　It warms the very sickness in my heart,
　　That I shall live and tell him to his teeth,
　　" Thus didest thou."

King.　　　　　　　　If it be so, Laertes,—
　　As how should it be so? how otherwise?—

---

41. *Of . . . them*] Q, omitted F.　46. asking your] F, asking you Q.
47. occasion] Q, occasions F; and more strange] F, omitted Q.　48. *Hamlet*]
F, omitted Q.　50. *abuse, and*] Q, *abuse? or* F.　54. *advise*] F, *deuise* Q.
55. *I'm*] F, *I am* Q.　57. *shall*] F, omitted Q.　58. *didest*] F, *didst* Q.

59. *As . . . otherwise*] If the King　speaks—how can he have returned?
refers to Laertes' feelings " should it　Yet how can it be otherwise with his
not" (or *but*) seems required.　But it　letter in my hand?　The doubt is
may be Hamlet's return of which he　continued in line 62.

Will you be ruled by me?

Laer.   Ay, my lord;   60
So you will not o'errule me to a peace.

King. To thine own peace.   If he be now return'd,
As checking at his voyage, and that he means
No more to undertake it, I will work him
To an exploit now ripe in my device,   65
Under the which he shall not choose but fall;
And for his death no wind of blame shall breathe;
But even his mother shall uncharge the practice,
And call it accident.

Laer.   My lord, I will be ruled;
The rather, if you could devise it so   70
That I might be the organ.

King.   It falls right.
You have been talk'd of since your travel much,
And that in Hamlet's hearing, for a quality
Wherein, they say, you shine; your sum of parts
Did not together pluck such envy from him   75
As did that one, and that, in my regard,
Of the unworthiest siege.

Laer.   What part is that, my lord?

King. A very riband in the cap of youth,
Yet needful too; for youth no less becomes
The light and careless livery that it wears   80

60. *Ay, my lord*] Q, omitted F.   61. *So you will*] Q, *If so you'l* F.
63. *checking at*] F, *the King at* Q, *liking not* Q 4.   69–82. *My lord . . .
graveness*] Q, omitted F.

63. *checking*] A hawk "checks"   artifice or stratagem. For *practice*,
when it forsakes its proper quarry and   see v. ii. 328.
follows some inferior game.   See   77. *siege*] rank (literally, seat), as
Twelfth Night, III. i. 71.   in *Othello*, I. ii. 22 : "men of royal
68. *uncharge the practice*] acquit,   siege."
free from accusation (charge), the

Than settled age his sables and his weeds,
Importing health and graveness.   Two months since,
Here was a gentleman of Normandy;—
I have seen myself, and served against, the French,
And they can well on horseback; but this gallant 85
Had witchcraft in 't; he grew unto his seat,
And to such wondrous doing brought his horse
As he had been incorpsed and demi-natured
With the brave beast; so far he topp'd my thought,
That I, in forgery of shapes and tricks,   90
Come short of what he did.

Laer.   A Norman was 't?

King. A Norman.

Laer. Upon my life, Lamord.

King.   The very same.

Laer. I know him well; he is the brooch indeed
And gem of all the nation.   95

King. He made confession of you,

---

82. *Two*] Q, *Some two* F;   *since*] Q, *hence* F.   84. *I have*] Q, *I've* F.
85. *can*] Q, *ran* F.   86. *unto*] Q, *into* F.   88. *he had*] Q 6; *had he* Q, F.
89. *topp'd*] Q, *past* F; *my*] F, *me* Q.   93. *Lamord*] Q, *Lamound* F.
95. *the*] Q, *our* F.

---

82. *health*] denoting an attention to health.   Schmidt understands *health* as prosperity. Warburton read "wealth." Furness takes "health" to refer to the livery of youth, and "graveness" to that of settled age.

85. *can*] are skilled.   Compare *Phœnix and Turtle*, 14: "the priest . . . That defunctive music can."

89. *topp'd*] exceeded, as in *Macbeth*, IV. iii. 57.

90. *forgery*] invention, as in *Midsummer Night's Dream*, II. i. 81.

93. *Lamord*] I retain the Q form of the name, having noticed in Cotgrave, "*Mords*, a bitt of a horse."   Several of Shakespeare's names for minor characters are significant; the word *mords* is masculine, but the printer of Q may be responsible for *La*. Pope has Lamond; Malone conjectured Lamode; Grant White has Lamont. C. E. Browne notes that Pietro Monte was the instructor of Louis VII.'s Master of the Horse.

94. *brooch*] ornament, as in Jonson's *Staple of News*, III. ii. : "Who is the very Brooch o' the Bench, Gem o' the city."

96. *confession*] the unwilling acknowledgment by a Frenchman of a Dane's superiority.

And gave you such a masterly report
For art and exercise in your defence,
And for your rapier most especially,
That he cried out, 'twould be a sight indeed   100
If one could match you; the scrimers of their nation,
He swore, had neither motion, guard, nor eye,
If you opposed them.   Sir, this report of his
Did Hamlet so envenom with his envy
That he could nothing do but wish and beg   105
Your sudden coming o'er, to play with him.
Now, out of this,—

Laer.   What out of this, my lord?

King. Laertes, was your father dear to you?
Or are you like the painting of a sorrow,
A face without a heart?

Laer.   Why ask you this?   110

King. Not that I think you did not love your father,
But that I know love is begun by time,
And that I see, in passages of proof,
Time qualifies the spark and fire of it.
There lives within the very flame of love   115
A kind of wick or snuff that will abate it;
And nothing is at a like goodness still,
For goodness, growing to a plurisy, *superabundance*

99. *especially*] F, *especial* Q.   101–103. *you . . . this*] Q, *you Sir.
This* F (omitting *the scrimers . . . opposed them.*)   106. *him*] F, *you* Q
and several editors.   107. *What*] Q, *Why* F.   115–124. *There . . .
ulcer*] Q, omitted F.

101. *scrimers*] fencers.   French,   113. *passages of proof*] well-estab-
escrimeurs.   lished instances.
102. *motion*] a fencing term ; used   117. *still*] constantly, as in II. ii.42.
by Vincentio Saviolo in his *Practise*   118, *plurisy*] plethora ; as if derived
(1595) ; see line 158 of the present   from *plus, pluris.* So *The Two Noble
scene.   Kinsmen,* v. 1 : " the plurisy of
                                                                people."

Dies in his own too-much; that we would do
We should do when we would; for this " would "
    changes,   120
And hath abatements and delays as many
As there are tongues, are hands, are accidents;
And then this " should " is like a spendthrift sigh,
That hurts by easing.   But to the quick o' the
    ulcer:
Hamlet comes back; what would you undertake 125
To show yourself your father's son in deed
More than in words?
Laer.   To cut his throat i' the church.
King. No place, indeed, should murder sanctuarize;
Revenge should have no bounds.   But, good
    Laertes,
Will you do this, keep close within your
    chamber.   130
Hamlet return'd shall know you are come home;
We 'll put on those shall praise your excellence,
And set a double varnish on the fame
The Frenchman gave you; bring you, in fine,
    together
And wager on your heads; he, being remiss,   135
Most generous and free from all contriving,
Will not peruse the foils, so that with ease
Or with a little shuffling, you may choose

---

123. *spendthrift*] Q 6, *spend-thirfts* Q.   126. *your . . . in deed*] F (with
indeed), *indeede your fathers sonne* Q.   130. *chamber.*] Steevens; comma
after *chamber* Q, F.   135. *on*] F, *o'er* Q.

123. *spendthrift sigh*] Alluding to
the notion that sighs shorten life by
drawing blood from the heart.   See
M. N. D., III. ii. 97.

128. *sanctuarize*] protect from pun-
ishment as a sanctuary does.

130. [A device to keep him from
coming to an explanation with
Hamlet.   N. C. S. cites Bradley to
this effect.   R. H. C.]

137. *peruse*] see II. i. 90.

A sword unbated, and in a pass of practice
Requite him for your father.

Laer.   I will do 't ;   140
And for that purpose I 'll anoint my sword.
I bought an unction of a mountebank,
So mortal that but dip a knife in it,
Where it draws blood no cataplasm so rare,
Collected from all simples that have virtue   145
Under the moon, can save the thing from death
That is but scratch'd withal ; I 'll touch my point
With this contagion, that, if I gall him slightly,
It may be death.

King.   Let 's further think of this ;
Weigh   what   convenience   both   of   time   and
          means   150
May fit us to our shape.   If this should fail,
And that our drift look through our bad performance,
'Twere better not assay'd ; therefore this project
Should have a back or second, that might hold,
If this should blast in proof.   Soft!—let me
          see—   ·   155
We 'll make a solemn wager on your cunnings ;
I ha 't :

141. *that*] F, omitted Q.   143. *that but dip*] Q, *I but dipt* F (*I = Ay*).
150. *convenience*] F, *conueiance* Q.   151. *shape. If . . . fail,*] Rowe ; Q
has no point except comma after *fayle* ; F has comma after *shape*, semicolon
after *faile*.   155. *should*] F, *did* Q.   156. *cunnings*] Q, *commings* F.

139. *unbated*] not blunted, as foils   155. *blast in proof*] suffer blight in
are by a button. *Love's Labour's Lost*,   the trial.
I. i. 6 : " bate his scythe's keen   156. *cunnings*] skill.   Caldecott
edge."   and Knight explain F *commings* as
139. *pass of practice*] treacherous   bouts at fence.   Cotgrave has *Venuĕ*,
thrust ; see line 68.   " A comming ; . . . also a vennie in
142. *mountebank*] quack-doctor, as   fencing."
in *Othello*, I. iii. 61.

When in your motion you are hot and dry,—
As make your bouts more violent to that end,—
And that he calls for drink, I 'll have prepared
him   160
A chalice for the nonce; whereon but sipping,
If he by chance escape your venom'd stuck,
Our purpose may hold there.   But stay! what
noise?—

Enter QUEEN.

How now, sweet queen!

Queen. One woe doth tread upon another's heel,   165
So fast they follow.—Your sister's drown'd,
Laertes.

Laer. Drown'd!   Oh, where?

Queen. There is a willow grows aslant a brook,
That shows his hoar leaves in the glassy stream;
There with fantastic garlands did she come,   170
Of crow-flowers, nettles, daisies, and long purples,
That liberal shepherds give a grosser name, *rampant widow.*

159. *that*] Q, *the* F.   160. *prepared*] F, *prefard* Q.   162. *stuck*] Q, F;
tucke Q 6.   163. *But . . . noise?*] Q, omitted F.   164. *How . . .
queen*] F 2, *how sweet Queene* F, omitted Q.   166. *they*] Q, *they'l* F.
168. *aslant a*] F, *ascaunt the* Q.   169. *hoar*] *hore* F, *horry* Q.   170.
There with . . . come] F, *Therewith . . . make* Q.

162. *stuck*] Dyce: "more properly *stock*, an abbreviation of *stoc-
cado*," or *stoccata*, a thrust.   So
Twelfth Night, III. iv. 303.   The
tucke of Q 6 means rapier.
168. *willow*] significant of forsaken
love.
171. *crow-flowers*] butter-cup, but
used formerly of ragged-robin.   In
Gerarde's *Herbal* identified with
"Wilde Williams, Marsh Gilloflours,
and Cockow Gellofloures."
171. *long purples*] According to
Ellacombe "the common purple or-

chises of the woods and meadows.
The name of Dead Men's Fingers was
given to them from the pale palmate
roots of some of the species."
172. *liberal*] free - spoken, as in
Richard II. II. i. 229, or licentious,
as in *Much Ado*, IV. i. 93.   Grosser
names are found in old Herbals.
"One," says Malone, "Gertrude had
a particular reason to avoid—*the rampant widow.*"   To find a significance
in each plant is perhaps to consider
too curiously; but see notes in Furness.

But our cold maids do dead men's fingers call
   them;
There, on the pendent boughs her coronet weeds
Clambering to hang, an envious sliver broke;   175
When down her weedy trophies and herself
Fell in the weeping brook. Her clothes spread
   wide,
And, mermaid-like, awhile they bore her up;
Which time she chanted snatches of old tunes,
As one incapable of her own distress,   180
Or like a creature native and indued
Unto that element; but long it could not be
Till that her garments, heavy with their drink,
Pull'd the poor wretch from her melodious lay
To muddy death.

Laer.   Alas, then, she is drown'd!   185
Queen. Drown'd, drown'd.
Laer. Too much of water hast thou, poor Ophelia,
   And therefore I forbid my tears; but yet
   It is our trick; nature her custom holds,
   Let shame say what it will; when these are
      gone   190

---

173. *cold*] F, *cull-cold* Q.   176. *her*] Q, *the* F.   179. *tunes*] Q 1, F; *laudes* Q.   181. *indued*] F, *indewed* Q.   183. *their*] Q, *her* F.   184. *lay*] Q, *buy* F.   185. *she is drown'd!*] Q (note of exclamation, Pope); *is she drown'd.* Qq 4, 5; *is she drown'd?* F, Q 6.

175. *sliver*] a branch; properly a branch slivered (split) from a tree. So in *Macbeth*, IV. i. 28: "slips of yew Sliver'd in the moon's eclipse."

179. *tunes*] The agreement of Q 1 and F argues strongly against the Q *lauds*, which some editors prefer, probably as heightening the pathos.

180. *incapable*] without capacity to apprehend; see *capable* in III. ii. 14.

181. *indued*] brought to a state or condition in harmony with that element. So in *Othello*, III. iv. 146, an aching finger "*indues*" our healthful members to a "sense of pain."

189. *trick*] way, as in *2 Henry IV.* I. ii. 240: "it was always yet the trick of our English nation."

I must weep

The woman will be out.—Adieu, my lord;
I have a speech of fire, that fain would blaze,
But that this folly douts it.   [*Exit.*
King.   Let's follow, Gertrude,
How much I had to do to calm his rage!
Now fear I this will give it start again;   195
Therefore let's follow.   [*Exeunt.*

much more frightened than he appeared to Laertes.

ACT V

SCENE I.—*A Churchyard.*

Enter two Clowns, with spades and mattocks.

First Clo. Is she to be buried in Christian burial
that wilfully seeks her own salvation?

Second Clo. I tell thee she is; and therefore make
her grave straight; the crowner hath sat on
her, and finds it Christian burial.   5

First Clo. How can that be, unless she drowned
herself in her own defence?

Second Clo. Why, 'tis found so.

First Clo. It must be *se offendendo*; it cannot be else.

192. *of fire*] F, *a fire* Q.   193. *douts*] Knight; *doubts* F; *drownes* Q, F 2.
Act V. Scene I.

A Churchyard] Capell, A Church Rowe.   2. *that*] F, *when she* Q.
3. *and*] F, omitted Q.   9. se offendendo] F, *so offended* Q.

193. *douts*] does out, extinguishes.
In *Henry V.* iv. ii. 11, where *dout*
seems to be the verb, F has *doubt*.

Act V. Scene I.

4. *straight*] straightway, immediately, as in ii. ii. 459. Johnson
supposed that it meant from east to
west ; Douce, that it meant not north

of the church, where suicides were
buried.

4. *crowner*] A form of "coroner"
found in Holinshed, Harrison, Pepys,
and others.

9. offendendo] The Clown's mistake for *defendendo*, as perhaps *salvation* in line 2 for its opposite.

For here lies the point: if I drown myself   10
wittingly it argues an act; and an act hath
three branches; it is, to act, to do, and to
perform: argal, she drowned herself wittingly.

Second Clo. Nay, but hear you, goodman delver,—

First Clo. Give me leave.   Here lies the water;   15
good: here stands the man; good: if the man
go to this water, and drown himself, it is, will
he nill he, he goes; mark you that: but if
the water come to him, and drown him, he
drowns not himself: argal, he that is not   20
guilty of his own death shortens not his own
life.

Second Clo. But is this law?

First Clo. Ay, marry, is 't; crowner's quest law.

Second Clo. Will you ha' the truth on 't?   If this   25
had not been a gentlewoman, she should have
been buried out o' Christian burial.

First Clo. Why, there thou say'st; and the more
pity that great folk should have countenance
in this world to drown or hang themselves   30
more than their even Christian.—Come, my

12. *to act*] Q, *an Acte* F.   13. *perform: argal*] F, *performe, or all;* Q.
18. *that:*] *that,* Q, *that?* F.   27. *o'*] Jennens, *a* Q, *of* F.   31. *Christian*] F, *Christen* Q.

12. *three branches*] Shakespeare
seems to have read or heard of
Plowden's report of Hales *v.* Petit.
Sir James Hales had drowned himself; the coroner's jury returned a
verdict of *felo de se.* Dame Hales's
counsel argued that the act of suicide
cannot be completed in a man's life-
time. Walsh, Serjeant, *contra* re-
plied that "the act consists of three
parts"—the imagination, the resolu-
tion, and the execution. Plowden's
Commentaries were not translated
from the French until the eighteenth
century.

13. *argal*] the Clown's perversion
of *ergo.*

24. *quest*] inquest.

31. *even Christian*] fellow Christian; found in Chaucer's *Parson's
Tale,* in Latimer, and elsewhere.

spade.   There is no ancient gentlemen but gardeners, ditchers, and grave-makers; they hold up Adam's profession.

Second Clo. Was he a gentleman?   35

First Clo. A' was the first that ever bore arms.   *coat & arms?*

Second Clo. Why, he had none.

First Clo. What, art a heathen?   How dost thou understand the Scripture?   The Scripture says Adam digged; could he dig without arms?   40 I'll put another question to thee; if thou answerest me not to the purpose, confess thyself—

Second Clo. Go to.

First Clo. What is he that builds stronger than   45 either the mason, the shipwright, or the carpenter?

Second Clo. The gallows-maker; for that frame outlives a thousand tenants.

First Clo. I like thy wit well, in good faith; the   50 gallows does well; but how does it well? it does well to those that do ill; now, thou dost ill to say the gallows is built stronger than the church: argal, the gallows may do well to thee.   To 't again; come.   55

36. *A'*] Q, *He* F.   The same difference occurs frequently in this scene, and elsewhere.   37-40. *Why . . . arms?*] F, omitted Q.   43. *thyself—*] F, *thy selfe.* Q.   48. *frame*] F, omitted Q.

34. *hold up*] maintain, continue, as in *Merry Wives*, v. v. 110.
35. *gentleman*] Adam's spade, says Douce, is set down in some of the books of heraldry as the most ancient form of escutcheon.

42, 43. *confess thyself—*] Malone: "'And be hanged,' the Clown would have said . . . a common proverbial sentence."

Second Clo. "Who builds stronger than a mason, a
     shipwright, or a carpenter?"
First Clo. Ay, tell me that, and unyoke.
Second Clo. Marry, now I can tell.
First Clo. To't.   60
Second Clo. Mass, I cannot tell.

Enter HAMLET *and* HORATIO, *at a distance.*

First Clo. Cudgel thy brains no more about it, for
     your dull ass will not mend his pace with
     beating; and when you are asked this ques-
     tion next, say "a grave-maker"; the houses   65
     that he makes last till doomsday. Go, get
     thee to Yaughan; fetch me a stoup of liquor.

                              [*Exit Second Clown*

61. Enter] F, after line 71 Q.   66. *that*] F, omitted Q; *last*] Q4; *lasts* Q,
F.   67. *to Yaughan*] F (*Yaughan* italicised), *in, and* Q; *stoup*] F, *soope* Q.

58. *unyoke*] after this great effort you
may unharness the team of your wit.

67. *Yaughan*] Unexplained; perhaps the name of a London tavern-
keeper. The alehouse of "deaf Iohn"
is mentioned in Jonson's *Alchemist*;
in *Every Man out of his Humour*, v.
vi., he mentions "a Jew, one Yohan,"
but not as a tavern-keeper. Yaughan
is said to be a common Welsh name.
Of several emendations recorded in
the *Cambridge Shakespeare*, the most
plausible is that of Mr. Tovey:
"Go to, y'are gone: get thee gone,
fetch." *Y'are gone* occurs, but in
another connection, in Q1, meaning
"you are out of it, you have failed to
solve the question"; *get thee gone*
occurs in the same Q after "the
gallowes dooes well to them that do
ill." Or we might read with Q "Go,
get thee in," and add, "y'are gone,"
as an emendation of "Yaughan." If
"Yaughan" was a printer's error of

F, the reader for the press, taking it
for a proper name, might have substituted "to" for "in," and so
produced the F reading. Why has
no ingenious gentleman suggested a
shake and jumble of the letters, with
an error of *a* for *o* (the boxes for these
letters being next each other in the
compositor's case)? The first Clown's
"confess thyself" was to be followed
by "and be hanged," but he was interrupted; he proceeds, however, to
say that the gallows may do well for
his comrade. Now *Yaughan* easily
yields us *You* (misprinted *Yau*); *ghan*
is *hang* with the last letter misplaced
as first. Read therefore, the ingenious gentleman might say, with Q,
"Go, get thee in," and add, "hang
you; fetch, etc." The F "to" may
be accounted for as mentioned above.

67. *stoup*] Jennens supposes that Q
soope is the Clown's pronunciation of
sup.

First Clown digs, and sings.

In youth, when I did love, did love,
 Methought it was very sweet,
To contract, Oh! the time, for, Ah! my
 behove,   70
 Oh! methought there was nothing meet.

Ham. Has this fellow no feeling of his business,
 that he sings at grave-making?

Hor. Custom hath made it in him a property of
 easiness.   75

Ham. 'Tis e'en so; the hand of little employment
 hath the daintier sense.

First Clo. [Sings.] *But age, with his stealing steps,*
 Hath claw'd me in his clutch,
 And hath shipp'd me intil the land,   80
 As if I had never been such.

        [*Throws up a skull.*

Ham. That skull had a tongue in it, and could
 sing once; how the knave jowls it to the

Knocks

70. for, *Ah*] for *a* Q, F.   71. there was nothing] F, there a was nothing
a Q.   73. *at*] F, *in* Q.   79. claw'd] Q, caught F.   80. intil] F, into
Q.   81. Throws . . .] Capell; omitted Q, F.

<table>
<tr><td>

68–71.] This and the two following stanzas are—with variations here—from a poem attributed to Lord Vaux, and printed in Tottel's *Miscellany* (p. 173, ed. Arber). The *Oh* and *Ah* are perhaps grunts of the digger at work; Clar. Press, however, take them to represent drawling notes, like the *stile-a* and *mile-a* of Autolycus in *Winter's Tale,* IV. iii., which may be right, and finds support from a similar example in the Tragedy of *Hoffman.* "To contract the time" seems to be

</td><td>

caught up from a later stanza of the poem "And tract of time," as "And shipp'd me intil the land" certainly is; the resulting nonsense being designed by Shakespeare. For the traditional music — the tune of *The Children in the Wood* — see Furness (from Chappell), p. 385.

74, 75. *property of easiness*] a peculiarity that now comes easily.

80. intil] into, as in Chaucer.

83. *jowls*] knocks (used specially of the head), as in *All's Well,* I. iii. 58.

</td></tr>
</table>

ground, as if it were Cain's jaw-bone, that
did the first murder! It might be the pate 85
of a politician, which this ass now o'er-reaches,
one that would circumvent God, might it
not?

Hor. It might, my lord.

Ham. Or of a courtier, which could say " Good 90
morrow, sweet lord! How dost thou, good
lord?" This might be my Lord Such-a-one,
that praised my Lord Such-a-one's horse, when
he meant to beg it, might it not?

Hor. Ay, my lord. 95

Ham. Why, e'en so; and now my Lady Worm's;
chapless, and knocked about the mazzard with
a sexton's spade. Here's fine revolution, an
we had the trick to see't. Did these bones
cost no more the breeding, but to play at 100
loggats with 'em? mine ache to think on't.

---

84. *it were*] F, *twere* Q.　　85. *It*] F, *This* Q.　　86. *now o'erreaches*] Q,
o're Offices F.　　87. *would*] Q, *could* F.　　91. *good*] F, *sweet* Q.
94. *meant*] F, *went* Q.　　97. *mazzard*] F, *massene* Q.　　98. *an*] Capell,
and Q, *if* F.　　101. *'em*] F, *them* Q.

84. *Cain's jaw-bone*] Prof. Skeat
(*Notes and Queries*, Aug. 21, 1880)
showed that Cain, according to the
legend, slew Abel with an ass's jaw-
bone. This is mentioned in *Cursor
Mundi*, I. p. 71, lines 1071–74 (Early
Eng. Text Soc.).

86. *politician*] Clar. Press: "con-
spirator, schemer, plotter. The word
is always used in a bad sense by
Shakespeare."

86. *o'er-reaches*] The F *o'er-offices*
may be right; *office*, as a verb, occurs
in *Coriolanus*, v. ii. 68, and in *All's
Well*, III. ii. 129. *O'er-offices* may
mean "treats as one holding a superior

office." *O'er-reaches* is used in the
literal sense, and for circumvent.

92.] Steevens compares *Timon of
Athens*, I. ii. 216–218.

97. *mazzard*] the head; a form of
mazar, a bowl; the later Qq alter the
misprint of Q *massene* to *mazer*.

101. *loggats*] The game of loggats is
described by Clar. Press; the players
throw the loggats (little logs), truncated cones of apple-wood, as near
the Jack, a wooden wheel, as possible;
the floor is strewn with ashes: "perhaps Hamlet meant to compare the
skull to the Jack at which the bones
were thrown."

First Clo. [Sings.] *A pick-axe, and a spade, a spade,*
           For and a shrouding sheet ;
        Oh, a pit of clay for to be made
           For such a guest is meet. 105
                          [*Throws up another skull.*

Ham. There's another ; why may not that be the
    skull of a lawyer ? Where be his quiddits
    now, his quillets, his cases, his tenures, and his
    tricks ? why does he suffer this rude knave
    now to knock him about the sconce with a 110
    dirty shovel, and will not tell him of his action
    of battery ? Hum ! This fellow might be in 's
    time a great buyer of land, with his statutes,
    his recognizances, his fines, his double vouchers,
    his recoveries ; is this the fine of his fines, and 115
    the recovery of his recoveries, to have his fine
    pate full of fine dirt ? will his vouchers vouch
    him no more of his purchases, and double ones
    too, than the length and breadth of a pair of

105. Throws . . .] Capell ; omitted Q, F.   106. *may*] Q, *might* F.
107. *quiddits*] F, *quiddities* Q.   108. *quillets*] F, *quillites* Q.   109. *rude*]
F, *madde* Q.   115, 116. *is this* . . . *recoveries*] F, omitted Q.   117. *his
vouchers*] F, *vouchers* Q.   118, 119. *double ones too*] F, *doubles* Q.

103. For and] and moreover ; so
Skelton, *Against Garnesche*, "Syr
Gawen, Syr Cayus, for and Syr
Olyvere" (ed. Dyce, i. 119) ; found
also in Middleton and Beaumont and
Fletcher.

107. *quiddits*] quiddities, subtleties,
from the Schoolmen's *quidditas*, the
what-ness, distinctive nature of a
thing.

108. *quillets*] frivolous distinctions ;
from *quidlibet*.

113. *statutes*] bonds, statutes-mer-
chant or statutes-staple, the nature of
which is explained in Thomas Blount's

Law Dictionary. "Recognizances,"
another form of bond. "Fines" and
"recoveries," modes of converting an
estate tail into a fee-simple. In a
recovery with double voucher, two
persons are *vouched*, or called on, to
warrant the tenant's title.

115. *fine of his fines*] end of his
fines.

117. *fine dirt*] Rushton (*Shakespeare, a Lawyer*) thinks that this
means the *last* dirt that will ever
occupy his pate.

119. 120. *pair of indentures*] conveyances or contracts, in duplicate,

indentures? The very conveyances of his 120
lands will hardly lie in this box; and must
the inheritor himself have no more, ha?

Hor. Not a jot more, my lord.

Ham. Is not parchment made of sheep-skins?

Hor. Ay, my lord, and of calf-skins too.   125

Ham. They are sheep and calves which seek out
assurance in that.   I will speak to this fellow.
—Whose grave's this, sirrah?

First Clo. Mine, sir.—

> *Oh, a pit of clay for to be made*   130
> *For such a guest is meet.*

Ham. I think it be thine, indeed, for thou liest in't.

First Clo. You lie out on't, sir, and therefore 'tis
not yours; for my part, I do not lie in't, and
yet it is mine.   135

Ham. Thou dost lie in't, to be in't, and say it is
thine; 'tis for the dead, not for the quick;
therefore thou liest.

First Clo. 'Tis a quick lie, sir; 'twill away again,
from me to you.   140

Ham. What man dost thou dig it for?

First Clo. For no man, sir.

Ham. What woman, then?

---

121. *hardly*] F, *scarcely* Q.   125. *calf-skins*] F, *Calves skinnes* Q.   126.
which] Q, *that* F.   128. *sirrah*] Q, *Sir* F.   129–131. *Mine . . . meet*]
F, Q (as prose), *Mine sir*, or a . . . made (omitting For . . . meet).
133. *'tis*] Q, *it is* F.   134, 135. *and yet*] F, *yet* Q.   136. *it is*] Q, *'tis* F.

the paper or parchment *indented,* so
as to be divided into two, which two
must fit together in proof of genuine-
ness.

122. *inheritor*] possessor, as in
Love's Labour's Lost, II. i. 5.
127. *assurance*] used in the ordinary
and the legal sense (conveyance of
land or tenements by deed).

First Clo. For none, neither.

Ham. Who is to be buried in 't? 145

First Clo. One that was a woman, sir ; but, rest her
  soul, she 's dead.

Ham. How absolute the knave is ! we must speak
  by the card, or equivocation will undo us. By
  the Lord, Horatio, these three years I have 150
  taken note of it ; the age is grown so picked
  that the toe of the peasant comes so near the
  heel of the courtier, he galls his kibe.—How
  long hast thou been a grave-maker ?

First Clo. Of all the days i' the year, I came to 't 155
  that day that our last King Hamlet o'ercame
  Fortinbras.

Ham. How long is that since ?

First Clo. Cannot you tell that ? every fool can tell
  that ; it was the very day that young Hamlet 160

150. *these*] F, *this* Q.   151. *taken*] F, *tooke* Q.   153. *heel*] Q, *heeles* F ;
the courtier] Q, *our Courtier* F.   154. *a*] F (and later Qq), omitted Q.
155. *all*] F, omitted Q.   156. *o'ercame*] F, *overcame* Q.   160. *the very*]
F, *that very* Q.

148. *absolute*] positive, decided, free
from conditions. See *Cymbeline*, IV.
ii. 106.

149. *card*] chart ; or perhaps the
card on which the points of the
mariner's compass were marked, as
in *Macbeth*, I. iii. 17.   The sense
"map" or "sea-chart" seems to be
the earlier. In any case "to speak
by the card" means to speak with
exactness to a point.

149. *equivocation*] ambiguity in the
use of terms, not necessarily with a
view to mislead.

150. *three years*] Q 1 has "this
seaven yeares." It is, perhaps, worth
asking whether any allusion can be
intended here to the great Poor Law
legislation of 1601, when the principle

of taxation for the relief of the poor
was fully and finally established. The
date is exactly three years before the
words appeared in 1604. The purses,
if not the kibes, of needy courtiers
were galled by the assessments of the
overseers. The Act is that of 43 Eliz. ;
the earlier Act of 39 Eliz. preceded the
second Q by seven years, the first Q
by six.

151. *picked*] spruce, smart, as in
Love's Labour's Lost, V. i. 14. Johnson and Steevens supposed that there
was an allusion to *picked* shoes, shoes
with long projecting points, "beaks
or pykes."

153. *kibe*] chilblain, as in *Tempest*,
II. i. 276.

13

was born; he that is mad, and sent into
England.

Ham. Ay, marry; why was he sent into England?

First Clo. Why, because a' was mad: a' shall recover his wits there; or, if a' do not, 'tis no 165
great matter there.

Ham. Why?

First Clo. 'Twill not be seen in him there; there
the men are as mad as he.

Ham. How came he mad? 170

First Clo. Very strangely, they say.

Ham. How " strangely "?

First Clo. Faith, e'en with losing his wits.

Ham. Upon what ground?

First Clo. Why, here in Denmark; I have been 175
sexton here, man and boy, thirty years.

161. *is*] Q, *was* F.   165. *'tis*] Q, *it 's* F.   168. *him there*] Q, *him* F.
176. *sexton*] Q 4, *Sexten* Q, *sixeteene* F, *Sexestone* F 2.

169. *as mad as he*] Clar. Press
quotes Marston, *Malcontent*, III. i.:
" Your lordship shall ever find . . .
amongst a hundred Englishmen four-
score and ten madmen." So also
Massinger, *A Very Woman*, III. i.:
" The fellow [an Englishman] is mad,
stark mad. Believe they are all so."

176. *thirty years*] Hamlet's age—
thirty—is here fixed in a twofold way
—by the date of the grave-digger's
service and by the number of years
since Yorick's death. Gonzago and
his wife, who represent the elder
Hamlet and Gertrude, have been
married thirty years. It is true, however, that passages in earlier scenes—
in particular the scene of Laertes
parting from Ophelia—lead us to
conceive Hamlet as younger. He is
a student of Wittenberg; but it is a
foreign university. Prof. Hales has
quoted a passage from Nash, *Pierce
Pennilesss's Supplication*, on the late
age at which the Danes commenced
education: " You shall see a great
boy . . . weeping under the rod
when he is thirty years old." In
Q 1 Hamlet's age is not fixed, and
he seems younger throughout. Perhaps in recasting the play Shakespeare felt that Hamlet's weight of
thought implied an age beyond that
of very early manhood, and failed
to harmonise the earlier and later pre-
sentations of his hero. His Troilus
is under twenty-three; Florizel looks
about twenty-one; Cymbeline's sons
are twenty-three and twenty-two;
Hamlet is surely older than these
youths. The heyday of Gertrude's
blood is tame; she may be forty-five

Ham. How long will a man lie i' the earth ere he
    rot?

First Clo. I' faith, if a' be not rotten before a' die,
    —as we have many pocky corpses now-a-days, 180
    that will scarce hold the laying in,—a' will
    last you some eight year or nine year; a
    tanner will last you nine year.

Ham. Why he more than another?

First Clo. Why, sir, his hide is so tanned with his 185
    trade that a' will keep out water a great
    while; and your water is a sore decayer of
    your whoreson dead body.   Here's a skull
    now; this skull has lain in the earth three and
    twenty years.   190

Ham. Whose was it?

First Clo. A whoreson mad fellow's it was; whose
    do you think it was?

Ham. Nay, I know not.

First Clo. A pestilence on him for a mad rogue! 195
    a' poured a flagon of Rhenish on my head
    once.   This same skull, sir, was Yorick's skull,
    the king's jester.

Ham. This?

179. *I' faith*] F, *Fayth* Q.   180. *now-a-days*] F, omitted Q.   188, 189.
Here's . . . in the] F, *heer's a skull now hath lyen you i' th* Q.   189, 190.
three and twenty] F, *23* Q, *this dozen yeare* Q 1 (but in a different connection, and perhaps not Yorick's skull).   197. *This same skull, sir*] Q, words
repeated F; *Yorick's*] F, *sir Yoricks* Q.

or forty-six: yet, like Gonzago's wife,   perhaps the Danish *Jörg* (George);
who is of that age, she may have   Magnússon (in Clar. Press): per-
the power to charm.   However we   haps a corruption of Rorick, Saxo's
account for the inconsistency, we   Roricus, Hamlet's maternal grand-
must accept dates so carefully de-   father. Furness notes that Jerick is
termined.   the name of a "Dutch Bowr" in
    197. *Yorick's*] Ainger: Yorick is   Cnapman's *Alphonsus.*

First Clo. E'en that.   200

Ham. Let me see.—   *[Takes the skull.*

Alas, poor Yorick!—I knew him, Horatio; a
fellow of infinite jest, of most excellent fancy;
he hath borne me on his back a thousand
times; and now, how abhorred in my imagina- 205
tion it is! my gorge rises at it. Here hung
those lips that I have kissed I know not how
oft.—Where be your gibes now? your gambols?
your songs? your flashes of merriment, that
were wont to set the table on a roar? Not 210
one now, to mock your own grinning? quite
chop-fallen? Now get you to my lady's
chamber, and tell her, let her paint an inch
thick, to this favour she must come; make her
laugh at that.—Prithee, Horatio, tell me one 215
thing.

Hor. What's that, my lord?

Ham. Dost thou think Alexander looked o' this
fashion i' the earth?

Hor. E'en so.   220

Ham. And smelt so? puh!   *[Puts down the skull.*

201. *Let me see*] F, omitted Q. Takes the skull] Capell (after *This?* line
199); omitted Q, F.   204. *borne*] F, *bore* Q.   205. *now*] Q, omitted F.   205,
206. *in my . . . it is*] Q, *my imagination is.* F.   210, 211. *Not one*] Q, *No
one* F.   211. *grinning*] Q, *leering* F.   213. *chamber*] Q 1, F; *table* Q.
221. *so? puh*] F, *so pah* Q, *so? pah* Q 6. Puts down . . .] Collier; omitted Q, F.

214. *favour*] commonly used for
appearance, aspect; also for beauty,
comeliness; also for the countenance,
the face.

218. *Alexander*] Perhaps Shakespeare thought of Alexander's beauty
and sweet smell as well as of his con-
quests. North's *Plutarch*: " Alexander had a very faire white colour

mingled also with red . . . his skin
had a marvellous good favour . . .
his bodie had so sweet a smell " that
his apparel " took thereof a passing
delightful savour." His corpse re-
mained " many days naked without
buriall, in a hote drie countrie," yet
was " still a cleane and faire corps as
could be " (*Life of Alexander*).

Hor. E'en so, my lord.

Ham. To what base uses we may return, Horatio!
    Why may not imagination trace the noble
    dust of Alexander, till he find it stopping 225
    a bung-hole?

Hor. 'Twere to consider too curiously, to consider so.

Ham. No, faith, not a jot; but to follow him
    thither with modesty enough, and likelihood
    to lead it ; as thus : Alexander died, Alexander 230
    was buried, Alexander returneth into dust;
    the dust is earth; of earth we make loam;
    and why of that loam, whereto he was con-
    verted, might they not stop a beer-barrel?

        Imperious Cæsar, dead and turn'd to clay,   235
        Might stop a hole to keep the wind away ;
        Oh, that that earth, which kept the world in awe,
        Should patch a wall t' expel the winter's flaw!
    But soft! but soft! aside: here comes the king,

Enter Priests, etc. in procession ; the Corpse of OPHELIA,
LAERTES *and Mourners following ;* KING, QUEEN,
their Trains, etc.

    The queen, the courtiers; who is this they follow? 240
    And with such maimed rites ?   This doth betoken
    The corse they follow did with desperate hand

230. *as thus*] Q I, F ; omitted Q.   231. *into*] F, *to* Q.   235. *Imperious*]
Q, *Imperiall* F.   238. *winter's*] F, *waters* Q.   239. Enter . . .] Malone.
Enter K. Q. Laertes and the corse Q.   Enter King, Queene, Laertes, and
a coffin, with Lords attendant F.   240. *this*] Q, *that* F.

229. *modesty*] moderation, freedom   238. *flaw*] gust. Dyce quotes Cot-
from exaggeration, as in III. ii. 22.   grave : " A flaw or gust of wind
   235. *Imperious*] Imperial, as in *Tourbillon de vent.*"
Troilus and Cressida, IV. v. 172 :
" most imperious Agamemnon."

Fordo it own life ; 'twas of some estate
Couch we awhile, and mark.

                         [Retiring with Horatio.

Laer. What ceremony else ?   245

Ham. That is Laertes, a very noble youth : mark.

Laer. What ceremony else ?

Priest. Her obsequies have been as far enlarged
      As we have warrantise ; her death was doubtful ;
      And, but that great command o'ersways the order,
      She should in ground unsanctified have lodged 251
      Till the last trumpet ; for charitable prayers,
      Shards, flints, and pebbles should be thrown on her ;
      Yet here she is allow'd her virgin crants,
      Her maiden strewments, and the bringing home 255
      Of bell and burial.

---

243. *it*] Q, F ; *its* Q 6 ; *it's* Ff 3, 4 ; *of*] Q, omitted F.   244. Retiring . . .]
Capell ; omitted Q, F.   248. Priest] F, Doct Q, First Priest Capell.
249. *warrantise*] Dyce, *warrantis* F, *warrantie* Q, *warranties* Caldecott
(ed. 2).   251. *have*] F, *been* Q.   252. *prayers*] Q, *prayer* F.   253.
Shards] F, omitted Q.   254. *crants*] Q ; *Rites* F, Q 6 and many editors.

243. *Fordo*] see II. i. 103 ; and for
it, see I. ii. 216.

244. *Couch*] conceal, lurk. Bar-
rough, *Meth. Physick*, 1610 : " If
the quantity of humour be great, it
sometime coucheth itself in some
principall member."

249. *warrantise*] The word occurs
in *Sonnets*, cl., and in *1 Henry VI.*
I. iii. 13. Clar. Press : " The rubric
before the Burial Office forbids it to
be used for persons who have laid
violent hands on themselves."

253. *Shards*] Potsherds.

254. *crants*] wreaths, garlands, or
perhaps singular, garland (German,
Krantz). *New Eng. Dict.* quotes
Greene in *Harl. Misc.* II. 246 :
" The filthy queane weares a craunce,"
and Nichol, *Progr. Q. Eliz.*, 1596.

Hardiman, *Our Prayer-Book*, 138,
says : " The crants were garlands
which it was usual to make of white
paper, and to hang up in the church
on the occasion of a young girl's
funeral. Some of these were hanging
up in Flamborough Church, York-
shire, as late as 1850." Many editors
give F *rites.* See Brand's *Popular
Antiquities*, II. 302.

255. *strewments*] Several passages
of Shakespeare refer to strewing the
corpse or the grave with flowers ; in
Cymbeline, IV. ii. 285, we have
" strewings fitt'st for graves."

255. *bringing home*] Clar. Press
compares *Romeo and Juliet*, IV. v.
85–90, adding : " the marriage-rites
in the case of maidens are sadly
parodied in the funeral rites."

Laer. Must there no more be done?

Priest.   No more be done;
    We should profane the service of the dead
    To sing a requiem and such rest to her
    As to peace-parted souls.

Laer.   Lay her i' the earth;— 260
    And from her fair and unpolluted flesh
    May violets spring!—I tell thee, churlish priest,
    A ministering angel shall my sister be,
    When thou liest howling.

Ham.   What, the fair Ophelia?

Queen. Sweets to the sweet; farewell!   265
                      [*Scattering flowers.*
    I hoped thou shouldst have been my Hamlet's
         wife;
    I thought thy bride-bed to have deck'd, sweet maid,
    And not have strew'd thy grave.

Laer.   Oh, treble woe
    Fall ten times treble on that cursed head
    Whose wicked deed thy most ingenious sense 270
    Deprived thee of.—Hold off the earth awhile,
    Till I have caught her once more in mine arms.
                    [*Leaps into the grave.*

---

259. *sing a requiem*] Q, *sing sage* Requiem F.   265. *Sweets . . . farewell*] *Sweets to the sweet, farewell,* Q, *Sweets, to the sweet farewell.* Ff 1, 2, *Sweets, to thee sweet farewell.* Ff 3, 4. Scattering flowers] Johnson; omitted Q, F.   268. *have*] Q, *t' have* F; *treble woe*] Q, *terrible woer* F, *terrible wooer* Ff 2-4, *treble woes.* Furness (S. Walker conject.).   269. *treble*] F, *double* Q.   272. Leaps . . .] F (with *in* for *into*), omitted Q.

259. *a requiem*] The "sage requiem" of F has been emended "sad requiem," Collier MS. "such requiem," Dyce conject., Grant White.

264. *howling*] Used also in *Romeo and Juliet,* III. iii. 48, of the outcries in hell: "the damned use that word [banished] in hell, Howlings attend it."

270. *ingenious*] quick in apprehension. Compare *Lear,* IV. vi. 287, 288. Q 6 reads "ingenuous."

Now pile your dust upon the quick and dead,
Till of this flat a mountain you have made
To o'er-top old Pelion or the skyish head   275
Of blue Olympus.

Ham. [*Advancing.*]   What is he whose grief
Bears such an emphasis? whose phrase of sorrow
Conjures the wandering stars, and makes them
          stand
Like wonder-wounded hearers?   This is I,
Hamlet the Dane.   [*Leaps into the grave.*

Laer.   The devil take thy soul!   280
                    [*Grappling with him.*

Ham. Thou pray'st not well.
I prithee, take thy fingers from my throat;
For, though I am not splenitive and rash,
Yet have I something in me dangerous,
Which let thy wisdom fear.   Hold off thy hand! 285

King. Pluck them asunder.

Queen.   Hamlet, Hamlet!

All. Gentlemen,—

Hor.   Good my lord, be quiet.
          [*The Attendants part them, and they come out
                              of the grave.*

---

276. Advancing] Capell; omitted Q, F; *grief*] Q, *griefes* F.   278.
Conjures] Q, *Conjure* F.   280. Leaps . . .] omitted Q, F; Hamlet
leaps in after Laertes Q 1; Grappling] Rowe; omitted Q, F.   283. *For*]
Q, *Sir* F; *and*] F, omitted Q.   284. *something in me*] F, *in me something*
Q.   285. *wisdom*] Q 1, Q; *wisenesse* F; *Hold off*] Q, *Away* F.   287.
All. *Gentlemen,—*] Malone, All. *Gentlemen.* Q, omitted F.   Hor.] Q, Gen.
F.   The Attendants . . .] Malone; omitted Q, F.

278. *wandering stars*] Clar. Press   283. *splenitive*] The spleen was the
quotes Cotgrave (under Planette):   seat of anger. Compare *1 Henry IV.*
"they be also called Wandering   v. ii. 19.
starres."

Ham. Why, I will fight with him upon this theme
      Until my eyelids will no longer wag.

Queen. O my son, what theme?   290

Ham. I loved Ophelia; forty thousand brothers
      Could not, with all their quantity of love,
      Make up my sum.—What wilt thou do for her?

King. Oh, he is mad, Laertes.

Queen. For love of God, forbear him.   295

Ham. 'Swounds, show me what thou 'lt do;
      Woo't weep? woo't fight? woo't fast? woo't tear
         thyself?
      Woo't drink up eisel? eat a crocodile?

vinegar

---

296. *'Swounds*] Q, *Come* F ; *thou 'lt*] F, *th 'owt* Q.   297. *woo't fast*] Q, omitted F.   298. *eisel*] Theobald, *Esill* Q, *Esile* (italicised) F.

289. *wag*] move ; free from its present trivial or ludicrous associations. So "the empress never wags," *Titus Andronicus*, v. ii. 87 ; and Spenser, *Faerie Queene*, iv. iv. 167.

292. *quantity*] see iii. iv. 75 ; used in depreciatory sense.

297. *Woo't*] Perhaps used to express Hamlet's hurried utterance ; but it occurs, *Ant. and Cleop.* iv. ii. 7, and iv. xv. 59, with no such significance. Q i has *Wilt*. For *Thou 'lt*, line 296, Q has *th 'owt*, possibly with the same intention.

298. *eisel*] Criticism has not advanced much beyond Theobald's suggestions of 1733, that the Q *Esill* and F *Esile* mean either eisel, vinegar, or some river ; and of the names of rivers none is more plausible than Theobald's " *Yssel*, in the German Flanders." Parallels for the hyperbole of drinking a river can be pointed out in several Elizabethan writers, in Greene's *Orlando Furioso*, in *Eastward Hoe*, and elsewhere. The proposal Nilus has only the crocodile to favour it. An English *Esill* has not been found, though there is an Iseldun

(according to Sharon Turner, the Down of the Yssel). On the other hand, it has been shown that "drink up" does not necessarily mean exhaust ; it may mean drink eagerly, quaff.   In *Sonnets*, cxi., Shakespeare names "potions of eisel" as a bitter and disagreeable remedy for "strong infection."   The word was used (see *New Eng. Dict.*) for the vinegar rejected by Christ upon the cross.   The chief objection to eisel, vinegar, seems to be, as Theobald puts it, that "the proposition was not very grand." This objection would be met if we could find any special propriety in the proposition.   Now vinegar, even in small quantities, as we learn from William Vaughan's *Directions for Health* (ed. 7, 1633, p. 47, first published about 1607), while it allays heat and choler, "hurteth them that be sorrowfull."   L. Joubert, Physician to the French King, in his *Seconde Partie des Erreurs Populaires* (Rouen, 1600, p. 135), notes the vulgar error : "Que le vinaigre est la mort de la colère et la vie de la mélancholie." There may be irony in Hamlet's choice

I 'll do 't.   Dost thou come here to whine?

To outface me with leaping in her grave?   300

Be buried quick with her, and so will I:

And, if thou prate of mountains, let them
    throw

Millions of acres on us, till our ground,

Singeing his pate against the burning zone,

Make Ossa like a wart! Nay, an thou 'lt mouth, 305

I 'll rant as well as thou.

Queen.   This is mere madness;

And thus awhile the fit will work on him;

Anon, as patient as the female dove,

When that her golden couplets are disclosed,

His silence will sit drooping.

Ham.   Hear you, sir; 310

What is the reason that you use me thus?

I loved you ever.—But it is no matter;

Let Hercules himself do what he may,

The cat will mew, and dog will have his day. [*Exit.*

299. *thou*] F, omitted Q.   305. *an*] Pope; *and* Q, F.   306. Queen] Q,
Kin. F.   307. *thus*] F, *this* Q.   309. *couplets*] Q, *cuplet* F.

of extravagant performances suggested
by Laertes' extravagance of grief:
Would you artificially heighten your
sorrow by a bitter potion of eisel?
Would you allay your anger?

298. *eat a crocodile*] Hamlet's challenge to revolting feats—half-passion-
ate, half-ironical—receives more point
if we remember that in current natural
history the crocodile was a monster
of the serpent tribe. See Topsell's
Historie of Serpents. T. Bright regards the crocodile's bite as poisonous,
like an asp's.

306. *madness*] Compare this with
Hamlet's apology to Laertes, v. ii.

243, spoken at Gertrude's suggestion.

309. *golden couplets*] The pigeon
lays two eggs, and the young, when
disclosed or hatched (see III. i. 174),
are covered with yellow down.

314. *dog . . . day*] "Bay" has
been proposed for *day*, but the saying
was proverbial; examples are found
both earlier and later than *Hamlet.*
The meaning is, "Laertes must have
his whine and his bark." Hamlet had
previously (I. ii. 153) contrasted himself with Hercules: if Hercules cannot
silence dogs, much less I, who am
little like that hero.

King. I pray you, good Horatio, wait upon him.—   315
                              [*Exit Horatio.*

[*To Laertes.*] Strengthen your patience in our last
    night's speech;
We'll put the matter to the present push.—   *instant forwarding*
Good Gertrude, set some watch over your son.—
This grave shall have a living monument:
An hour of quiet shortly shall we see;   320
Till then, in patience our proceeding be.   [*Exeunt.*

SCENE II.—*A Hall in the Castle.*

Enter HAMLET *and* HORATIO.

Ham. So much for this, sir; now let me see the other;
    You do remember all the circumstance?
Hor. Remember it, my lord?
Ham. Sir, in my heart there was a kind of fighting   *journey to England*
    That would not let me sleep; methought I lay   5
    Worse than the mutines in the bilboes. Rashly,—
    And praised be rashness for it, let us know,

315. *you*] F, *thee* Q.   320. *shortly*] F, *thirtie* Q, *thereby* Qq 3-6.

                        Scene II.

1. *let me*] F, *shall you* Q.   2. *circumstance?*] Theobald; *circumstance.*
Q, F.   3. *lord?*] F, *Lord.* Q.   6. *bilboes*] F, *bilbo* Q.   6, 7. *Rashly,—*
. . . *know,*] Furness, *rashly, And praysd . . . it: let us know,* Q, *rashly,*
(*And . . . it*) *let us know,* F.

317. *present push*] instant forwarding.
319. *living*] enduring. Moberly:
"a statue like life itself." Clar. Press
suggests a double meaning, *enduring*
(meant for Gertrude), the life of Hamlet (for Laertes).

            Scene II.

4. *fighting*] So Arden of Feversham,
III. vi.: "This fighting at my harte."
6. *mutines in the bilboes*] mutineers

(as in *King John*, II. i. 378) in the
fetters. Bilbo (of uncertain deriva-
tion, perhaps named from Bilboa in
Spain) was a long iron bar, with
sliding shackles, to confine the ankles,
a lock fixing one end to the floor.
The earliest example of the word in
New Eng. Dict. is of 1557 from
Hakluyt's *Voyages*. See App. III.
6, 7. *Rashly*] Pope read *Rashness*,
Tyrwhitt, retaining *Rashly*, and read-

Our indiscretion sometimes serves us well

When our deep plots do pall; and that should teach us

There's a divinity that shapes our ends,　　　10

Rough-hew them how we will.

Hor.　　　　　　　　　　　　That is most certain.

Ham. Up from my cabin,

My sea-gown scarf'd about me, in the dark

Groped I to find out them; had my desire,

Finger'd their packet, and in fine withdrew　　15

To mine own room again; making so bold,

My fears forgetting manners, to unseal

Their grand commission; where I found, Horatio,—

O royal knavery!—an exact command,

Larded with many several sorts of reasons　　20

Importing Denmark's health, and England's too,

With, ho! such bugs and goblins in my life,

---

8. *sometimes*] F, *sometime* Q.　　9. *deep*] Q, *deare* F; *pall*] Q, F, *fall* Qq 3–6; *teach*] F, *learn* Q.　　13. *me, in the dark*] Q 6, no point in Q, comma only after *darke* F.　　17. *unseal*] F, *unfold* Q.　　19. *O*] F, *A* Q.　　20. *reasons*] Q, *reason* F.

ing *for it lets*, would place *And praised* to *certain*, line 11, in a parenthesis, thus connecting *Rashly* with "up from my cabin."

9. *pall*] Pope read *fail*, and is followed by Capell, Dyce (ed. 2), Furness, Hudson. Ingleby, citing several examples, maintains that *fall* was used by Elizabethan writers where we should use *fail*, and *fall* is the reading here of Qq 3–6.　*Pall*, however, to grow vapid and so worthless, occurs in *Ant. and Cleop.* II. vii. 88, "pall'd fortunes," and has here the authority of both Q and F.

10, 11. *ends, Rough-hew*] To *rough-hew*, perhaps originally a carpenter's word, extended its meaning. Thus Florio: "*Abbozzare*, to rough-hew or cast any first draught, to bungle up

ill-favouredly." We do not need the assistance of the dealer in skewers who told Farmer that his nephew could rough-hew them, but that he had himself to shape their ends.

13. *sea-gown*] Singer quotes Cotgrave: "*Esclavine* . . . a sea-gowne, or a coarse, high-collered, and short-sleeved gowne, reaching down to the mid-leg, and used most by sea-men and saylors."

20. *Larded*] see IV. v. 36.

21. *Importing*] concerning. Compare *Love's Labour's Lost*, IV. i. 57.

22. *bugs*] bugbears, as in *Taming of the Shrew*, I. ii. 211. In Chapman's *Gentleman Usher*, enter "Sylvan, with a Nymph, a man Bugge and a woman."

That, on the supervise, no leisure bated,

No, not to stay the grinding of the axe,

My head should be struck off.

Hor.   Is't possible?   25

Ham. Here's the commission: read it at more leisure.

But wilt thou hear me how I did proceed?

Hor. I beseech you.

Ham. Being thus be-netted round with villanies,—

Ere I could make a prologue to my brains,   30

They had begun the play,—I sat me down,

Devised a new commission, wrote it fair;

I once did hold it, as our statists do,

A baseness to write fair, and labour'd much

How to forget that learning; but, sir, now   35

It did me yeoman's service.   Wilt thou know

The effect of what I wrote?

Hor.   Ay, good my lord.

27. *me*] F, *now* Q.   28. *I*] *Ay* Capell and several editors.   29–31.
villanies . . . I] Dyce, *villaines, Or . . . play, I* Q, *villaines, Ere . . .
Play. I* F.   37. *effect*] Q, *effects* F.

23. *bated*] deducted; no leisure time
is to be taken out of the interval
between the supervisal of the commission and Hamlet's execution. *Promp-
torium Parvulorum*, "Baten or abaten
of weyte or mesure, *subtraho.*"

29. *villanies*] For instances of
the confusion of *villaine* and *villanie*
in F, see Sidney Walker, *Criticism on
Shakespeare*, ii. 44.

30, 31.] Hamlet's brains operate
without any scheme assigned to them
by his conscious self. They proceed
as players without an argument to the
play. See the prologue to *Romeo and
Juliet*, where the action of the play is
set forth. Theobald, taking *They* as
referring to Hamlet's enemies, read
(in parenthesis):

"(Ere I could make a prologue, to my
    Bane
They had begun the Play :)."
33. *statists*] statesmen, as in *Cymbeline*, II. iv. 16.   Ritson quotes
Florio's *Montaigne*, 1603, p. 125:
" I have in my time seene some who
by writing did earnestly get both their
titles and living, to disavow their ap-
prentise age, marre their pen, and
affect the ignorance of so vulgar a
qualitie."

36. *yeoman's service*] Stevens: "The
ancient yeomen were famous for their
military valour. 'These were the
good archers in times past' says Sir
Thomas Smith, 'and the stable
troop of footmen that affraide all
France.'"

Ham. An earnest conjuration from the king,
    As England was his faithful tributary,
    As love between them like the palm should flourish, 40
    As peace should still her wheaten garland wear,
    And stand a comma 'tween their amities,
    And many such-like *As*es of great charge,
    That, on the view and knowing of these contents,
    Without debatement further, more or less,   45
    He should the bearers put to sudden death,
    Not shriving-time allow'd.

Hor.   How was this seal'd ?

Ham. Why, even in that was heaven ordinant.
    I had my father's signet in my purse,
    Which was the model of that Danish seal;   50
    Folded the writ up in the form of the other,
    Subscribed it, gave 't the impression, placed it safely,

---

40. *like*] Q, *as* F ; *should*] F, *might* Q.   43. A*s*es] Furness, *as sir* Q, A*ss*is F.   44. *knowing of*] Q, *know of* F.   46. *the*] F, *those* Q.   48. *ordinant*] Q, *ordinate* F.   51. *the form*] Q, *form* F.   52. *Subscribed*] F, *Subscribe* Q.

---

42. *comma*] Theobald substitutes *commere* ; Hanmer, *cement* ; other suggestions are *co-mate, column, counter.* No emendation is required ; the obscurity has arisen through forgetting an earlier meaning of *comma,* a phrase or group of words forming a short member of a sentence or period. The *New Eng. Dict.,* which gives several examples, so explains *comma* in the only other instance in which it is used by Shakespeare—*Timon of Athens,* I. i. 48 : " no levelled malice Infects one comma in the course I hold." Here amity begins and amity ends the period, and peace stands between like a dependent clause. Clar. Press, following Johnson, explains otherwise : "comma is used here as opposed to 'period' or full stop, and in this view a mark of connection, not division " ; but there is no suggestion of a full stop here, and a comma in this sense always marks a division ; nor is the idea that peace *connects* amities, but that it derives its force through dependence on mutual love. [See Appendix III.]

43. *As*es] A quibble, as Johnson notices, between "as" (pronounced *ass* in Warwickshire) and *ass* the beast of burden or *charge* ; charge being used in the double sense of material burden and moral weight. See *Twelfth Night,* II. iii. 184, 185. The quibble of *as, ass* is amusingly introduced in Chapman's *Gentleman Usher,* near close of Act III.

50. *model*] counterpart. Malone refers to *Richard II.* III. ii. 153.

The changeling never known.   Now, the next day
Was our sea-fight, and what to this was sequent
Thou know'st already.   55

Hor. So Guildenstern and Rosencrantz go to 't.

Ham. Why, man, they did make love to this employ-
    ment;
They are not near my conscience; their defeat
Does by their own insinuation grow.
'Tis dangerous when the baser nature comes   60
Between the pass and fell incensed points
Of mighty opposites.

Hor.   Why, what a king is this!

Ham. Does it not, thinks 't thee, stand me now upon—
He that hath kill'd my king and whored my
    mother,
Popp'd in between the election and my hopes,   65
Thrown out his angle for my proper life,
And with such cozenage—is 't not perfect conscience
To quit him with this arm? and is 't not to be
    damn'd
To let this canker of our nature come
In further evil?   70

54. *sequent*] Q, *sement* F.   56. *So . . . to't*] Q; in F comma before
go.   57. *Why . . . employment*] F, omitted Q.   58. *defeat*] Q, *debate* F.
59. *Does*] Q, *Doth* F.   62. *this !*] Q, *this ?* F.   63. *thinks 't*] S. Walker
conject., Dyce, *thinke* Q, *thinkst* F; *upon—*] Boswell, *uppon?* Q, *vpon* F.
68–80. *To quit . . . here ?*] F, omitted Q.

59. *insinuation*] Malone: "By   63. *thinks 't thee*] Walker's cor-
their having insinuated or thrust   rection of F; seems it to thee.
themselves into the employment."   63. *stand me now upon*] is it not
61. *pass*] thrust, as in line 170.   incumbent on me, as in *Richard II.*
Dyce and other editors hyphen *fell-* II. iii. 138.
incensed.   70. *In*] Into, as in v. i. 300.
62. *opposites*] opponents, as in
Twelfth Night, III. iv. 253.

Hor. It must be shortly known to him from England
    What is the issue of the business there.

Ham. It will be short; the interim is mine;
    And a man's life's no more than to say " One."
    But I am very sorry, good Horatio,   75
    That to Laertes I forgot myself; *He seeks*
    For, by the image of my cause, I see *revenge too*
    The portraiture of his; I'll court his favours;
    But, sure, the bravery of his grief did put me
    Into a towering passion.

Hor.   Peace! who comes here? 80

generosity

Enter OSRIC.

Osr. Your lordship is right welcome back to Denmark.

Ham. I humbly thank you, sir.—[*Aside to Hor.*] Dost
    know this water-fly?

Hor. [*Aside to Ham.*] No, my good lord.

Ham. [*Aside to Hor.*] Thy state is the more   85
    gracious, for 'tis a vice to know him.   He hath
    much land, and fertile; let a beast be lord of
    beasts, and his crib shall stand at the king's
    mess: 'tis a chough, but, as I say, spacious in
    the possession of dirt. *land*   90

73. *is*] Hanmer, *'s* F.   74. *life's*] F, *life* Reed and many editors.
78. *court*] Theobald, *count* F.   80. Enter *Osric*] F 2; Enter a Courtier
Q; Enter young *Osricke* F.   81. (and later) Osr.] F, Cour. Q.   89.
say] Q, *saw* F.

79. *bravery*] bravado, or ostentation.   Examples of each meaning
are common.
    83. *water-fly*] Because the water-
fly is a little, skipping, burnished
creature, seeming busily idle. See
Troilus and Cressida, v. i. 38.
    89. *chough*] If the Cornish chough
(which Ritson says is "pronounced

by the natives *chow*") or red-legged
crow, be meant, the following, from
Carew's *Survey of Cornwall*, 1602
(p. 110, ed. 1811), may be quoted:
"His state, when he is kept tame,
ungracious, in filching and hiding of
money, and such short ends, and
somewhat dangerous in carrying
sticks of fire." Camden also notices

Osr. Sweet lord, if your lordship were at leisure, I
should impart a thing to you from his majesty.

Ham. I will receive it, sir, with all diligence of spirit.
Put your bonnet to his right use; 'tis for the head.

Osr. I thank your lordship, 'tis very hot. *He is too refined to put his hat on.* 95

Ham. No, believe me, 'tis very cold; the wind is northerly.

Osr. It is indifferent cold, my lord, indeed. *Cf. Polonius' agreement.*

Ham. But yet methinks it is very sultry and hot
for my complexion. *He teases him.*

Osr. Exceedingly, my lord; it is very sultry,—as 100
'twere,—I cannot tell how. But, my lord, his
majesty bade me signify to you that he has
laid a great wager on your head. Sir, this is
the matter—

Ham. I beseech you, remember— 105

[*Hamlet moves him to put on his hat.*

Osr. Nay, good my lord; for mine ease, in good

91. *lordship*] Q, *friendship* F. 93. *sir*] Q, omitted F. 94. *Put*] F,
omitted Q. 95. *'tis*] F, *it is* Q. 98. *But yet*] Q, omitted F ; *sultry*] F,
sully Q. 98, 99. *hot for my complexion*] F, *hot, or my complection* Q, *hot, or
my complexion*—Warburton and many editors. 101. *But*] F, omitted Q.
104. *matter*—] Rowe ; *matter.* Q, F. 105. Hamlet moves . . .] Johnson ;
omitted Q, F. 106. *good my lord*] Q, *in good faith* F ; *mine*] F, *my* Q.

his money-loving and his incendiary
practices. Chough's "chat" and
"gabble" are spoken of in *Tempest*,
II. i. 266, and *All's Well*, IV. i. 22.
But Caldecott may be right in thinking that here *chuff* may be meant.
Furness quotes Cotgrave : "*Franc-
goutier*, A substanciall yonker,
wealthie chuffe," and "*Maschefouyn*,
a chuffe, boore . . . one that is fitter
to feed with cattell than to conuerse
with men."

95–103.] Theobald noted the parallel
in Juvenal, *Sat.* iii. : "igniculum
brumæ si tempore poscas, Accipit
endromidem ; si dixeris, æstuo, sudat."

105. *remember*] So *Love's Labour's*

Lost, v. i. 103 : "I do beseech thee,
remember thy courtesy ; I beseech
thee, apparel thy head." The meaning of the phrase (found also in Jonson and elsewhere) is Remember that
you have already complied with the
requirement of courtesy ; so cover
your head.

106. *for mine ease*] the conventional
form of reply, when remaining un-
covered. Examples are cited from
Marston's *Malcontent* (Induction),
and Florio's *Second Frutes* : that
from Marston (given to Shakespeare's
fellow-player William Sly) is one of
several reminiscences of Hamlet.
Malone inferred that Sly had played

14

faith. Sir, here is newly come to court
Laertes; believe me, an absolute gentleman,
full of most excellent differences, of very soft *quality*
society and great showing; indeed, to speak 110
feelingly of him, he is the card or calendar
of gentry, for you shall find in him the continent of what part a gentleman would see.

absurd
metaphors

Ham. Sir, his definement suffers no perdition in
you; though, I know, to divide him inven- 115
torially would dizzy the arithmetic of
memory, and yet but yaw neither, in respect

move unsteadily

Brilliant skit
on Euphuism.
Wit-snapping. Hamlet
enjoys it

107-147. *Sir, here . . . unfellowed*] Q, omitted F, which abbreviates by
reading *Sir, you are not ignorant of what excellence* Laertes *is at his weapon.*
116. *dizzy*] Q 4, *dosie* Q.

Osric ; but Sly also asks Sinklo to
"sit between my legs" (a reminiscence of Hamlet and Ophelia), to
which Sinklo replies, "the audience
will then take me for a viol-de-gambo,
and think that you play upon me"
(a reminiscence of Hamlet and the
two courtiers).

108. *absolute*] consummate, perfect,
as in *Merry Wives*, III. iii. 66: "an
absolute courtier."

109. *differences*] characteristics
(which difference one person from
others). In heraldry a difference
(alteration of or addition to a coat
of arms) distinguishes a junior member
or branch of a family from the chief
line.

111. *feelingly*] with just perception.
Compare *Twelfth Night*, II. iii. 172.
Q misprints *sellingly*.

111, 112. *card . . . gentry*] card,
chart or map (as in v. i. 149) "by
which a gentleman should direct his
course ; the calendar by which he is
to choose his time" (Johnson).
Gentry, courtesy, as in II. ii. 22.
Perhaps *card* here means the card of
the mariner's compass ; *calendar* (use-
ful in navigation with its astronomical

data) was used figuratively as example, model.

112, 113. *continent*] summary, sum
and substance of the qualities a gentleman would desire to contemplate,
with a play on the geographical
meanings of continent and part,
suggested by *card.* Nicholson proposes *parts,* as in IV. vii. 74.

114. *definement*] definition. Hamlet uses an affected preciosity ; no
other example of the word in this
sense earlier than 1867 is recorded in
New Eng. Dict. ; no other example
in any sense before 1643.

116. *arithmetic*] "The two metaphors (arithmetic and quick sail),"
says Clar. Press, "are a little difficult
to separate." Perhaps they should
rather be united. The *card* and *continent* suggest a voyage to discover
Laertes' parts. The arithmetic of
memory may be the computations
made in a navigator's head ; in 1625
T. Addison published his *Arith-
metical Navigation.* Q *dosie* is only
an obsolete form of *dizzy* (see *New
Eng. Dict., dozy*).

117. *yaw*] Qq 3-6 have *raw,*
which Johnson explains : "the best

of his quick sail. But, in the verity of extol-
ment, I take him to be a soul of great article,
and his infusion of such dearth and rareness, 120
as, to make true diction of him, his semblable
is his mirror, and who else would trace him,
his umbrage, nothing more.

Osr. Your lordship speaks most infallibly of him.

Ham. The concernancy, sir? why do we wrap the 125
gentleman in our more rawer breath?

Osr. Sir?

Hor. Is't not possible to understand in another
tongue? You will do't, sir, really.

125. *sir? why*] Capell, *sir, why* Q.   127. *Sir?*] Capell, *Sir.* Q.   129.
tongue?] Theobald, *tongue.* Q; *You . . . really*] Qq 3–6; *You will too't
sir really* Q.

account of him would be *imperfect*";
Heath explains—Laertes was but
young (*raw*) in proportion to his progress in accomplishments. To yaw,
used of a ship, means to move unsteadily, to diverge from their course;
"huc illuc vacillare," says Coles's
Dictionary. But neither means "for
all that" (examples in Schmidt's *Sh.
Lexicon,* under *neither*). *In respect
of* has two meanings in Shakespeare:
(1) with regard to, (2) in comparison
with. "*His* quick sail" may possibly,
as Deighton holds, mean *its.* These
are the data for an explanation of
Hamlet's jargon; to which it should
be added that for *yet* Dyce and
others read *it; yt, it,* being easily
mistaken for *yet*; and that Staunton
conjectures *wit* for *yet.* The explanation of the text as it stands may be:
To enumerate in detail the perfections
of Laertes would bewilder the computations of memory, yet for all that
—in spite of the calculations—the
enumeration would stagger to and
fro (and so fall behind) in comparison
with Laertes' quick sailing (or, pos-

sibly, considering *its* quick sail, which
ought to steady the ship).

119. *article*] business, concern;
"of great article," of great moment
or importance. See *New Eng. Dict.,
article,* 10.

120. *infusion . . . rareness*] the
qualities infused into him; something
higher than acquisition. Sir T.
Browne (*Religio Medici,* II. § viii.)
would sometimes shut his books,
thinking the pursuit of knowledge a
vanity, when, wait a little and we
shall enjoy knowledge by "instinct
and infusion." *Dearth,* dearness.
Bishop Barlow, *Three Sermons*
(1596): "Dearth is that, when all
things . . . are rated at a high price."

122. *trace*] follow, as in *1 Henry
IV.* III. i. 48.

125. *concernancy*] concernment;
another affected word; no other example given in *New Eng. Dict.*

125. *why . . .*] Theobald took
these words as spoken of Osric to
Horatio; no doubt, erroneously.

128, 129. *Is't . . . tongue*] Johnson
conjectured "a mother tongue."

Ham. What imports the nomination of this gentle- 130
man?

Osr. Of Laertes?

Hor. [*Aside to Ham.*] His purse is empty already;
all's golden words are spent.

Ham. Of him, sir. 135

Osr. I know you are not ignorant—

Ham. I would you did, sir; yet, in faith, if
you did, it would not much approve me.
Well, sir?

Osr. You are not ignorant of what excellence Laertes 140
is—

Ham. I dare not confess that, lest I should compare
with him in excellence; but, to know a man
well were to know himself.

Osr. I mean, sir, for his weapon; but in the im- 145
putation laid on him by them, in his meed he's
unfellowed.

Ham. What's his weapon?

Osr. Rapier and dagger.

132. *Laertes ?*] Q 6, *Laertes.* Q.   136. *ignorant*—] Theobald, *ignorant* Q.
138, 139. *me. Well, sir ?*] Globe Sh., *me, well sir.* Q, *me. Well, sir.*
Theobald.   141. *is*—] Malone, *is.* Q.   145. *for his*] Q 6, *for this* Q.
146. *them, in his meed*] Steevens, *them in his meed,* Q.

Jennens: "understand? In another
tongue you" (addressed to Osric).
Malone conjectured: "Is 't possible
not to understand in a mother tongue?"
(addressed to Hamlet). The words
are surely addressed to Osric, and
mean "Might you not understand
if you used a less affected dialect?"
Moberly explains: "Can't you understand your own absurd language on
another tongue."
   129. *You . . . really*] Theobald
read *rarely.* Heath: "You do 't, sir,

rarely." The words are an ironical
encouragement to Osric to talk like a
rational human being—Believe me
you will succeed.
   138. *approve*] commend.
   143. *to know . . . himself*] to know
another implies self-knowledge, the
height of human wisdom.
   145, 146. *imputation*] repute, as in
Troilus and Cressida, I. iii. 339.
   146. *meed*] merit, as in *3 Henry VI.*
IV. viii. 38.

Ham. That's two of his weapons; but, well.   150

Osr. The king, sir, hath wagered with him six Barbary horses; against the which he has imponed, *staked*
as I take it, six French rapiers and poniards,
with their assigns, as girdle, hangers, and so:
three of the carriages, in faith, are very dear to 155
fancy, very responsive to the hilts, most delicate
carriages, and of very liberal conceit.

Ham. What call you the carriages?

Hor. [*Aside to Ham.*] I knew you must be edified
by the margent ere you had done.   160

Osr. The carriages, sir, are the hangers.

Ham. The phrase would be more ~~germane~~ to the
matter if we could carry cannon by our sides; *why not stick to*
I would it might be hangers till then. But, *"hangers"*
on: six Barbary horses against six French 165
swords, their assigns, and three liberal-conceited
carriages; that's the French bet against the
Danish. Why is this " imponed," as you call it?

---

151. *hath wagered*] Q, *ha's wag'd* F.   152. *he has imponed*] Theobald, *hee has impaund* Q, *he impon'd* F.   154. *hangers*] F, *hanger* Q;
and so] Q, *or so* F.   159, 160. Hor. . . . *done*] Q, omitted F.   161. *carriages*] F, *carriage* Q.   162. *germane*] F 3, *Ierman* Q, *Germaine* F.
163. *cannon*] F, *a cannon* Q.   164. *might be*] F, *be* Q.   165. *on:*] Pope,
on, Q, *on* F.   167. *bet*] Q, *but* F.   168. *this " imponed" as*] F, *this all* Q.

152. *imponed*] staked. Perhaps
Osric's affected pronunciation of *im-
pawned.* Johnson suggested *deponed.*
Minsheu gives *deponere* as Latin for
stake.

154. *assigns*] appurtenances. No
other example of this sense in *New
Eng. Dict.*

154. *hangers*] straps by which the
rapier hung from the girdle—often
richly ornamented, as that described
by Jonson's Matthew (*Every Man
in his Humour*, I. iv.), "a hanger . . .

both for fashion and workmanship . . .
most peremptory beautiful."

156. *very responsive*] closely corresponding.

157. *liberal conceit*] elaborate design.

160. *margent*] Explanatory notes
often in old books printed in the
margin.

163. *cannon*] Knolles, *History of
the Turks*, 1603: "He commanded
the great ordnance to be laid upon
carriages."

Osr. The king, sir, hath laid, sir, that in a dozen
passes between yourself and him, he shall not 170
exceed you three hits; he hath laid on twelve
for nine; and it would come to immediate trial
if your lordship would vouchsafe the answer.

Ham. How if I answer No?

Osr. I mean, my lord, the opposition of your person 175
in trial.

Ham. Sir, I will walk here in the hall; if it please
his majesty, 'tis the breathing time of day with
me; let the foils be brought, the gentleman
willing, and the king hold his purpose, I will 180
win for him if I can; if not, I will gain nothing but my shame and the odd hits.

Ors. Shall I re-deliver you e'en so?

Ham. To this effect, sir; after what flourish your
nature will. 185

169. *sir, that*] Q, *that* F. 170. *yourself*] Q, *you* F. 171, 172. *laid*
. . . *nine*] Q, *one twelve for mine* F. 172. *it*] Q, *that* F. 177, 178. *hall;*
. . . *majesty, 'tis*] F, *hall,* . . . *majestie, it is* Q. 180. *purpose,*] Theobald; *purpose;* Q, F. 181. *if I*] F, *and I* Q; *I will*] Q, *Ile* F.
183. *re-deliver* . . . *so*] F, *deliver you so* Q.

171, 172. *twelve for nine*] The word
passes seems to mean *passes which
count*, the same as hits; the encounter
is to continue until one party has
made a dozen hits. The King wagers
that Laertes—famous as a fencer, and
therefore able to afford his rival odds
— will not have made his twelve
hits until Hamlet's hits are nine; if
Hamlet falls short of nine, Laertes
wins. Other explanations will be
found in Furness. In Q 1 Hamlet
asks "And howe's the wager?" The
"Bragart Gentleman" replies:
　"Mary sir, that yong Leartes in
　　twelve venies
　　At Rapier and Dagger do not get
　　three oddes of you."

Venue or venny was sometimes used
for a hit; more commonly, a bout
or a thrust.

173. *answer*] Osric uses the word
for encounter. So in the *Paston
Letters*, "My Lord the Bastard took
upon him to answer xxiv knyts and
gentylmen . . . at jostys of pese."

178. *breathing time*] Clar. Press:
"the time of relaxation and rest."
Breathing time was so used; but this
time of relaxation was also the time for
recreative exercise. "To breathe"
came to mean to exercise briskly
(from the quickening of the respiratory
organs); so breathing time means a
time of intermission from compelled
toil and a time of voluntary exercise.

Osr. I commend my duty to your lordship.

Ham. Yours, yours.— [*Exit Osric.*

He does well to commend it himself; there
are no tongues else for's turn.

Hor. This lapwing runs away with the shell on his 190
head. *conceited youngster* *eggshell.*

Ham. He did comply with his dug before he sucked
it. Thus has he, and many more of the same
bevy that I know the drossy age dotes on, *Generalising*
only got the tune of the time and outward 195 *again*
habit of encounter; a kind of yesty collection
which carries them through and through the
most fond and winnowed opinions; and do *have no criticism*
but blow them to their trial, the bubbles are
out. 200

187, 188. *Yours . . . does*] F (yours ; hee), *Yours doo's* Q. 189. *turn*]
Q, *tongue* F. 192. *He . . . with*] F, *A did sir with* Q, *A did so sir with*
Qq 3–6. 193. *has*] Q, *had* F ; *many*] Q, *mine* F, *nine* F 2. 194. *bevy*]
F (*beauy*), *breede* Q. 195. *and outward*] F, *and out of an* Q. 196. *yesty*]
F, *histy* Q, *misty* Qq 4–6. 198. *fond and winnowed*] F, *prophane and
trennowed* Q. 199. *trial*] Q, *tryalls* F.

190. *lapwing*] So Meres, *Wit's
Treasury* : "As the lapwing runneth
away with the shell on her head as soon
as she is hatched"; hence a forward,
conceited youngster. Clar. Press
adds insincere, the lapwing crying far
from its nest to mislead intruders.
See *Measure for Measure*, i. iv. 32.

192. *comply with*] see ii. ii. 394.

195, 196. *outward . . . encounter*]
exterior manner of address.

196. *yesty collection*] frothy aggre-
gation (of empty knowledge, like a
mass of bubbles).

198. *fond and winnowed opinions*]
Warburton's emendation *fann'd* is apt,
and has found many supporters.
Tschischwitz proposes *profound* for Q
prophane. Q trennowed becomes *tren-*

nowned in later Quartos, and *renowned*
in Q 1676. Fleay proposes *fond un-
winnowed.* Moberly explains : "frothy
expressions suited to express the
absurdest and most over-refined no-
tions"; Clar. Press : "The metaphor
is a mixed one . . . Osric, and others
like him, are compared to the chaff
which mounts higher than the sifted
wheat, and to the bubbles which rise to
the surface through the deeper water."
The metaphor in "winnowed" seems
to me incidental and latent; the
meaning is "Their frothy acquisitions
carry them successfully through the
slight judgments of the most exquisite
arbiters *elegantiarum.*" If we read
fanned, the same remains the
meaning.

Enter a Lord.

Lord. My lord, his majesty commended him to
you by young Osric, who brings back to him
that you attend him in the hall; he sends to
know if your pleasure hold to play with Laertes,
or that you will take longer time.   205

Ham. I am constant to my purposes; they follow
the king's pleasure; if his fitness speaks, mine
is ready; now or whensoever, provided I be
so able as now.

Lord. The king, and queen, and all are coming 210
down.

Ham. In happy time.

Lord. The queen desires you to use some gentle
entertainment to Laertes before you fall to
play.   215

Ham. She well instructs me.   [*Exit Lord.*

Hor. You will lose this wager, my lord.

Ham. I do not think so; since he went into France,
I have been in continual practice; I shall win
at the odds. But thou wouldst not think how 220
ill all's here about my heart; but it is no
matter.

Hor. Nay, good my lord,—

Trying to persuade him not to?

201–216. Enter . . . *instructs me*] Q, omitted F.   214. *fall*] Q, *gve* Qq
4–6.   220. *But*] F, omitted Q.   220, 221. *how ill all's*] Q, *how all* F.
223. *lord,*—] Capell ; *lord.* Q, F.

206. *purposes*] Walker : "note the
double meaning." Tschischwitz :
"Hamlet's *purpose* is unchanged to
kill the King . . . when the King is
fit for it in the hour of his unholy
pleasure."

212. *In happy time*] like *à la bonne
heure*; as in *Othello*, III. i. 32.
220. *odds*] Malone : "With the
advantage that I am allowed."

Ham. It is but foolery; but it is such a kind of
gain-giving as would perhaps trouble a woman. 225
Hor. If your mind dislike any thing, obey it; I will
forestall their repair hither, and say you are
not fit.
Ham. Not a whit; we defy augury; there's a special
providence in the fall of a sparrow. If it be 230
now, 'tis not to come; if it be not to come, it
will be now; if it be not now, yet it will come;
the readiness is all; since no man has aught
of what he leaves, what is 't to leave betimes?
Let be.   235

Enter KING, QUEEN, LAERTES, *Lords,* OSRIC, *and
Attendants with foils and gauntlets: a table and
flagons of wine on it.*

King. Come, Hamlet, come, and take this hand from me.

[*The King puts the hand of Laertes into that
of Hamlet.*

225. *gain-giving*] F, *gamgiving* Q, *game-giving* Qq 4–6.   226. *it*]
Q, omitted F.   229. *there's a*] F, *there is* Q.   231. *now*]F, omitted Q.
233–235. *the readiness . . . Let be*] Caldecott; *The readines is all, since no
man of ought he leaves, knowes what ist to leave betimes, let be.* Q; *The
readinesse is all, since no man ha's ought of what he leaves. What is't to
leave betimes?* F.   235. Enter King . . .] F (substantially); A table
prepared, Trumpets, Drums, and Officers with Cushions, King, Queene, and
all the state, Foiles, daggers, and Laertes. Q.   236. The King . . .]
Johnson (substantially); omitted Q, F.

225. *gain - giving*]   misgiving;
formed like *gainsay.*
   233, 234. *since . . . betimes*]
Many editors follow Warburton, who
punctuates Q thus : "Since no man,
of ought he leaves, knows, what."
Johnson read " knows aught of."
The Q certainly gives a fine and
characteristic meaning : since no man
knows what life may bring, since no

man can solve its mysteries. But the
idea of F is vulgarised by reducing it
to " If a man cannot carry away with
him life's goods"; it is rather : If we
possess nothing except our personality,
what matters it to leave the adventi-
tious things of life soon or late.
Hanmer read " Since no man owes
aught of what he leaves."

Ham. Give me your pardon, sir; I 've done you wrong;
But pardon 't, as you are a gentleman.
This presence knows,
And you must needs have heard, how I am
    punish'd   240
With sore distraction.   What I have done,
That might your nature, honour and exception
Roughly awake, I here proclaim was madness.
Was 't Hamlet wrong'd Laertes?   Never Hamlet;
If Hamlet from himself be ta'en away,   245
And when he 's not himself does wrong Laertes,
Then Hamlet does it not; Hamlet denies it.
Who does it then?   His madness; if 't be so,
Hamlet is of the faction that is wrong'd;
His madness is poor Hamlet's enemy.   250
Sir, in this audience,
Let my disclaiming from a purposed evil
Free me so far in your most generous thoughts,
That I have shot mine arrow o'er the house,
And hurt my brother.

237. *I've*] F, *I have* Q.   241. *sore*] F, *a sore* Q.   248. *madness ;*]
madnesse. Q, *Madnesse?* F.   251. *Sir . . . audience*] F, omitted Q.
254. *mine*] F, *my* Q.   255. *brother*] Q 1, Q; *Mother* F.

239. *presence*] royal and courtly assembly; frequent in Shakespeare.
242. *exception*] disapproval. Compare *All's Well* I. ii. 40.
255. *brother*] The F *mother* is almost certainly a mere printer's error; yet it is worth considering that Hamlet has been requested by his mother to "use some gentle entertainment to Laertes"; that the speech, in complying with her request, merely develops her words in the last scene, "This is mere madness, etc."; that it is spoken not without the characteristic irony of adopting another's point of view; that Hamlet twice before has pointed his indifference to the King by expressed deference to his mother; and that he might ironically apologise for his apology (which Johnson thought unworthy of him as lacking sincerity) by hinting at the close why it was made and made in the desired form—"And hurt—my mother" (with a slight salutation towards Gertrude). Can it be that this reading of F was an afterthought of Shakespeare? [See Appendix III.]

Laer.   I am satisfied in nature, 255
 Whose motive, in this case, should stir me most
 To my revenge; but in my terms of honour
 I stand aloof, and will no reconcilement,
 Till by some elder masters of known honour
 I have a voice and precedent of peace,   260
 To keep my name ungored. But till that time
 I do receive your offer'd love like love,
 And will not wrong it.

Ham.   I embrace it freely,
 And will this brother's wager frankly play.—
 Give us the foils.—Come on.

Laer.   Come, one for me. 265

Ham. I 'll be your foil, Laertes; in mine ignorance
 Your skill shall, like a star i' the darkest night,
 Stick fiery off indeed.

Laer.   You mock me, sir.

Ham. No, by this hand.   269

King. Give them the foils, young Osric.—Cousin Hamlet,
 You know the wager?

 Ham.   Very well, my lord;
 Your grace hath laid the odds o' the weaker side.

---

261. *keep*] F, omitted Q ; *ungored*] Q, *ungorg'd* F ; *till*] F, *all* Q.   263. *I*]
Q, *I do* F.   265. *Come on*] F, omitted Q.   267. *darkest*] Q, F ; *brightest*
Ff 2-4.   271. *wager?*] Capell ; *wager.* Q, F.   272. *hath*] F, *has* Q.

255. *nature*] Hamlet has referred
to "nature" and "honour"; Laertes
replies as to each point.
 260. *voice and precedent*] authori-
tative pronouncement, justified by
precedent, on the question whether
an insult by one distracted should be
formally resented. Laertes' words—
spoken by an assassin—are wholly
insincere.

268. *Stick fiery off*] stand out
brilliantly. For "darkest," changed
in F 2 to "brightest," see *Ant. and
Cleop.* I. iv. 13.
 272. *odds*] three points given to
Hamlet, who is assumed to be the
less skilled. Supposed, erroneously,
by some to refer to the greater value
of the King's stake.

King. I do not fear it; I have seen you both;
     But since he is better'd, we have therefore odds.
Laer. This is too heavy; let me see another.   275
Ham. This likes me well.—These foils have all a
     length?   [*They prepare to play.*
Osr. Ay, my good lord.
King. Set me the stoups of wine upon that table.—
     If Hamlet give the first or second hit,
     Or quit in answer of the third exchange,   280
     Let all the battlements their ordnance fire;
     The king shall drink to Hamlet's better breath;
     And in the cup an union shall he throw,
     Richer than that which four successive kings
     In Denmark's crown have worn. Give me the
     cups;   285
     And let the kettle to the trumpet speak,
     The trumpet to the cannoneer without,
     The cannons to the heavens, the heaven to
     earth,
     "Now the king drinks to Hamlet!"—Come,
     begin;—
     And you, the judges, bear a wary eye.   290
Ham. Come on, sir.
Laer.   Come, my lord.   [*They play.*

274. *better'd*] F, *better* Q.   276. *length?*] Rowe; *length.* Q, F.
283. *union*] F, *Vnice* Q, *Onixe* Qq 3-6.   286. *trumpet*] Q, *trumpets* F.
289.] Trumpets the while (stage direction) Q, omitted F.   291. *Come, my lord*] Q, *Come on sir* F.

274. *better'd*] not naturally superior, trained by Parisian fencers.
280. *quit*] pay off scores.
283. *union*] Malone quotes Florio: "*Vnione* . . . Also a faire, great, orient pearle, called an vnion."

Steevens quotes Holland's *Pliny*: "Vnions, as a man would say, Singular, and by themselves alone." Pliny tells of Cleopatra's dissolving a pearl in vinegar, and drinking it.
286. *kettle*] see I. iv. 11.

Ham.   One.

Laer.   No.

Ham.   Judgment.

Osr. A hit, a very palpable hit.

Laer.   Well; again.

King. Stay; give me drink.—Hamlet, this pearl is
    thine;

    Here's to thy health.—

        [*Trumpets sound, and cannons shot off within.*

             Give him the cup.

Ham. I'll play this bout first; set it by awhile.— 295

    Come.   [*They play.*

        Another hit; what say you?

Laer. A touch, a touch, I do confess.

King. Our son shall win.

Queen.   He's fat, and scant of breath.—

    Here, Hamlet, take my napkin, rub thy brows;

    The queen carouses to thy fortune, Hamlet.   300

Ham. Good madam!

King.   Gertrude, do not drink!

Queen. I will, my lord; I pray you, pardon me.

King. [*Aside.*] It is the poison'd cup! it is too late!

Ham. I dare not drink yet, madam; by and by.

---

294. Trumpets . . .] Malone.   Drum, trumpets and shot.   Florish, a
peece goes off. Q (after *hit*, line 292), Trumpets sound, and shot goes off. F
(after *cup*).   295. *set it*] Q, *set* F.   296. *Come.*] Come: F, *Come,* Q.
297. *A touch, a touch,*] F, omitted Q; *confess*] F, *confest* Q.   299. *Here
. . . napkin*] Q, *Heere's a napkin* F.   301. *madam!*] Dyce; *Madam.* Q,
F; *Madam—* Rowe.   303, 307. Aside] Rowe.

293. *pearl*] In fact the poison. See
line 337.
  298. *fat*] Clar. Pres.: "There is
a tradition that this line was appropriate to Richard Burbage, who first
acted the character of Hamlet." H.
Wyeth proposes *faint*; Plehwe, referring to IV. vii. 158, conjectures *hot.*
  299. *napkin*] handkerchief, as in
Othello, III. iii. 290.

Queen. Come, let me wipe thy face.   305
Laer. My lord, I 'll hit him now.
King.   I do not think 't.
Laer. [*Aside.*] And yet 'tis almost 'gainst my conscience.
Ham. Come, for the third, Laertes: you but dally;
  I pray you, pass with your best violence;
  I am afeard you make a wanton of me.   310
Laer. Say you so? come on.   [*They play.*
Osr. Nothing, neither way.
Laer. Have at you now!

> [*Laertes wounds Hamlet; then, in scuffling,*
> *they change rapiers, and Hamlet wounds*
> *Laertes.*

King.   Part them! they are incensed.
Ham. Nay, come, again.   [*The Queen falls.*
Osr.   Look to the queen there, ho!
Hor. They bleed on both sides. — How is it, my
  lord?   315

307. *'tis . . . 'gainst*] F, *it is . . . against* Q.   308. *third . . . you*]
Steevens, *third Laertes, you doe* Q, *third. Laertes, you* F.   310. *afeard*] F,
sure Q.   313. *Laertes wounds . . .*] Rowe, omitted Q.   In scuffling
they change Rapiers F; They catch one anothers Rapiers, and both are
wounded, Leartes falles downe, the Queene falles downe and dies Q 1.
314. *come, again*] F; *come againe* Q, Ff 2-4.   The Queen falls] Capell;
omitted Q, F.   315. *is it*] Q, *is 't*] F.

310. *wanton*] treat me like an
indulged boy.
313. Stage direction] Of several
methods of exchanging rapiers adopted
by actors, or described by commentators, that suggested by H. von
Friesen (*Sh. Jahrbuch*, 1869) seems
to accord best with the stage direction of Q 1. The writer derives it
from his recollections of the fencing-
school. "As soon as your opponent
has made a pass, and is about to
return to his guard, you strike the
most powerful *battute* possible (*i.e.* a

blow descending along the blade of
your opponent) . . . advance the left
foot close to the outer side of the right
foot of your opponent, seize with the
left hand the guard of your opponent's
rapier. . . . The opponent meets the
attack with the same manœuvre, and
gets his assailant's weapon in his
hand in the same way." The com-
batants change places, and continue
to fight. (Furness's translation ab-
breviated.) [See Appendix III.]
314. *ho!*] Supposed by Staunton
to be a signal to stop the combat.

Osr. How is't, Laertes?

Laer. Why, as a woodcock to mine own springe, Osric;

I am justly kill'd with mine own treachery. *Admits his own treachery.*

Ham. How does the queen?

King.   She swounds to see them bleed.

Queen. No, no, the drink, the drink,—O my dear Hamlet,—   320

The drink, the drink!—I am poison'd. [*Dies.*

Ham. O villany!—Ho! let the door be lock'd: *realizes the treachery*

Treachery! seek it out! [*Laertes falls.* *fears for them all.*

Laer. It is here, Hamlet. Hamlet, thou art slain;

No medicine in the world can do thee good; 325

In thee there is not half an hour of life;

The treacherous instrument is in thy hand,

Unbated and envenom'd; the foul practice

Hath turn'd itself on me; lo, here I lie,

Never to rise again; thy mother's poison'd; 330

I can no more.—The king, the king's to blame.

Ham. The point envenom'd too!—⎤ *action. Short lines*

Then, venom, to thy work! ⎦ [*Stabs the King.*

All. Treason! treason!

King. Oh, yet defend me, friends; I am but hurt. 335

317. *mine own*] Q, *mine* F.   321. Dies] Rowe; omitted Q, F.   322. *Ho!*] Theobald, *how* Q, *hoe* Q 4, *How?* F.   323. Laertes falls] Capell; omitted Q, F.   324. *here, Hamlet. Hamlet*] F, *heere Hamlet,* Q. 326. *hour of*] F, *houres* Q.   327. *thy*] F, *my* Q.   333. Stabs the King] Rowe, Hurts the King F, omitted Q.

317. *woodcock*] see I. iii. 115.
328. *Unbated*] see IV. vii. 139.
328. *practice*] artifice, stratagem. See IV. vii. 68.
332. *The point*] Staunton supposes

Hamlet first to note that the button is gone, and reads, "The point — envenom'd too!"
333. *to thy work*] Theobald (ed. 2) read "do thy work."

Ham. Here, thou incestuous, murderous, damned Dane,

Insists on murdering him twice.

Drink off this potion !   Is thy union here?

Follow my mother !   [*King dies.*

Laer.   He is justly served ;

It is a poison temper'd by himself.——

Trace of generosity

Exchange forgiveness with me, noble Hamlet ; 340

Mine and my father's death come not upon thee,

Nor thine on me !   [*Dies.*

free of the guilt of my death

Ham. Heaven make thee free of it !   I follow thee.——

I am dead, Horatio.——Wretched queen, adieu !——

You that look pale and tremble at this chance,   345

That are but mutes or audience to this act,

Had I but time (as this fell sergeant, death,

Is strict in his arrest) oh, I could tell you——

But let it be.——Horatio, I am dead ;

Thou livest ; report me and my cause aright   350

To the unsatisfied.

Hor.   Never believe it ;

wishes to commit suicide

I am more an antique Roman than a Dane ;

Here 's yet some liquor left.

Ham.   As thou 'rt a man,

Give me the cup : let go ; by heaven, I 'll have 't.——

forces it from him

336. *Here*] F, *Heare* Q (= here ?) ; *murderous*] F, omitted Q.   337. *off*]
F, *of* Q (= off ?) ; *union*] Q 1, F ; *the Onixe* Q.   338. King dies] F,
omitted Q.   342. Dies] F, omitted Q.   348. *you*—] Pope, *you*, Q, *you.*
F.   350. *cause aright*] Q, *causes right* F.   351. *Never believe*] Q, F ;
Never ; believe Hanmer.

337. *union*] see line 283. Caldecott suggests a play on the word ; the
potion effects the union of the King
and Queen.

346. *mutes*] performers in a play
who have no words. The word occurs
in the stage direction for the dumb-
show preceding the play, Act III. ii.
146.

347. *sergeant*] Malone compares
Silvester's *Du Bartas* : "And Death,
drad Serjant of th' eternall Iudge,"
and Shakespeare's *Sonnets*, lxxiv. :
" when that fell arrest Without all
bail shall carry me away." " Ser-
geants" is of frequent occurrence in
Elizabethan literature as the name for
officers who arrest debtors.

O good Horatio, what a wounded name,   355
Things standing thus unknown, shall live behind
　　me!
If thou didst ever hold me in thy heart,
Absent thee from felicity awhile,   *do not seek death*
And in this harsh world draw thy breath in
　　pain,
To tell my story.—
　　　　　　[*March afar off, and shot within.*
　　　　　What war-like noise is this?   360

Osr. Young Fortinbras, with conquest come from
　　Poland,
　　To the ambassadors of England gives
　　This war-like volley.

Ham.　　　　　Oh, I die, Horatio;
The potent poison quite o'er-crows my spirit;
I cannot live to hear the news from England;   365
But I do prophesy the election lights
On Fortinbras; he has my dying voice;   *vote*
So tell him, with the occurrents, more and less,
Which have solicited—the rest is silence.   [*Dies.*

355. *good Horatio*] F, *god Horatio* Q, *God Horatio* Qq 4-6, *God!—Horatio*
Capell.   356. *live*] F, *I leave* Q; *me!*] Jennens, *me?* Q, *me.* F.   360. March
. . .] Steevens, A march a farre off Q, March afarre off, and shout within F.
369. *solicited—*] Jennens, *solicited,* Q, *solicited.* F; *silence.*] Q, *silence.
O, o, o, o.* F; Dies] F, omitted Q.

356. *shall live*] Staunton in support
of F cites *Much Ado,* III. i. 110:
"No glory lives behind the back of
such."
364. *o'er-crows*] triumphs over (as a
victorious cock). To several examples
cited by Steevens and Malone, add
The Spanish Mandevile, 1618, p.
135: "Being somewhat haughtie,
and suffering no man to overcrow

him." Qq 4-6, Pope, and other
editors read *ore-growes.*
368. *occurrents*] occurrences, inci-
dents.   Beaumont and Fletcher,
Beggar's Bush, I. i.: "kept me
stranger . . . to all the occurrents of
my country."
369. *solicited*] invited, prompted,
as in *Richard II.* I. ii. 2.

simple epitaph.

Hor. Now cracks a noble heart.—Good night, sweet
　　prince,　　　　　　　　　　　　　　　　　　370
　　And flights of angels sing thee to thy rest !—
　　Why does the drum come hither? [*March within.*

Outside world comes in.

Enter FORTINBRAS, *the English Ambassadors, with drum,
colours, and attendants.*

For. Where is this sight?

Hor.　　　　　　　　　　　What is it ye would see?
　　If aught of woe or wonder, cease your search.

For. This quarry cries on havoc.—O proud Death! 375
　　What feast is toward in thine eternal cell,
　　That thou so many princes at a shot
　　So bloodily hast struck?

First Amb.　　　　　　　　　The sight is dismal;
　　And our affairs from England come too late;
　　The ears are senseless that should give us hearing, 380
　　To tell him his commandment is fulfill'd,
　　That Rosencrantz and Guildenstern are dead.
　　Where should we have our thanks?　　*Claudius*

Hor.　　　　　　　　　　　Not from his mouth,
　　Had it the ability of life to thank you;
　　He never gave commandment for their death. 385

370. *cracks*] Q, *cracke* F.　　372. March within] Capell; omitted Q, F.
Enter Fortinbras . . .] F (substantially).　　Enter Fortenbrasse, with the
Embassadors. Q.　　373. *ye*] F, *you* Q.　375. *This*] Q, *His* F.　378. First]
Capell; omitted Q, F.

370. *cracks*] So *Coriolanus*, v. iii.
9: "with a crack'd heart."
371. *sing*] Warburton reads *wing*.
375. *This quarry . . . havoc*] *His*
of F may refer to Death. White's
explanation seems right: "This heap
of dead proclaims an indiscriminate
slaughter." For "cry on" compare

Othello, v. i. 48, *Richard III.* v. iii.
231. Clar. Press: "This pile of
corpses urges to merciless slaughter."
376. *toward*] see I. i. 77.
376. *eternal*] Perhaps used in the
sense which expresses abhorrence;
see note on I. v. 21.
383. *his mouth*] The King's mouth.

But since, so jump upon this bloody question,   *exactly*
You from the Polack wars, and you from England,
Are here arrived, give order that these bodies
High on a stage be placed to the view ;
And let me speak to the yet unknowing world 390
How these things came about; so shall you hear
Of carnal, bloody, and unnatural acts,
Of accidental judgments, casual slaughters, *killing of Polonius.*
Of deaths put on by cunning and forced cause, *Hamlet*
And, in this upshot, purposes mistook 395
Fall'n on the inventors' heads: all this can I *Laertes, Claudius*
Truly deliver.

For.   Let us haste to hear it,
And call the noblest to the audience. *hearing*
For me, with sorrow I embrace my fortune;
I have some rights of memory in this kingdom, 400
Which now to claim my vantage doth invite me,

Hor. Of that I shall have also cause to speak,
And from his mouth whose voice will draw on *give you more causes.*
     more ;
But let this same be presently perform'd,
Even while men's minds are wild; lest more
     mischance, 405

---

390. *to the yet*] F, *to yet* Q.   394. *forced cause*] F, *for no cause* Q.
400. *rights*] Q, *Rites* F.   401. *now to*] Q, *are to* F.   402. *shall have
also*] Q, *shall have alwayes* F.   403. *on more*] F, *no more* Q.   405.
while] Q, *whiles* F.

386. *jump*] see I. i. 65.
392. *carnal*] changed to *cruell* in
Qq 4, 5. This line refers to the
King's incestuous marriage and the
murder of his brother ; the next, to
the death of Ophelia (accidental
judgments) and of Polonius (casual
slaughter) ; that which follows, to the

deaths of Rosencrantz and Guildenstern.
394. *put on*] instigated. Compare
Coriolanus, II. i. 272 ; for other
examples see Schmidt.
400. *of memory*] traditional and
remembered.

15*

On plots and errors, happen.

For.   Let four captains
Bear Hamlet, like a soldier, to the stage ;
For he was likely, had he been put on,
To have proved most royally : and for his passage,
The soldiers' music and the rites of war   410
Speak loudly for him.—
Take up the bodies.—Such a sight as this
Suitable for battle field. Becomes the field, but here shows much amiss.—
Go, bid the soldiers shoot.

[*A dead march.   Exeunt, bearing off the bodies ;
after which a peal of ordnance is shot off.*

409. *royally*] F, *royall* Q.   410. *rites*] F, *right* Q.   412. *bodies*] Q,
body F.   414. Stage direction] Capell (substantially) ; Exeunt Q ; Exeunt
Marching : after the which, a Peale of Ordenance are shot off. F.

406. *On*] Perhaps "as the conse-   408. *put on*] set to work (as King),
quence of " ; perhaps "on the top   brought to trial.
of."   409. *passage*) departure, as in III.
                                                              iii. 86.

APPENDIX I

The "Travelling" of the Players (II. ii. 347).

Q 1 (1603) reads as follows:

Ham. How comes it that they travell? Do they grow
    restie?
Gil. No my Lord, their reputation holds as it was wont.
Ham. How then?
Gil. Yfaith my Lord, noveltie carries it away,
    For the principall publike audience that
    Came to them, are turned to private playes,
    And to the humour of children.

Q (1604):

Ham. How chances it they trauaile? their residence both
    in reputation, and profit was better both wayes.
Ros. I thinke their inhibition, comes by the meanes of the
    late innouasion.
Ham. Doe they hold the same estimation they did when
    I was in the Citty; are they so followed.
Ros. No indeed are they not.

F (1623) repeats Q (1604) so far, and adds all that
follows as given in the text (pp. 79–81) to and including
the words "Hercules and his load too."

The discussion of this matter by Prof. W. Hall Griffin
in *The Academy*, April 25, 1896, seems to me highly
satisfactory. At Michaelmas 1600 Henry Evans took
possession of the Blackfriars Theatre,—a private theatre,—
which he leased from Richard Burbage, and there he set
up "a companie of boyes," who became exceedingly
popular. This is referred to in Q. 1.

Q (1604) refers to an inhibition and an innovation. Probably this is a veiled allusion to the popularity of the children, an innovation,[1] which had almost the effect of an inhibition. If we must find an express inhibition, that due to the visitation of the Plague, 1603, may answer the purpose. In January 1604 the children became "the Children of her Majesty's Revels"; in 1603 Shakespeare's company became the King's servants. It was inexpedient that the King's servants should censure the Queen's children. Hence the omission of any reference to boy actors in Q 1604.

The passage in F refers not only to boy actors, but probably also to the "war of the theatres," in which Jonson, Marston, Dekker took prominent parts. The children performed *Cynthia's Revels*, 1600, and *The Poetaster*, 1601. Jonson admits that he had "tax'd" the players, but only some of them, and that "sparingly" (see Apologeticall Dialogue appended to *The Poetaster*). A far less probable suggestion as to the "inhibition" is, that it refers to the disgrace of Shakespeare's company at court in 1601, owing to the share they had taken, by a performance of *Richard II.*, in the conspiracy of Essex. See S. Lee's *Life of Shakespeare*, pp. 213-217.

[See, for a new view, an article (" The Date of Shakespeare's *Hamlet* ") in *Shakespeare's Workshop*, 1928, in which Mr. W. J. Lawrence argues that " the tragedians of the city " (II. ii. 346) have been wrongly identified with the Lord Chamberlain's men, " who never travelled save under the compulsion of the plague," and that Rosencrantz's explanation, " I think their inhibition comes by the means of the late innovation," was inspired by the Privy Council order of June 22, 1600, " limiting the number of playhouses to two, and forbidding all acting in London (*i.e.* all professional acting : the boys were looked upon as amateurs) save by the Globe and Fortune players, under penalty of imprisonment," in

---

[1 Though the word is elsewhere in Shakespeare used only for a political uprising, this is not a sufficient reason for confining it to that sense here. R. H. C.]

consequence of which "there must have been an immediate exodus into the country." When, as events showed, the order was not enforced, it was necessary, in Mr. Lawrence's view, to give another reason "for the travelling of the tragedians," which was done "none too aptly," by imputing it to the rivalry of the children. If, however, this is not too apt in respect of "inhibition," it accords very well with loss of "estimation." Mr. Lawrence regards the F passage (ll. 355–383) as an interpolation for this purpose, which "could not have been written before May or June 1601," and, as further proof of interpolation, argues that Hamlet's speech, "It is not very strange," etc., is not a reply to Rosencrantz's last, "Ay, that they [the boys] do, my lord ; Hercules and his load too," but rather to line 354, "No, indeed, they are not." From Hamlet, however, the answer seems to me to be probable enough, and the thought of the boys may have called up in his mind the thought of the King's "picture in little." R. H. C.]

APPENDIX II

Some Passages from the Quarto of 1603

IT may be of interest to give a few passages from the Quarto of 1603, which differ considerably from the received text, or are wholly absent from it. For II. i. 77–100 the Q 1603 gives:

Of. O yong Prince *Hamlet*, the only floure of *Denmark*,
Hee is bereft of all the wealth he had,
The Iewell that ador'nd his feature most
Is filcht and stolne away, his wit 's bereft him,
Hee found mee walking in the gallery all alone,
There comes hee to mee with a distracted looke,
His garters lagging downe, his shooes untide,
And fixt his eyes so stedfast on my face,
As if they had vow'd, this is their latest obiect.
Small while he stoode, but gripes me by the wrist,
And there he holdes my pulse till with a sigh
He doth unclaspe his holde, and parts away
Silent, as is the mid time of the night :
And as he went, his eie was still on mee,
For thus his head over his shoulder looked,
He seemed to finde the way without his eies :
For out of doores he went without their helpe,
And so did leave me.

III. ii. 53. The Quarto 1603 adds to Hamlet's criticism of the Stage Clown the following :

And then you have some agen, that keepes one sute
Of ieasts, as a man is knowne by one sute of
Apparell, and Gentlemen quotes his ieasts downe
In their tables, before they come to the play, as thus ;

Cannot you stay till I eate my porrige? and, you
  owe me
A quarters wages : and, my coate wants a cullison :
And your beere is sowre : and, blabbering with his
  lips,
And thus keeping in his cinkapase of ieasts,
When, God knows, the warme Clowne cannot make a
  iest,
Vnlesse by chance, as the blinde man catcheth a
  hare :
Maisters tell him of it.

Dr. B. Nicholson has argued that Kemp is the clown
specially hit at ; he had left Shakespeare's company.
When he returned, these specialised jests were omitted.
Dr. Nicholson further argues that the praise of Yorick is
the praise of Tarlton, who died in 1588, and that on
Kemp's return to the company the praise of Tarlton was
made less pointed by altering the period during which
Yorick's skull had lain in the earth from twelve to twenty-
three years.

III. iii. 36–72.   Q. 1603 reads :
King. O that this wet that falles upon my face
  Would wash the crime cleere from my conscience !
  When I looke up to heaven, I see my trespasse,
  The earth doth still crie out upon my fact,
  Pay me the murder of a brother and a king,
  And the adulterous fault I have committed :
  O these are sinnes that are unpardonable :
  Why say thy sinnes were blacker then is ieat,
  Yet may contrition make them as white as snowe :
  I but still to persever in a sinne,
  It is an act gainst the universall power,
  Most wretched man, stoope, bend thee to thy prayer,
  Aske grace of heaven to keepe thee from despaire.

III. iv. 136.   From *Exit Ghost* to the close of the scene
Q 1603 gives the following :
Queene. Alas, it is the weaknesse of thy braine,
  Which makes thy tongue to blazon thy hearts griefes :

But as I have a soule, I sweare by heaven,
I never knew of this most horride murder:
But Hamlet, this is onely fantasie,
And for my love forget these idle fits.

Ham. Idle, no mother, my pulse doth beate like yours,
It is not madnesse that possesseth Hamlet.
O mother, if ever you did my deare father love,
Forbeare the adulterous bed to night,
And win your selfe by little as you may,
In time it may be you wil lothe him quite:
And mother, but assist mee in revenge,
And in his death your infamy shall die.

Queene. Hamlet, I vow by that majesty,
That knowes our thoughts, and lookes into our hearts,
I will conceale, consent, and doe my best,
What stratagem soe're thou shalt devise.

Ham. It is enough, mother, good night:
Come sir, I 'le provide you a grave,
Who was in life, a foolish prating knave.

The following is absent from the later texts, but the information here given by Horatio to the Queen is given by Hamlet to Horatio in the received text in v. ii. This scene follows IV. v.:

Enter HORATIO *and the* QUEENE.

Hor. Madame, your sonne is safe arriv'de in *Denmarke*,
This letter I even now receiv'd of him,
Whereas he writes how he escap't the danger,
And subtle treason that the king had plotted,
Being crossed by the contention of the windes,
He found the Packet sent to the king of *England*,
Wherein he saw himselfe betray'd to death,
As at his next conversion with your grace,
He will relate the circumstance at full.

Queene. Then I perceive there's treason in his lookes
That seem'd to sugar o're his villanie:
But I will soothe and please him for a time,
For murderous mindes are alwayes jealous,
But know not you *Horatio* where he is?

Hor. Yes Madame, and he hath appoynted me
 To meete him on the east side of the Cittie
 To morrow morning.

Queene. O faile not, good *Horatio,* and withall, com-
 mend me
 A mothers care to him, bid him a while
 Be wary of his presence, lest that he
 Faile in that he goes about.

Hor. Madam, never make doubt of that:
 I thinke by this the news be come to court:
 He is arriv'de, observe the king, and you shall
 Quickely finde *Hamlet* being here,
 Things fell not to his minde.

Queene. But what became of *Gilderstone* and *Rossencraft?*

Hor. He being set ashore, they went for *England,*
 And in the Packet there writ down that doome
 To be perform'd on them that poynted for him:
 And by great chance he had his fathers seale,
 So all was done without discoverie.

Queene. Thankes be to heaven for blessing of the prince,
 Horatio once againe I take my leave,
 With thowsand mothers blessings to my sonne.

Hor. Madam adue.

APPENDIX III

Mr. W. J. Craig, who in knowledge of the language of Shakespeare is, I believe, unsurpassed by any living student, has read the proof-sheets of this edition (not always agreeing with my interpretations), has noted omissions, and has sent me a mass of valuable illustrations and additions, from which I make a scanty selection.

I. i. 106 : *head*, source, as in *All's Well*, I. iii. 178, "Your salt tears' head." Hence origin, cause. Compare II. ii. 55.

I. i. 166 : *russet*, probably gray turning to gold or to red. Latham's *Johnson's Dictionary* notices that Sir I. Newton uses russet for gray.

I. ii. 4 : *one brow of woe*. Brow, aspect, look. See Schmidt's *Lexicon*.

I. ii. 100 : *peevish*, foolish, silly, as in *Comedy of Errors*, IV. i. 93.

I. iii. 56 : *shoulder of your sail*. Shoulder, the back. See Schmidt's *Lexicon*.

I. v. 48 : *dignity*, worth, excellence. See *Love's Labour's Lost*, IV. iii. 236.

I. v. 97 : *globe*. Schmidt thinks this may mean the world; Mr. Craig suggests this little world of man. Compare *Lear*, III. i. 10.

I. v. 116. Compare Marston, *The Dutch Courtezan*, I. ii. "Wha, ho, ho! come, bird, come."

I. v. 133: *whirling words.* Schmidt defines whirling "giddy." Mr. Craig prefers F *hurling.* But compare *1 Henry VI.* I. v. 19, "My thoughts are whirl'd like a potter's wheel."

I. v. 150: *truepenny.* Mr. Craig notes "old truepenny" as occurring in *The Returne from Pernassus,* II. iv., and Beaumont and Fletcher, *The Loyal Subject,* I. iii.; he adds that Truepenny is the name of a character in *Ralph Roister Doister,* and is defined in Bailey's *Dictionary* (1721), "a name given by way of taunt to some sorry fellow."

II. ii. 63: *preparation,* used specially for a force ready for combat, as in *Coriolanus,* I. ii. 15.

II. ii. 339: *the humorous man.* Mr. Sidney Lee notes a mention in *Henslowe's Diary,* p. 183, of "The honorable lyfe of the humorous Earle of Gloster with his conquest of Portugalle." [See note to Introduction, p. xv.]

II. ii. 381: *carry it away.* Mr. Craig compares *Romeo and Juliet,* III. i. 77, and notices an example earlier than any in *New English Dictionary,* Nash, *The Unfortunate Traveller* (1594), Grosart's *Nash,* v. 42.

II. ii. 402, 403. Mr. Craig quotes from *Apollo Shroving* (1627), "It lifts a man up till he grow lesse and lesse like a hawk after a hernshaw."

II. ii. 605: *John-a-dreams.* Mr. Craig notices "Johndreaming" as an epithet in Hall's translation of *Homer,* 1581, b. ii.

III. iv. 135. Compare Jonson, *The Fortunate Isles,* "Enter Skogan and Skelton, in like habits as they lived."

IV. ii. 33: *Hide fox,* defined as "hide and seek, a child's play," by Pegge, *Alphabet of Kenticisms,* 1735.

IV. vii. 139: *unbated.* Compare "unrebated swords" in North's *Plutarch,* "Coriolanus," p. 241, ed. 1603.

v. ii. 6 : *bilboes*. Mr. Craig notes an earlier example than any in *New English Dictionary* : Elyot, *Latin Dictionary* (1538), " *arca*, the pillory, stocks, or bilboes." v. ii. 298 : *fat and scant of breath*. Mr. Craig understands *fat* to mean not reduced to athletic condition by a fencer's training.

I make the following additions to the first edition :—

[I. i. 21. The "awe" of Marcellus and the "incredulity" of Horatio are remarked in the note here, and that the Ghost was no devil in "a pleasing shape" in that on I. v. 138 ; but when the significance of these things is pointed out as by Professor J. Dover Wilson in N. C. S., their effect is expanded and the subsequent doubts of Hamlet become much more intelligible. In brief, while Marcellus shares the belief of the time in ghosts and would whole-heartedly accept the Ghost's account of purgatory in I. v. 10–13, and while Horatio reflects the scepticism that finds voice in Scot's *Discoverie of Witchcraft*, 1584, Hamlet, fresh from the protestant University of Wittenberg, is neither sceptic nor believer in purgatory, but uncertain whether angels or more probably devils might not assume the shapes of the departed to mislead and betray. Hence his address in I. iv. 40 to "spirit of health" or "goblin damn'd" bringing "air from heaven" or "blasts from hell," and hence, after temporary conviction, his later uncertainties. R. H. C.]

[I. i. 120 : *almost to doomsday*. N. C. S. cites Herford : "almost to the point of complete darkness, alluding to the biblical prophecy that at the second coming of Christ ' the moon shall not give her light ' (*Matt.* xxiv. 29)." R. H. C.]

I. ii. 129, *solid* : The case in favour of *sallied*, meaning *sullied*, is strengthened by the fact that in *Love's Labour's Lost*, v. ii. 352, we have in Folio and Quartos *unsallied lily*. [" Sullied " has received further support from Dr. W. W. Greg (*Principles of Emendation in Shakespeare*, 1928) and Mr. J. Dover Wilson, not without provoking pleas for " solid " on literary grounds. See *Times Literary Supplement*, Oct. 4, 11, 25, etc., 1928. R. H. C.]

[I. iv. 7. *What . . . mean, my lord?* Inconsistencies which have been pointed out in connection with Horatio, such as, *e.g.*, his ignorance here compared with his knowledge of Danish affairs in I. i. 79, are justly defended in N. C. S. and *What Happens in Hamlet*, pp. 233, 4, as allowable in a character designed not for the study but the stage, and, in the hands of a skilful dramatist, impressive enough to impose itself on spectators so strongly that it can be employed to meet the needs of more than one situation without any danger of inconsistency being noticed. R. H. C.]

I. iv. 8–10. Compare Marlowe's *Faustus*, ed. Bullen, I. p. 300 : " He took his rouse with stoups of Rhenish wine."

I. v. 68, 69. T. Bright in his book on Melancholy describes the brain (p. 13) as being " as tender as a *posset curd.*"

II. i. 63 : *carp of truth*. So Chapman, *For stay in Competence*, " caught with carps of sophistry."

II. ii. 103. Compare C. Hollyband, *The Italian Schoolmaister*, 1597, " When the effect is defective." sig. R. 5.

II. ii. 174. *fishmonger*. Add " Such arrant honest women as are fishe for every man [*i.e.* harlots.] " B. R. *Herodotus*, 1584 (reprint, ed. Lang, p. 131).

II. ii. 201, 202 : Compare from *Greene's Tu Quoque* (Hazlitt, Dodsley, xi. p. 282), " Surely I was begotten in a plum-tree, I ha' such a deal of gum about mine eyes."

II. ii. 342 : *sere*. Compare " whose tongue grew all too glibbe upon the seare." N. Breton, *Pasquil's Fooles-Cap* (1600).

II. ii. 381. So Nash, *The Unfortunate Traveller* (ed. Grosart, v. 74), " from all the world hee *carries it awaie.*"

[II. ii. 454 : *chopine*. N. E. D. has : " The English writers *c.* 1600 persistently treated the word as Italian, even spelling it *cioppino*, pl. *cioppini*, and expressly associated it with Venice, so that, although not recorded in Italian dictionaries, it was apparently temporarily fashionable there." R. H. C.]

[II. ii. 586. Mr. Ross D. Waller, writing to the *Times Literary Supplement*, Nov. 17, 1932, records a parallel (curious, even if due to coincidence only) between Drayton's *Piers Gaveston*, 1593 or 1594, ll. 995, 6, and II. ii. 586 in *Hamlet*, where Q1 reads : " Why what a dunghill idiote slave am I ? " and Q2 : " Oh what a rogue and pesant slave am I ? " These versions of the line, together, recall the three words " dunghill," " pesant " and " slavery " found in Drayton's couplet, and are " spoken there by one who like Hamlet was ' born a king ' " :

" Base dunghill mind, that doest such slavery bring,
To live a pesant, and be borne a king." R. H. C.]

[III. ii. 102 : *I eat the air*, etc. N. C. S. sees here a quibble on *heir* and *air*, and in the whole speech another hint of the ambitious designs which the King feared in Hamlet, and which Hamlet wished him to suspect. R. H. C.]

[III. ii. 146 : If the dumb-show stood alone, we might follow Professor J. Dover Wilson in attributing the King's apparent indifference to his being too busy discussing Hamlet's behaviour to Ophelia with Polonius and the Queen ; but he is similarly unmoved by the protracted allusion to his marriage, being too clever and too hardened to give himself away at the first challenge. R. H. C.]

III. iii. 80. Mr. C. Crawford (to whom I owe the note on II. i. 63) points out to me a parallel in Bacon's *Charge against Frances, Countess of Somerset* (1615) : " But it [the murder] hath three circumstances, which make it grievous beyond other murders ; whereof the first is, that it takes away a man in full peace, in God's and the King's peace ; he thinketh no harm, but is comforting of nature

with refection and food, so that, as the Scripture saith,
' his table is made a snare.' "

[III. iv. 53. If Mr. W. J. Lawrence is right (see
" *Hamlet* as Shakespeare Staged It," in *Pre-Restoration
Studies*, 1927, the pictures hung side by side as in the
print referred to in the note, p. 140 *ante*, and were covered
with curtains (in a manner once common) which Hamlet
drew aside in turn. R. H. C.]

[IV. ii. 14 : *replication*. N. C. S. points out that this
is a legal term = an answer to a charge, and refers to
N. E. D.2. R. H. C.]

IV. ii. 20 : *like an ape*. Compare Cotgrave under
Sphinge : " having eaten meat ynough, he reserves his
chaps-full to feed on when he feeles himselfe hungrie
againe."

V. i. 67. A " Master Youghan " is named in Hakluyt
(ed. Maclehose, viii. 332, W. J. Craig).

V. i. 151. Compare Cyril Tourneur, *The Transformed
Metamorphosis* (1600) :—

" Now earth's baddest good
Makes ev'ry peasant seem of gentle blood."

The date is not distant from that of *Hamlet*.

[V. ii. 42 : *comma*. N. C. S. (xxxiv note and p. 242)
points out that N. E. D. places this passage under *comma*
2c, *fig.* = Break of continuity, interval, pause, which
Dowden is supposed to have overlooked. I am not
satisfied that Dowden would have preferred this meaning
to the one he gives from *comma* 1. N. C. S. quotes an
" exact parallel " from N. E. D. *comma* 2c : " Though
a truce may give a comma or colon to the war, nothing
under a peace can put a perfect period thereuntoo " (1661
Fuller's *Worthies* (1840)); but here a war is in question
(not the amity of two nations) in which a truce is compared to a comma and a peace to a full stop. In our text
peace is not a full stop but a comma. Comma can mean
" pause " if *amities* is ironical, as Professor Dover Wilson

says, but England, at any rate, is not to suspect irony, but a persuasive argument. R. H. C.]

[v. ii. 237–255 : Professor Dover Wilson acquits Hamlet of irony and insincerity (see note on l. 255 *ante*), accepting his plea as made in all good faith. The attendant circumstances gave the slaying of Polonius the stamp of sanity, yet it may be that Hamlet looks back upon the deed as an act of madness. R. H. C.]

[v. ii. 313 : Stage Direction. In v. ii. 149 the contest was to be with " Rapier and dagger," and the S. D. in Q1, l. 235, mentions daggers, as recorded on p. 217 *ante*. It is probable, then, that when *Hamlet* was first produced the play was with rapier and dagger, for which the explanation given in the note *ad loc.* does not suffice. That given by Professor Dover Wilson in *What Happens in Hamlet*, 1935, p. 286, is more to the point. He refers to a letter in *T. L. S.*, Jan. 25, 1934, from Mr. Evan John : Hamlet " closes with him [Laertes], beats aside his dagger with the dagger in his own left hand, and suddenly dropping to the ground the foil in his right, seizes with the empty hand the hilt of the sword he covets and wrests it from his enemy's grasp." R. H. C.]

PRINTED BY MORRISON AND GIBB LTD., LONDON AND EDINBURGH